OCCASIONAL PAPER 243

Central America: Global Integration and Regional Cooperation

Edited by Markus Rodlauer and Alfred Schipke

INTERNATIONAL MONETARY FUND

Washington DC

2005

© 2005 International Monetary Fund

Production: IMF Multimedia Services Division
Typesetting: Alicia Etchebarne-Bourdin

Cataloging-in-Publication Data

Central America: global integration and regional cooperation/edited by Markus
   Rodlauer and Alfred Schipke—Washington, D.C.: International Monetary
   Fund, 2005.

            p. cm.—(Occasional paper); 243

Includes bibliographical references.
ISBN 1-58906-446-1

   1. Central America—Economic integration. 2. Central America—Economic
conditions—Statistics. 3. Free trade—Central America. 4. Foreign exchange
rates—Central America. 5. Poverty—Central America. I. Rodlauer, Markus.
II. Schipke, Alfred, 1959– III. Occasional paper (International Monetary Fund);
no. 243.

HC141.C36 2005

Price: US$25.00
(US$22.00 to full-time faculty members and
students at universities and colleges)

Please send orders to:
International Monetary Fund, Publication Services
700 19th Street, N.W., Washington, DC 20431, U.S.A.
Tel.: (202) 623-7430   Telefax: (202) 623-7201
E-mail: publications@imf.org
Internet: http://www.imf.org

recycled paper

Contents

Tables

Figures

Foreword

Central America has come a long way since it emerged from the so-called lost decade of the 1980s. Peace and democracy have been firmly reestablished; governments have implemented important economic and social reforms; and, as a result, the region enjoyed relatively strong growth and improved macroeconomic stability in the 1990s.

Nevertheless, Central America still faces important economic, social, and political challenges. Poverty remains high in most countries, as institutional weaknesses have tended to undermine growth and governments' ability to deliver on the high expectations associated with the peace process; and weak fiscal positions and financial sectors have left economies vulnerable to shocks and natural disasters to which the region is particularly exposed.

In the face of these challenges, recent years have seen a renewed effort at adjustment and reform across the region, geared toward boosting growth and reducing poverty in a lasting way. Central America is also becoming increasingly integrated, as a region and globally, and there is growing recognition, at home and abroad, that increased regional cooperation is key to each country's success as it tries to compete in the global economy.

This study looks at these challenges and how Central America is attempting to meet them, with particular emphasis on issues and challenges arising from the growing integration under way in the region. By focusing on the policy implications of increased trade and financial integration, the study should help policymakers make the best of Central America's considerable potential and set the region on a path of sustainable rapid growth. The IMF stands ready to continue to assist the region in its efforts to meet these challenges.

Rodrigo de Rato
Managing Director
International Monetary Fund

Issues raised by Central America's growing economic integration are at the center of this study coordinated by our team in the Western Hemisphere Department. A core theme is the need to intensify regional collaboration in a number of areas to maximize the benefits offered by globalization in terms of sustained growth, poverty reduction, and broader social progress. In particular, the study provides a framework for deepening cooperation in banking supervision and regulation, tax policy and administration, and economic statistics. It also notes that integration must be anchored in strong domestic economic policies, especially fiscal reforms to ensure sustainable public debt levels and structural reforms to raise productivity and competitiveness. The study is especially timely as the Free Trade Agreement with the United States (CAFTA-DR) will provide a new impetus for economic integration in the region and its ability to compete successfully in the global economy.

Anoop Singh
Director, Western Hemisphere Department
International Monetary Fund

Preface

This Occasional Paper is the product of a team effort led by Markus Rodlauer and Alfred Schipke, both staff members of the IMF's Western Hemisphere Department. The team includes authors from a number of other departments in the IMF, as well as an outside co-author from the region.

The authors would like to express their deep appreciation for the valuable guidance provided by Olav Gronlie, who—as the head of the Central American Division—was instrumental in moving the project forward as part of the IMF's increased emphasis on regional issues and those related to regional integration. They would like to thank and acknowledge the comments received from Agustín Carstens. Also, the authors are grateful to Tamim Bayoumi, Michael Keen, Anoop Singh, Teresa Ter-Minassian, and Philip Young for their comments and advice.

Particular thanks go to Susan McCuskey and Hildi Wicker Deady, who worked extremely hard to ensure the timely publication of this paper, and to Mauricio Bourdin for valuable research assistance. The authors would like to thank the authorities of the respective countries in Central America and the Dominican Republic, the Central American Monetary Council, and the participants of an internal IMF Workshop on Central America for helpful comments and suggestions. Marina Primorac of the External Relations Department coordinated the production of the publication.

The opinions expressed in this paper are solely those of its authors and do not necessarily reflect the views of the International Monetary Fund, its Executive Directors, or the authorities in the respective Central American countries and the Dominican Republic.

Abbreviations and Acronyms

ASCM	Agreement on Subsidies and Countervailing Measures
BIS	Bank for International Settlements
CABEI	Central American Bank for Economic Integration
CACM	Central American Common Market
CACS	Central American Council of Superintendents of Banks, Insurance, and Other Financial Institutions
CAFTA	Central American Free Trade Agreement
CAFTA-DR	Central American–Dominican Republic Free Trade Agreement
CAMC	Central American Monetary Council
CBERA	Caribbean Basin Economic Recovery Act
CBTPA	Caribbean Basin Trade Partnership Act
CBI	Caribbean Basin Initiative
CET	Common external tariff
CGE	Computable general equilibrium
CPI	Consumer price index
DQAF	Data Quality Assessment Framework
DSGE	Dynamic stochastic general equilibrium [model]
EMU	European Monetary Union
FDI	Foreign direct investment
FSAP	Financial Sector Assessment Program
FSSA	Financial System Stability Assessment
GDDS	General Data Dissemination System
GFS	Government Finance Statistics
GSP	Generalized System of Preferences
GTAP	Global Trade Analysis Project
HIPC	Heavily indebted poor countries
IDB	Inter-American Development Bank
IIP	International Investment Position
MFN	Most favored nation
MOU	Memorandum of understanding
NAFTA	North American Free Trade Agreement
OECD	Organization for Economic Cooperation and Development
PPI	Producer price index
PRGF	Poverty Reduction and Growth Facility
PRSP	Poverty Reduction Strategy Paper
ROSC	Report on the Observance of Standards and Codes
SIECA	Secretariat for Central American Economic Integration
SDDS	Special Data Dissemination System
SNA	System of National Accounts
UN	United Nations
VaR	Value-at-Risk
VAR	Vector autoregressive system
VAT	Value-added tax
WTO	World Trade Organization

I   Introduction and Overview

Markus Rodlauer and Alfred Schipke

Central America has received growing attention in recent years as a region that is integrating successfully into the global economy. A decade and a half after the end of civil conflicts and serious economic dislocation in parts of the region, Central America has seen great progress on many fronts: peace and democracy have been firmly established, economies have stabilized and important market-oriented reforms have been implemented, and trade and financial openness have increased notably. As a result, growth has returned and social indicators have improved. At the same time, the glass can also be seen as half empty: poverty is still widespread in most countries; economic and social progress remains constrained by weak institutions and political difficulties; and the institutional framework of regional cooperation and integration is still at an early stage. There is concern that these problems, if unaddressed, could inhibit sustained growth and therefore undermine domestic consensus on the stability and market-oriented policy frameworks now being followed throughout the region. The key task facing policymakers in Central America is thus how to entrench and strengthen the virtuous cycle of good policies and strong institutions, solid growth that is more widely shared across societies, and domestic consensus on the policy framework. The vigorous embrace by the Central American countries and the Dominican Republic of the Free Trade Agreement with the United States (CAFTA-DR) is clear testimony of their commitment to a strategy of outward-looking and market-oriented integration to meet these challenges. This paper looks at the progress that has been made, the challenges ahead, and the region's efforts to meet them.

Background

Although the Central American countries are relatively small, they are quite large as a group and face many common policy challenges. With about 40 million people, Central America accounts for about 7 percent of the population in Latin America and the Caribbean and 4½ percent of total output.[1] In addition to a shared history and a common language, the Central American economies are characterized by small domestic markets, significant—albeit diminishing—dependence on traditional exports, and close economic ties to the United States. In addition, they face a major challenge from increased global competition in some of their key export products—such as from the recent expiry of quotas in world textiles trade—and are exposed to shocks such as natural disasters and terms-of-trade changes.

After the so-called lost decade of the 1980s, economic growth returned in the 1990s, reflecting improved domestic and external conditions. Economic progress was severely constrained in the 1980s by adverse external conditions and, in some of the countries, by civil conflicts and misguided economic policies. Following the resolution of the conflicts, in the 1990s the region enjoyed a significant peace dividend, and policymakers sharpened their focus on economic growth, macroeconomic stabilization, and structural reforms such as privatization, trade liberalization, and financial sector deregulation. As a result, the region grew by 4.5 percent a year during the 1990s (1.8 percent in per capita terms), spurred by increased foreign investment and greater export diversification. Substantial progress was also made on inflation, which has been reduced to single digits. However, despite the recovery in output, the benefits of growth often were not widely shared and the gains in per capita income were not sufficient to make significant inroads against poverty (Figure 1.1). Furthermore,

---

[1]In this paper, Central America is generally defined to include Costa Rica, El Salvador, Guatemala, Honduras, Nicaragua, and Panama; certain sections also include the Dominican Republic. This broader definition mirrors the membership of the Dominican Republic in the Central American Monetary Council and the Central American Council of Bank Superintendents, as well as the Dominican Republic's participation in CAFTA-DR. Including the Dominican Republic, the total population of Central America makes up about 9 percent of the population in Latin America and the Caribbean and about 6 percent of total output.

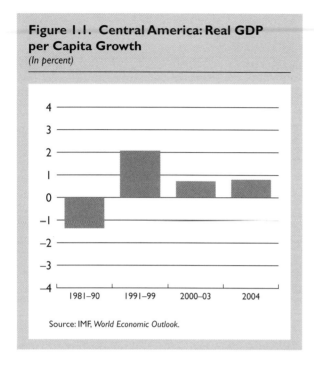

Figure 1.1. Central America: Real GDP per Capita Growth
(In percent)

Source: IMF, *World Economic Outlook.*

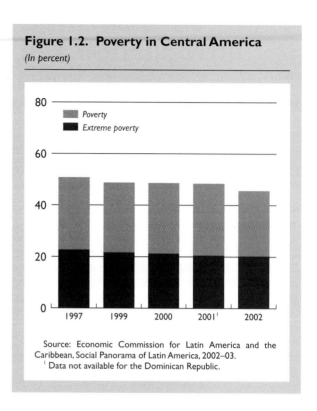

Figure 1.2. Poverty in Central America
(In percent)

Source: Economic Commission for Latin America and the Caribbean, Social Panorama of Latin America, 2002–03.
¹ Data not available for the Dominican Republic.

growth slowed in many countries in 2001, partly reflecting deteriorating external conditions but also because of difficulties in some countries in sustaining the reform momentum. Weak institutions and political uncertainty in some countries continue to undermine confidence and depress the investment climate.

Recent Developments

Political and Social Environment

Notwithstanding the great improvement in Central America's political conditions during the 1990s, economic policymaking remains hampered by weaknesses in the political process. To be sure, several rounds of peaceful elections over the past decade show that democracy has taken firm root in the region, supported by an active civil society and a free press. Nevertheless, the political landscape in many countries remains highly fragmented, and many governments (such as those in El Salvador, Guatemala, Honduras, and Nicaragua) are facing parliaments with an opposition party majority. Short election cycles also complicate sustained implementation of economic reform programs, and after just having gone through a series of elections in recent years, most countries in the region are about to enter another round of elections (presidential, legislative, or municipal) in 2005–06. In addition, vested interest groups pursuing their own agendas often wield disproportionate influ-

ence, complicating macroeconomic and structural policy implementation. At the same time, however, there appears to be a groundswell of support throughout the region for the basic overall principles of macroeconomic discipline, low inflation, market orientation, and openness—evidenced, for example, in the fairly broad support in Honduras for maintaining the economic programs supported by the Poverty Reduction and Growth Facility (PRGF), notwithstanding the difficult political situation and various pressure groups' desire for a bigger share of the budget. It remains to be seen whether the political process can deliver a critical mass of reforms, stability, and investor confidence over the next few years—which in turn will produce the kind of growth and social progress necessary to maintain broad domestic support for the policy framework.

Recent economic progress has not been mirrored by a similar improvement of social conditions, and much of the region continues to face widespread poverty (except in Costa Rica and Panama). About half the population lives in poverty, while some 20 percent faces extreme poverty (Figure 1.2). In part, poverty is associated with low-wage employment in the informal sector and is concentrated in rural areas where access to public services remains limited. Similar to inequalities elsewhere in Latin America, Central America's income distribution remains very uneven.

Recent years have seen renewed efforts across the region to address corruption and governance problems. New governments in Costa Rica, El Salvador, Guatemala, and Nicaragua have made fighting corruption a centerpiece of their policy platforms, and governance issues also figure prominently in Honduras' reform program supported by the IMF and other international financial institutions. Sustained progress in strengthening governance and reducing corruption will require continued focus on building institutions such as an independent and strong judiciary, transparency and accountability in public resource management, and reliable supervisory and regulatory bodies in the financial systems.

Recent Economic Developments

In 2003–04, Central America emerged from a period of sluggish growth to face a more favorable short-term outlook. Driven initially by a pickup in exports due to firming external demand conditions and commodity prices, the recovery in 2004 spilled over to domestic demand—despite the dampening effect of the oil price shock. Real GDP growth increased from 2¼ percent in 2002 to 3½ percent in 2004. The near-term outlook is also favorable, with regional growth in 2005 projected at 3¼ percent, although longer-term growth faces several challenges, including increased competition from China, especially in textiles, and rising world interest rates.

After a decline in inflation through 2003, recent increases in oil prices and stronger demand conditions caused inflation to rise throughout the region in 2004 to an average of 8½ percent. Assuming oil prices stabilize, inflation is expected to return to a downward path, supported by prudent fiscal and monetary policies.

External positions have continued to improve. Export growth in 2004 averaged over 14 percent in 2004, driven by strong U.S. demand and a recovery in commodity prices, especially that of coffee. While current account deficits remained largely unchanged (near 6 percent of GDP in 2004), in part reflecting the higher oil import bill, strong capital inflows have boosted international reserves.

Progress was made in reducing fiscal deficits. While most countries in Central America saw debt-to-GDP ratios rise over the past decade, the current cyclical upturn has allowed countries to strengthen policies and improve fiscal accounts: fiscal deficits declined from an average of near 6 percent of GDP in 2002 to 3 percent in 2004, helped by buoyant revenue collections that reflected both a growth dividend and ongoing reforms of tax policy and administration. Nevertheless, in several countries (Costa Rica, El Salvador, and Nicaragua), public debt remains high or has been on an upward trend. In Guatemala,

while public debt and fiscal deficits remained well contained, government efforts to strengthen the tax effort—and thus achieve the Peace Accord target of a tax-to-GDP ratio of 12 percent—were stalled by court decisions and opposition in congress. The 12 percent target was included as a key element in the 1996 Peace Accords to provide more resources for social programs and spending.

Regional Integration

Regional integration in Central America is gaining momentum. The past decade has witnessed growing linkages among the Central American economies as well as with their largest trading partner, the United States. While trade among the Central American countries has risen relatively slowly, trade with the United States increased fivefold in dollar terms during 1994–2003. On the other hand, the region has seen a significant increase of intraregional financial sector linkages. Central America has an open trade regime, with a tariff structure that is largely determined by the common external tariff of the Central American Common Market.[2] Although Central America has already preferential access to the U.S. market in the context of the Caribbean Basin Initiative,[3] the Central American Free Trade Agreement (CAFTA-DR), signed in 2004, should make this access permanent and extend it further in some areas leading to continued deepening of trade integration with the United States.

Economic policy coordination, however, is still at an early stage. The Central American countries continue to pursue independent fiscal policies, and while there is a regular consultation process among central banks, monetary and exchange rate policies evolve largely independently of each other.[4] Nevertheless, the region has a set of regional institutions that are increasingly involved in information sharing, harmonization of regulation, and policy coordination, particularly in areas such as banking supervision, central banking, and trade (Box 1.1).

Looking Ahead

What are the economic policy priorities for Central America to support a virtuous cycle of growth, strong policies and institutions, and domestic support?

---

[2]See Box 1.1 for the CET rates. The origins of economic integration efforts date back to the 1961 General Treaty of Economic Integration, which initiated the creation of a Central American Common Market.

[3]The Caribbean Basin Initiative would expire in 2008.

[4]The monetary policy stance in the officially dollarized economies (Panama and El Salvador) reflects, of course, that in the United States.

Box 1.1. Regional Economic Institutions

Central American Monetary Council (CAMC). The council was created in 1964 to coordinate the development of a Central American monetary union. The goal of setting up a monetary union has been abandoned, and the focus is now on policy coordination and technical assistance in monetary and credit policy and financial sector issues. The council meets every three months and has four standing committees: monetary policy, exchange and clearing policies, financial operations, and capital market and legal issues. The council comprises the central bank presidents of Costa Rica, El Salvador, Guatemala, Honduras, Nicaragua, and the Dominican Republic (which joined the council as a full member in 2002); Panama participates in meetings as an observer.

Central American Council of Superintendents of Banks, Insurance, and Other Financial Institutions (CACS). The principal objective of the council is to foster cooperation and the exchange of information among the superintendencies. One of its main projects is to facilitate consolidated supervision and standardization. The council was established in 1974 and includes the superintendents from Costa Rica, Guatemala, Honduras, El Salvador, Nicaragua, the Dominican Republic, and Panama. The council meets 2–3 times a year.

Central American Bank for Economic Integration (CABEI). The bank supports regional economic integration and development. Lending operations are directed mainly to infrastructure, industry, agriculture and livestock, social development, and the environ-ment. The bank began operations in 1961 and was opened to non-regional members in 1992. The bank's capital is currently subscribed by the regional members (Costa Rica, El Salvador, Guatemala, Honduras, and Nicaragua) and non-regional members (Argentina, China, Colombia, Mexico, and Spain). Under a special agreement, El Salvador, which is officially dollarized, could borrow funds for liquidity purposes.

Secretariat for Central American Economic Integration (SIECA). The general treaty for economic integration, signed in 1959, envisaged the creation of the Central American common market (CACM), which became effective in December 1960. The establishment of the CACM initially suffered a series of setbacks, but important progress has been made since 1985 with the adoption of (1) the Brussels tariff nomenclature (September 1985); (2) a tariff system based on the international harmonization system (January 1993);[1] (3) regional free trade (March 1993); and (4) a common external tariff (February 2001). The CACM comprises Costa Rica, El Salvador, Guatemala, Honduras, and Nicaragua (Panama is an observer). The common external tariff has four rates: zero (capital and intermediate goods, and raw materials not produced in the region); 5 percent (raw materials regionally produced); 10 percent (capital and intermediate goods regionally produced); and 15 percent (final goods).

---

[1]The Central American external tariff (CET) currently covers more than 90 percent of the region's trade and has an average tariff of 4.9 percent.

There is no single blueprint of reform for the region, as what is most needed and works best depends on the specific circumstances of each country. Nevertheless, the common history, similar features, and growing integration of the Central American countries suggest some key priorities that need to be addressed for sustained growth and social progress in the region.

- *Completion and implementation of CAFTA-DR.* The region has rightly set high expectations for this important trade agreement; the task is now to complete the agreement through ratification by members' parliaments and to implement the range of supporting reforms and institutional arrangements foreseen in it.[5]

- *Fiscal reforms.* The recent improvement in fiscal balances needs to continue, to ensure sustainable debt dynamics. Experience has shown that fiscal consolidation will endure only if it is based on a broad agenda to raise growth and implement structural reforms, especially institutional reforms to strengthen fiscal systems and make them more resilient against shocks and political pressures. Thus, efforts need to continue to strengthen countries' tax efforts, reduce budget rigidities, and improve budgets so that they better reflect the priorities in infrastructure, human capital, and support for the poor. Broader reforms to the overall fiscal framework may also be helpful in entrenching fiscal discipline, such as legislation to improve the budget process and/or impose sustainable debt limits.

- *Sound new credit flows.* Banking reforms in each country have already strengthened systems and made them more resilient against shocks. These reforms must continue to ensure new credit flows in an environment of sound prudential and supervisory standards. As part of this effort, regional coordination of regulations and supervision needs to be stepped up to keep pace with the

---

[5]El Salvador was the first country to ratify the agreement, at the end of 2004, followed by Honduras and Guatemala.

accelerating financial integration among Central American countries.

- *Investment climate.* The region is keenly aware of the need to improve the investment climate to increase its attractiveness for foreign direct investment. This may require further work to identify specific impediments in individual countries; typically, it will involve continuing improvements in infrastructure, including through private sector participation, strengthening the rule of law, and lowering the cost of doing business.

- *Transparency and governance.* Governments in the region recognize that fostering transparency in government and fighting corruption are top priorities if they are to effectively improve the investment climate and sustain domestic support for their policies. These goals must continue to pervade the full range of economic reforms being implemented, and governments should press ahead with establishing a preventive strategy and, in a given case, punishing wrongdoing wherever it occurs.

- *Regional collaboration.* Competing successfully in the global economy calls for further collaboration among countries in the region to maximize the benefits offered by economic integration, while minimizing its risks, such as those from cross-border financial transactions. In particular, increased coordination is needed in the areas of banking supervision and regulation, tax policy and administration, economic statistics, and large public investment projects.

Overview

The sections that follow bring together recent analysis by IMF staff, which focuses on six broad areas: the implications of CAFTA-DR, fiscal sustainability and related policy issues, exchange rate regimes, financial sector issues, macroeconomic statistics, and the political economy of reforms in Central America. In addressing these topics, the paper highlights the regional perspective and the need to match increasing economic integration with efforts to step up policy coordination and institution-building at the regional level.

- Section II analyzes the *macroeconomic implications of CAFTA-DR*, both for growth and the dynamics of macroeconomic fluctuations. Although Central America is already highly integrated with the United States, the section finds that CAFTA-DR will likely provide a further boost to trade, foreign direct investment, and growth in the region—a boost that will help meet the growing

competition the region is facing in some of its key export items, notably textiles. CAFTA-DR should also reduce macroeconomic volatility in the region as its economies integrate further with the U.S. economy. For the growth and stability benefits of CAFTA-DR to materialize, however, the agreement needs to be supported by reforms to strengthen key institutions such as regulatory bodies, dispute resolution and property rights, and labor market flexibility.

- In reviewing the *fiscal implications of trade liberalization*, Section III expects a near-term (direct) loss of customs revenues due to tariff reductions in the range of 0.1 to 0.3 percent of GDP. However, this impact should be mitigated over time by the (indirect) positive effect on revenue through higher growth and import volumes. Looking forward, the section argues that the growing regional trade integration heightens the need for greater cooperation on tax policy and administration—in particular, to avoid a "race to the bottom" among countries trying to compete for foreign direct investment through additional tax incentives.

- Section IV, on *fiscal sustainability*, uses a value-at-risk (VaR) approach to complement traditional assessments of sustainability. The analysis underscores the need for fiscal adjustment in most of the Central American countries—except Guatemala—to ensure sustainable debt dynamics. The section also shows the usefulness of the VaR approach in designing a country's debt management strategies.

- Section V looks at the implications of *exchange rate systems and the ongoing regional integration process*—as affected further by CAFTA-DR—on the kind of exchange rate regime that countries might consider in the long run. (The section notes that, in the short run, other important considerations may condition the choice of regime.) The empirical analysis suggests that Central America is still less suitable for a common currency (an independent Central American currency or the U.S. dollar) than Western Europe was in the 1970s, even after taking into account the predicted integration effects of CAFTA-DR. The analysis shows that during 1993–2003, the Central American countries have become relatively more suitable to dollarization, reflecting increased synchronization of business cycles, reduced inflation differentials, and rising trade flows with the United States. Similarly, looking ahead, the section posits that dollarization would probably bring more relative benefits for the region than a common currency that floats independently—although, again, neither of these two options is advisable in the near future. For countries that are already officially dollarized, the priority is to implement policies that ensure the sustainability of the regime, including prudent fiscal and wage policies and structural reforms to strengthen competitiveness and growth.

• Section VI, on *regional integration and financial systems*, notes the substantial progress made in recent years in strengthening financial systems. However, it also points to remaining weaknesses such as limited access to credit, high informal dollarization, portfolio problems, gaps in supervision and regulation, and underdeveloped capital markets. By addressing the accelerating regional financial integration and cross-border activities, the section underscores the need for stepped-up regional coordination in financial regulation and supervision; in particular, it highlights the significance of implementing effective consolidated supervision at both the domestic and regional level.

• Section VII, which discusses *macroeconomic statistics from a regional perspective*, calls for improvements and greater convergence of statistical systems in Central America, to support better economic analysis and policy design as well as deeper economic integration and policy coordination. It finds that the region has a fairly solid base of economic statistics, with most countries

either already subscribing or preparing to subscribe to the IMF's Special Data Dissemination System (SDDS) or the General Data Dissemination System (GDDS). Moves toward greater comparability of data and methodological convergence should be anchored on an advanced level, guided by those countries that already subscribe to the SDDS.

• Finally, Section VIII looks at the *political economy of reforms in Central America*. It summarizes the substantial progress made by the region over the past decade and a half in building stable democracies, implementing significant economic and social reforms, and entrenching a shared vision of the overall goals of economic growth, stability, and poverty reduction. At the same time, it highlights the challenges still being faced by the region in building the institutional framework for sustained sound economic policymaking and structural reforms. It concludes by noting the risks and constraints imposed by current institutional weaknesses for the implementation of ambitious economic reform programs, while also emphasizing the imperative of broadly engaging the political process in efforts to build domestic consensus on reforms. The section also notes the important contribution that economic policy and reforms can make in advancing the goals and principles that characterize successful political systems.

II Macroeconomic Implications of CAFTA-DR

M. Ayhan Kose, Alessandro Rebucci, and Alfred Schipke

Five Central American countries (Costa Rica, El Salvador, Guatemala, Honduras, and Nicaragua) and the United States signed the Central American Free Trade Agreement (CAFTA) in May 2004. The Dominican Republic (DR) joined the negotiations at the beginning of 2004 and signed the agreement (CAFTA-DR) in August 2004. The agreement will go into effect after the respective legislative bodies have ratified it.[1]

CAFTA-DR negotiations were seen as a boost in regional cooperation because Central America negotiated as a region and most of the issues were addressed within a single framework. Schedules for market access, however, were negotiated bilaterally between the United States and the individual Central American countries. In many respects, the agreement is modeled on other bilateral free trade agreements the United States has recently signed, such as those with Chile and Singapore.[2] Though the Central American countries already have strong trade and investment relations with the United States and enjoy preferential access in the context of the Caribbean Basin Initiative (CBI), CAFTA-DR is substantially more comprehensive and changes the form of trade relations from the unilateral preferential arrangement defined under the CBI to a permanent bilateral agreement.[3] For the Central American countries, the main expected benefits of the agreement are enhanced access to their largest export market, increased foreign direct investment, and institutional strengthening across a range of trade- and investment-related areas.

CAFTA-DR's main objective is to eliminate all tariffs and substantially reduce nontariff barriers between the United States and the Central American countries.[4] CAFTA-DR also includes a provision to foster trade flows between the Central American countries. During the past 10 years, the Central American countries have already significantly decreased tariffs for intraregional trade, and the common external tariff (CET) of the Central American Common Market is generally low and covers about 95 percent of imports to the region (Table 2.1).[5] In addition, these countries have taken various steps to reduce the dispersion of tariffs. Immediately after CAFTA-DR enters into force, tariffs on all nonagricultural and nontextile exports from Central America to the United States, and tariffs on about 80 percent of nonagricultural and nontextile exports from the United States to Central America, will be reduced. Tariffs on other goods will be phased out incrementally over a 5- to 20-year period. Though a significant proportion of exports from the Central American countries have already had tariff-free access to the U.S. market under the CBI, CAFTA-DR would further reduce various restrictions and eliminate compliance costs necessary to qualify for preferential access (Griswold and Ikenson, 2004).

In the case of agriculture and textiles, CAFTA-DR provides some enhanced market access, but its

---

[1]As of June 2005, the congresses of El Salvador, Guatemala, and Honduras have ratified the agreement. In 1998 the Dominican Republic had already signed a free trade agreement with Central American countries that went into effect with El Salvador, Guatemala, and Honduras in 2001 and with Costa Rica in 2002.

[2]In addition to Israel (1985), NAFTA (1994), and Jordan (2001), the United States has free trade agreements in effect with Chile and Singapore (both 2003) and Australia (2005). The United States has also signed free trade agreements with Bahrain and Morocco and has begun negotiations with several other countries, including Colombia, Ecuador, Oman, Panama, Peru, Thailand, United Arab Emirates, and the five nations of the Southern African Customs Union.

[3]The CBI currently provides 24 beneficiary countries with duty-free access to the U.S. market for most goods. It was first launched in 1983 through the Caribbean Basin Economic Recovery Act (CBERA) and expanded in 2000 through the U.S.–Caribbean Basin Trade Partnership Act (CBTPA).

[4]It was estimated that nearly 80 percent of Central American products enter the United States duty free, partly because of unilateral preference programs, including the CBI and Generalized System of Preferences (GSP) (see USTR, 2005a). Hornbeck (2004) provides a detailed discussion about the provisions of CAFTA-DR. Salazar-Xirinachs and Granados (2004) discuss economic and political objectives of the Central American countries in CAFTA. The full text of the agreement is available on the web page of the United States Trade Representative: http://www.ustr.gov/Trade_Agreements/Bilateral/CAFTA/CAFTA-DR_Final_Texts/Section_Index.html.

[5]Section III provides a detailed discussion of tax and tariff policies of the Central American countries.

Table 2.1. Tariffs in Central America, 1980–99
(In percent)

	Average Tariffs			Tariff Dispersion		
	1980s	1990s	1999	1980s	1990s	1999
Costa Rica	24.7	11.4	3.3	13.0	7.1	7.8
Dominican Republic	88.0	18.1	14.5	...	9.8	7.9
El Salvador	20.3	11.3	5.7	10.8	6.4	3.4
Guatemala	33.2	12.6	7.6	17.4	7.4	4.4
Honduras	41.9	9.4	8.1	21.8	6.3	7.8
Nicaragua	37.5	9.9	10.9	19.6	6.5	7.3

Source: Inter-American Development Bank.

extent is more limited than initially expected. The agreement envisages transition periods of up to 20 years for several agricultural goods, and it maintains import tariffs on sensitive items such as sugar and corn while increasing related import quotas. A wide range of agricultural products, including beef, butter, cheese, milk, and peanuts, continues to be protected by rather prohibitive tariff rate quotas. Although several of the Central American countries are major producers of sugar, CAFTA-DR does not open the U.S. markets to sugar imports from these countries. The agreement slightly increases their quotas on sugar imports, but the quota tariff on sugar remains very high, which is likely to prevent any sizable increase in sugar exports from the region.[6]

For textiles—compared with the current situation, in which Central America enjoys preferences under the CBI—the main changes will be the permanent nature of those preferences, and some easing of the rules of origin. CAFTA-DR also provides more comprehensive coverage of certain fabrics from Canada and Mexico and provisions for declaring certain fabrics in short supply, which would allow sourcing from third countries. However, rules-of-origin provisions require that exports of textile and apparel products of the Central American countries be produced using local components to qualify for duty-free access to the U.S. market.[7]

CAFTA-DR includes various provisions about flows of investment and financial services, government purchases, and protection of intellectual property rights. CAFTA-DR provides for strict observance of rules on intellectual property rights, investment, government procurement, and competition policies. In addition, it provides for broad access to several other markets, including services. Labor provisions are slightly tighter than under previous agreements because they offer a platform for examining the quality of legislation rather than merely ensuring its implementation.[8] Dispute resolution provisions of CAFTA-DR are modeled on NAFTA, promoting cooperative settlement of disputes but also providing dispute resolution by panels on both the governmental and the investor-state levels. The agreement would create a permanent committee on trade capacity building to help the Central American countries in trade negotiations.[9]

Although CAFTA-DR's provisions ease restrictions on investment flows, they do not contain balance of payments safeguards for transfers related to a wide range of financial and direct investments. In particular, the agreement (like the Singapore and Chile free trade agreements) contains a general prohibition on the use of capital controls for transactions covered by the agreement and restricts the use of capital controls *in extremis* by omitting a balance

---

[6]For the details of sugar provisions in CAFTA-DR and their implications for trade flows between the member countries, see Jurenas (2003) and USTR (2005b). Elliott (2005) discusses how the U.S. agricultural policies, including those protecting the sugar industry, affect free trade agreements like CAFTA-DR.

[7]Griswold and Ikenson (2004) argue that these rules-of-origin requirements are restrictive, since the size of the textile industry is very small in the region, implying that the Central American countries have to rely on U.S. textile components to gain duty-free access for their exports.

[8]Elliott (2004) provides a detailed account of the labor market provisions of CAFTA-DR and the potential implications for labor standards in the region. USTR (2005c) argues that the labor provisions are comparable to those in other agreements the United States signed, including with Jordan and Morocco.

[9]The United States and the other members of CAFTA-DR also signed supplemental agreements, including an Environmental Cooperation Agreement, to implement environmental provisions of CAFTA-DR and to coordinate the efforts to strengthen environmental cooperation in the region.

of payments safeguard exception. Although these restrictions could help protect U.S. investors from potential costs associated with capital controls that otherwise could be imposed by Central American countries during periods of financial crises, they may be premature given the still underdeveloped domestic financial systems in the region. In particular, they could limit policy options during financial crises when controls may be useful if implemented on a short-term basis in conjunction with other appropriate adjustment and reform measures.[10]

CAFTA-DR will likely have significant macroeconomic implications for Central America. The remainder of this section examines some of the key macroeconomic issues associated with the agreement. It next focuses on the impact of CAFTA-DR on trade flows and foreign direct investment (FDI). The section then addresses the question of whether the agreement is likely to give the region a boost in economic growth. Finally, it discusses how increased openness of trade and greater economic integration with the United States will affect countries' business cycles.

Implications for Trade and Investment Flows

Though similar preferential trade agreements are relatively recent—therefore providing little empirical evidence—Mexico's experience under the North American Free Trade Agreement (NAFTA) provides some insights on how CAFTA-DR could affect Central America. Signed by the United States, Canada, and Mexico a decade ago, NAFTA was the first major trade agreement to include a developing country and highly developed economies.[11] CAFTA-DR and NAFTA share a number of common characteristics, as both agreements envisage comprehensive tariff reductions, cover a broad spectrum of sectors, and include provisions for dispute settlement.

There are, of course, some caveats in analyzing the potential impact of CAFTA-DR in light of Mexico's NAFTA experience. For example, isolating the effects of NAFTA on Mexico is complicated given the other significant external and policy shocks that have occurred over the past decade. Also, Mexico differs from the Central American countries in that it shares a common border with the United States and has a larger and more diverse economy and higher per capita GDP than all Central American countries except Costa Rica (Table 2.2). Moreover, there have been some differences in the evolution of U.S. trade relations with Mexico and with the Central American countries. For example, the Central American countries have developed strong trade relations with the United States through their preferential access to the U.S. market under the CBI since 1983.[12] Before the advent of NAFTA, roughly 50 percent of Mexico's exports to the United States were duty free, whereas 80 percent of exports from Central America had duty-free access to the U.S. market in 2003.

Nevertheless, Mexico's experience under NAFTA provides some guidance in analyzing the potential implications of CAFTA-DR because of the common characteristics noted above. The following subsections analyze the evolution of trade, finance, and macroeconomic data of the CAFTA-DR members and Mexico covering the period 1980–2003. This period can be partitioned into three segments: 1980–93 represents the pre-NAFTA period; 1994–2003 is the NAFTA period; and 1996–2003 is the period following Mexico's peso crisis. This demarcation is useful because it helps isolate the impact of Mexico's peso crisis when analyzing Mexico's experience with NAFTA before and after its implementation.

Dynamics of Trade Flows

The United States is already the most important trading partner for Central America. In contrast, and counting the European Union as a single market, CAFTA-DR was only the United States' thirteenth-largest export market in 2003. However, within Latin America, Central America is the United States' second largest trading partner behind Mexico, as measured by the dollar value of U.S. trade in 2003. Imports from the Central American countries constituted less than 1.4 percent of total U.S. imports in 2003. Therefore, although the impact of CAFTA-DR

---

[10]There has been intensive debate about the relative costs and benefits of capital controls. Birdsall (2003) examines the implications of limiting the use of capital controls in the context of the U.S.-Chile FTA. Birdsall concludes that this could be viewed as a bad precedent for future preferential trade agreements since there is scope for limited market intervention even in financially developed markets during periods of crises. Forbes (2004) argues that the costs of blocking capital market integration are much greater than generally realized, because such controls could make it very difficult for small firms to obtain financing for productive investment. Rogoff (2002) provides a summary of various views about the costs and benefits of capital controls. In the case of CAFTA-DR, further research is necessary to understand the implications of the provisions on transfers and capital controls, including an assessment of adequacy of prudential exemptions in the financial services chapter of the agreement (see Section VI).

[11]Kose, Meredith, and Towe (2005) provide a review of NAFTA's impact on the Mexican economy.

[12]One could also argue that the macroeconomic implications of CAFTA-DR should be less extensive than those of NAFTA, since Central American countries have already reacted to NAFTA and undertaken some economic and institutional reforms to be able to compete with Mexico in the U.S. market during the past 10 years.

Table 2.2. Selected Economic Indicators: Central America and Mexico, 2004

	Costa Rica	Dominican Republic	El Salvador	Guatemala	Honduras	Nicaragua	Mexico
GDP (billions of U.S. dollars)	18.4	18.4	15.8	26.1	7.4	4.6	676.5
GDP growth (percent)[1]	4.2	2.0	1.5	2.7	4.6	5.2	4.4
GDP per capita (at PPP)	9,886.6	6,761.0	4,378.9	4,008.7	2,682.2	2,677.1	9,666.3
Inflation (percent)	13.1	28.9	5.5	9.2	9.2	9.3	5.2
Current account balance (percent of GDP)	−4.8	5.8	−4.4	−4.3	−5.2	−18.3	−1.3
Human development index (HDI) rank[2]	45.0	98.0	103.0	121.0	115.0	118.0	53.0

Sources: IMF, *World Economic Outlook*; and United Nations, *Human Development Report* (2004).

[1]Average annual percent growth.

[2]HDI is a composite measure (education, income, and life expectancy) of average achievement in human development. A lower ranking is better: for example, United States (7), Italy (21), and South Korea (30). The 2004 report reflects data for the year 2002.

on Central America could be substantial, its overall effect on the U.S. economy is likely to be limited.[13]

Central America has historically been very open, even more so than Mexico. Moreover, some of the Central American countries experienced a surge in international trade during the past 10 years (Figure 2.1). For example, the average share of trade (merchandise exports and imports) was more than 75 percent of GDP in Central America during 1994–2003, compared with about 55 percent in Mexico. While Central America has been quite open, with an average openness ratio of roughly 60 percent during 1980–2003, there has been some variation across countries. For example, from 1980 to 2003, the average openness ratio was less than 50 percent in El Salvador and Guatemala, but above 75 percent in Honduras and Nicaragua.

Since the launching of NAFTA, Mexico's trade with the United States has increased substantially. For example, Mexico's trade with the United States more than doubled in dollar terms between 1993 and 2003, while the share of trade in Mexico's GDP rose from less than 40 percent in the 1980–93 period to 58 percent during the NAFTA period (Figure 2.2).[14]

After the start of NAFTA, exports to (imports from) the United States as a percent of GDP increased to about 23 (21) percent from 7 percent during the 1980–93 period (Figures 2.3 and 2.4).

Several studies find that NAFTA contributed to the impressive growth of trade between Mexico and the United States. Some of these studies employ gravity models (Krueger, 1999, 2000), whereas others use export and import demand equations to analyze the impact of NAFTA on trade dynamics using aggregate trade data (CBO, 2003).[15] These studies conclude that the effect of NAFTA on trade linkages was substantial. Other studies using sectoral data series also find a more significant impact of NAFTA on trade flows (Romalis, 2002) than those employing aggregate trade data.[16]

Trade linkages between the United States and Central America have grown rapidly over the past decade. As a group, Central American countries'

[13]For extensive discussions about the impact of the agreement on the U.S. economy, see Hornbeck (2004). The U.S. International Trade Commission (USITC, 2004; and USTR, 2005a) estimates that the impact of the agreement on U.S. GDP will be less than 0.01 percent.

[14]Following the strong performance in the late 1990s, Mexico's trade with the United States began to fall off during the period 2000–03 (Figure 2.2). This appears to reflect a combination of both cyclical and structural factors. The U.S. economy has grown less rapidly in recent years than in the second half of the 1990s, especially in the industrial sector, which is the destination for most of Mexico's exports. In addition, Mexico has faced increased competition from other emerging market economies. In particular, China has been rapidly expanding its market share in

the United States, and some of the lower value-added segments of Mexico's export sector, such as textiles, have shifted production to elsewhere in the region, including Central America. The real appreciation of the peso in the late 1990s may also have affected Mexico's competitiveness, although this effect would be expected to unwind given the subsequent downward adjustment.

[15]Krueger (1999, 2000) points out that NAFTA was not trade diverting, since the categories in which Mexican exports to the United States registered the largest increase for the period 1990–96 overlapped with those in which they rose most rapidly with the rest of the world.

[16]Other studies use general equilibrium models to analyze the impact of NAFTA on the dynamics of trade and economic growth. Studies employing static computable general equilibrium (CGE) models estimate NAFTA's long-run impact on Mexico's exports to the United States at between 3 and 16 percent (CBO, 2003). In dynamic versions of these models, the impact of NAFTA on trade flows is found to be larger. For example, using a dynamic CGE model, Kouparitsas (1997) finds that the increase in Mexico's trade flows associated with NAFTA is about 20 percent.

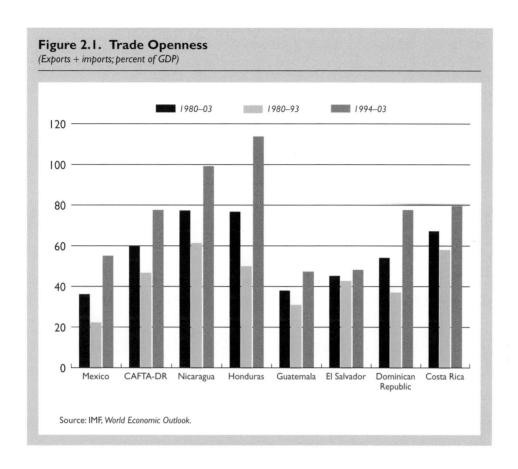

Figure 2.1. Trade Openness
(Exports + imports; percent of GDP)

Source: IMF, *World Economic Outlook.*

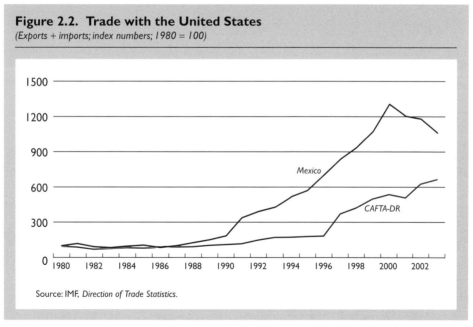

Figure 2.2. Trade with the United States
(Exports + imports; index numbers; 1980 = 100)

Source: IMF, *Direction of Trade Statistics.*

trade with the United States increased fivefold in dollar terms in the period 1994–2003. However, the extent of trade linkages with the United States differed substantially across the respective countries. Between 1994 and 2003, Honduras sent more than 55 percent of its total exports to the United States;

Figure 2.3. Exports to the United States
(Share of GDP; percent)

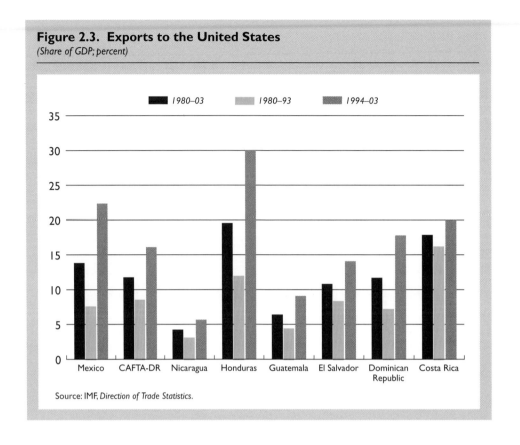

Source: IMF, *Direction of Trade Statistics.*

Figure 2.4. Imports from the United States
(Percent of GDP)

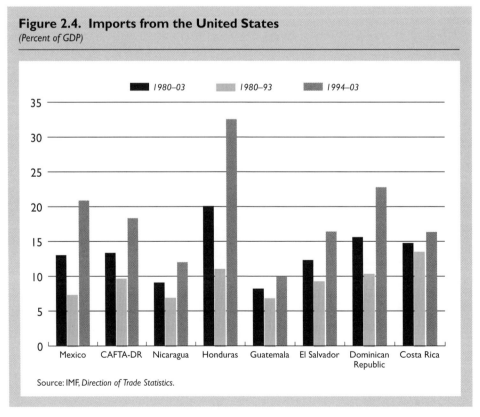

Source: IMF, *Direction of Trade Statistics.*

Table 2.3. Growth of Exports and Imports
(Average, in percent)

	Mexico	Emerging Markets	CAFTA-DR Average	Costa Rica	Dominican Republic	El Salvador	Guatemala	Honduras	Nicaragua
Exports									
1980–2003	9.35	7.72	3.90	9.33	3.93	4.55	3.42	1.09	4.69
1980–93	7.56	7.98	1.77	11.20	3.69	−0.18	3.22	−0.22	−0.01
1994–2003	11.67	7.38	6.67	7.83	4.24	10.72	3.61	2.80	10.80
1996–2003	8.58	6.13	5.72	7.92	3.73	10.48	2.52	2.60	7.07
Imports									
1980–2003	8.10	6.31	4.08	8.29	2.83	6.18	6.89	1.60	3.25
1980–93	6.42	6.75	2.41	12.04	1.55	4.34	7.23	0.34	−1.39
1994–2003	10.28	5.75	6.24	5.28	4.49	8.58	6.55	3.25	9.29
1996–2003	12.07	3.06	5.03	5.59	4.71	6.19	6.62	3.56	3.52

Sources: IMF, *World Economic Outlook*; and IMF staff calculations.

the corresponding figure for Costa Rica was 27 percent. The Dominican Republic commanded the largest share of the region's exports to the United States, accounting for more than 25 percent of the dollar value of exports in 2003; Nicaragua's share was the smallest, at less than 5 percent. The region's imports from the United States also increased substantially over the same period and, on average, accounted for more than 20 percent of GDP of the Central American countries during 1994–2003.

CAFTA-DR's Potential Impact on Trade Flows

Although both Mexico and the Central American countries have increased their trade linkages with the United States substantially during the NAFTA period, Mexico's trade with the United States grew much faster than Central America's. For example, the U.S. share in Mexico's exports rose from an annual average of 66 percent in 1980–93 to 86 percent during the period 1994–2003. The increase in the average export share of the Central American countries was less than 4 percentage points during the same period. Moreover, the average growth rate of total Mexican exports after the inception of NAFTA was roughly twice that of Central American exports (Table 2.3). Mexico's export growth rate was also much higher than the average growth rate of exports of several emerging market economies over the same period.[17]

Recent research suggests that trade flows between the United States and the Central American coun-

tries were not affected significantly by NAFTA. Since the United States has been the major trading partner for both Mexico and the Central American countries, Mexico's preferential treatment under NAFTA could have changed the dynamics of trade flows between the Central American countries and the United States. However, as documented by Lederman, Perry, and Suescún (2002), the extent of trade diversion from the Central American countries to Mexico was minimal after the inception of NAFTA. They argue that the Central American countries were effective in using the preferential access to the U.S. market under the CBI. They also find that NAFTA's rules-of-origin requirements limited Mexico's preferential access for sensitive export items of the Central American countries, such as apparel and textile products. Moreover, the liberalization programs implemented by the Central American countries during the 1990s were instrumental in boosting exports to the United States.[18]

Mexico's experience under NAFTA suggests that trade flows between the Central American countries and the United States could increase rapidly after the inception of CAFTA-DR.[19] Employing a multicountry computable general equilibrium (CGE) model, Hilaire and Yang (2003) find that the Central American countries' exports to the United States could increase by 28 percent after the inception of CAFTA-DR. This finding is consistent with

---

[17]The emerging market countries in the sample started undertaking trade and financial liberalization programs at about the same time Mexico did during the 1980s.

[18]Lederman, Maloney, and Serven (2003) also provide empirical evidence that NAFTA did not adversely affect trade flows between the Central American countries and the United States.

[19]These estimates do not take into account the possible impact of the expiry on January 1, 2005, of the world trade quotas of textiles and clothing. See also footnote 26.

Table 2.4. Top Eight U.S. Merchandise Imports from Central America, 2003
(In millions of U.S. dollars)

Product and HTS Number	Total	Costa Rica	Honduras	Guatemala	El Salvador	Nicaragua	Dominican Republic
Total U.S. imports	16,862	3,362	3,312	2,945	2,019	769	4,455
Knit apparel (61)	5,595	309	1,887	1,076	1,318	147	858
Woven apparel (62)	3,629	282	680	686	403	337	1,241
Edible fruit and nuts (08)	1,022	519	150	337	1	15	...
Electrical machinery (85)	1,364	814	98	2	34	39	377
Optical/medical equipment (90)	939	480	0	9	0	0	450
Spices, coffee, tea (09)	453	126	26	216	45	40	...
Fish and seafood (03)	303	69	124	21	19	70	...
Mineral fuel, oil (27)	187	4	0	177	6	0	...
Other	3,370	759	347	421	193	121	1,529
Top eight imports as percent of total	83	71	90	83	89	81	82

Sources: U.S. Department of Commerce; Harmonized Tariff Schedule (HTS); and Hornbeck (2004).

Mexico's experience under NAFTA, since Mexico's exports to the United States also rose by more than 50 percent in dollar terms in less than two years after the inception of NAFTA. They also find that the main sources of the increase in CAFTA-DR's exports to the United States are textiles, clothing, and processed crops.[20]

CAFTA-DR also could lead to an increase in trade flows through its impact on productivity and specialization patterns. Because the agreement includes various provisions about the flows of investment, financial services, and intellectual property, these gains could be substantial. Kehoe (2003) argues that static CGE models severely underestimated the impact of NAFTA on the volume of regional trade, because these models were unable to account for much of the increase in sectoral trade flows. Yet another potential problem associated with these models is that they do not capture the effects of productivity changes associated with trade agreements and they do not allow endogenous changes in specialization patterns. Thus, static CGE models, such as those used in Hilaire and Yang (2003), might show that the largest increase in trade would take place in those sectors that already have intensive trade linkages, though in fact the opposite could be true, as in the case of NAFTA.[21] Overall, these findings imply that CAFTA-DR's positive effect on trade flows between the Central American countries and the United States could be larger than suggested by the static CGE models.

CAFTA-DR's Potential Impact on the Composition of Trade

The Central American countries' major exports to the United States include agricultural products (bananas and coffee), apparel, and electrical machinery. The shares of coffee and bananas in total exports declined during the past decade and stood at about 6 percent and 3 percent, respectively, in 2003. However, apparel remained the main export item for all countries except Costa Rica (Table 2.4). The Dominican Republic, El Salvador, and Honduras accounted for almost 75 percent of the Central American countries' total apparel exports to the United States. The preferential market access provided by the CBI program played an important role in the rapid growth of apparel exports.

Roughly 60 percent of total exports of electrical machinery from the Central American countries to the United States was produced in Costa Rica, which has been able to attract sizable FDI flows to build plants for the production of computer parts in the past three years. The Central American countries' major

---

[20]Using a CGE model, USITC (2004) estimates that U.S. imports from the region will increase by 12.5 percent after the advent of CAFTA-DR. Brown, Kiyota, and Stern (2005) also use a CGE model to analyze the implications of CAFTA-DR. They find that production in textiles, wearing apparel, and leather products and footwear industries would increase substantially in Central American countries after the agreement because of their comparative advantage in these sectors.

[21]Kehoe and Ruhl (2003) document that the trade share of least-traded goods before NAFTA has almost tripled following the inception of NAFTA.

Table 2.5. Top Eight U.S. Merchandise Exports to Central America, 2003
(In millions of U.S. dollars)

Product and HTS Number	Total	Costa Rica	Honduras	Guatemala	El Salvador	Nicaragua	Dominican Republic
Total U.S. exports	15,074	3,414	2,845	2,274	1,824	503	4,214
Electrical machinery (85)	2,091	1,237	84	177	111	51	431
Knit apparel (61)	1,166	103	423	36	252	8	344
Machinery (84)	1,206	307	224	220	195	48	212
Knit/crocheted fabric (60)	664	34	340	16	266	8	...
Plastic (39)	817	256	81	147	79	11	243
Cotton yarn (52)	818	13	307	165	74	11	248
Woven apparel (62)	736	141	254	37	33	36	235
Cereals (10)	447	109	77	107	104	50	...
Other	7,129	1,214	1,055	1,369	710	280	2,501
Top eight exports as percent of total	54	64	63	40	61	44	54

Sources: U.S. Department of Commerce; Harmonized Tariff Schedule (HTS); and Hornbeck (2004).

Table 2.6. Diversification of Exports
(Average, in percent of total)

	Mexico	Emerging Markets	CAFTA-DR Average	Costa Rica	Dominican Republic	El Salvador	Guatemala	Honduras	Nicaragua
Manufacturing									
1980–2001	53.3	44.9	28.0	32.9	43.3	37.9	27.7	14.1	11.8
1980–93	37.1	38.9	24.2	25.4	43.6	33.5	25.1	8.6	9.2
1994–2001	81.6	55.5	34.4	46.1	42.6	45.4	32.2	23.8	16.2
Agriculture and food									
1980–2001	10.1	32.5	66.8	62.7	44.0	57.3	68.8	82.1	86.1
1980–93	11.9	35.7	72.4	69.3	55.4	62.3	71.9	86.9	88.6
1994–2001	7.0	26.8	55.7	51.0	15.6	48.5	63.5	73.6	81.9
Fuel and ores									
1980–2001	36.5	20.2	2.7	1.6	0.7	4.7	3.5	3.7	1.8
1980–93	50.9	22.6	2.7	1.7	0.9	4.1	3.0	4.4	2.0
1994–2001	11.2	15.8	2.6	1.5	0.2	5.7	4.3	2.4	1.6

Sources: World Development Indicators; and IMF staff calculations.

import items from the United States included electrical machinery, apparel, and fabric (Table 2.5).

Mexico's export base shifted toward manufactured goods following NAFTA's introduction. Although the share of manufactures in total exports had been increasing since at least 1980, the pace of diversification accelerated after the inception of NAFTA (Table 2.6). As a result, Mexico's export and import bases have become among the most diversified of emerging market economies. After the incep-

tion of NAFTA, vertical specialization has increased, with member countries increasingly specializing in particular stages of the production process. The prime example of this change has been the *maquiladora* trade along Mexico's northern border, where firms import inputs from the United States, process them, and re-export products back to the United States. *Maquiladora* firms often specialize in the manufacture of electronics, auto parts, and apparel. The growth of the *maquiladora* industry

Table 2.7. Gross Foreign Direct Investment Flows

	Mexico	CAFTA-DR Average	Costa Rica	Dominican Republic	El Salvador	Guatemala	Honduras	Nicaragua
				(Fraction of GDP, in percent)				
Gross FDI flows								
1980–2003	1.9	2.2	2.5	2.4	1.1	1.2	1.6	8.2
1980–93	1.3	1.2	2.0	1.3	0.7	1.2	0.8	0.0
1994–2003	2.9	3.5	3.2	4.0	2.0	1.1	2.7	8.2
				(Fraction of fixed investment, in percent)				
Gross FDI flows								
1980–2003	10.1	9.2	12.9	10.7	6.8	8.0	7.2	9.7
1980–93	6.8	5.8	10.0	5.8	5.7	8.5	4.6	0.0
1994–2003	14.8	14.0	17.0	17.5	8.3	7.2	10.8	23.2

Sources: IMF, *World Economic Outlook*; and IMF staff calculations.

accelerated during the 1990s, as the average annual growth rate of real value added produced by the *maquiladora* sector was about 10 percent in the period 1990–2002, over three times the average growth rate of real GDP during the same period (Hanson, 2002). Intra-industry trade between Mexico and the United States also rose significantly as the share of intra-industry trade in Mexico's manufacturing sector rose from 62.5 percent in the period 1988–91 to 73.4 percent in 1996–2000 (OECD, 2002). Moreover, NAFTA boosted intrafirm trade and resulted in a substantial increase in the variety of products traded between Mexico and the United States (Hillberry and McDaniel, 2002).

During the period 1994–2001, the Central American countries substantially diversified their trade bases. For example, the share of manufacturing exports rose from less than 25 percent in 1980–93 to approximately 34 percent over the period 1994–2001. Costa Rica, El Salvador, Honduras, and Nicaragua significantly increased their manufacturing exports. However, agricultural and food products still accounted for almost 60 percent of total exports during the period 1994–2001. Moreover, the extent of diversification was much lower in the Central American countries than in Mexico. During the period 1994–2001, the average share of manufactured exports of the Central American economies was less than half that of Mexico.

Mexico's experience under NAFTA suggests that CAFTA-DR could further accelerate diversification of Central America's trade base. There was a major change in the nature of goods exported from Mexico to the United States as these two countries developed stronger trade linkages during the past two decades. As discussed above, NAFTA was instru-

mental in the rapid growth of intra-industry and vertical trade between Mexico and the United States in the past 10 years. Compared with Mexico, the extent of the Central American countries' intra-industry trade with the United States—except Costa Rica's—has been much smaller. However, the Central American countries have recently begun expanding the scope of both vertical and intra-industry trade. For example, most of their imports of electrical machinery and apparel from the United States have been used as intermediate inputs in the production of other goods that have been re-exported back to the United States.[22]

Foreign Direct Investment Flows

The Central American countries were able to increase FDI flows significantly in the period 1994–2003. In Costa Rica, the Dominican Republic, and Nicaragua, gross FDI flows relative to GDP were larger than in Mexico over the same period, although the dollar amount of these flows was much smaller than that received by Mexico, given the larger size of the Mexican economy (Table 2.7). However, these flows were significant relative to

---

[22]Intra-industry trade within Central American countries is greater than between the Central American countries and the United States. However, there has been a change in recent years as intra-industry trade involving, in particular, apparel and electronic components has risen substantially. For example, apparel exports from the region to the United States have been increasing rapidly during the past 10 years. Costa Rica has been able to increase its exports of electronic components and to expand the scope of intra-industry trade because of U.S. investment in the production of electronic components and medical equipment (Taccone and Nogueira, 2004).

Table 2.8. Foreign Direct Investment Inflows from the United States
(In millions of U.S. dollars)

	1999	2000	2001	2002
Mexico	37,151	39,352	56,554	58,074
Costa Rica	1,493	1,716	1,677	1,602
Dominican Republic	968	1,143	1,233	1,123
El Salvador	621	540	361	580
Guatemala	478	835	389	391
Honduras	347	399	242	184
Nicaragua	119	140	157	242
Total CAFTA-DR countries	4,026	4,773	4,059	4,122

Source: U.S. Department of Commerce, Bureau of Economic Analysis.
Note: Data reflect stock of FDI historical-cost basis (Hornbeck, 2004).

total domestic investment, representing about 14 percent of domestic investment on average. The United States is the largest source of FDI flows to each Central American economy. About one-third of FDI flows from the United States went to Costa Rica between 1999 and 2002 (Table 2.8), and about one-fourth went to the Dominican Republic.

FDI flows between Mexico and its partners strengthened after NAFTA. The agreement contained various provisions that improved the relative standing of investors from the partner countries in Mexico and expanded the sectors in which they could operate. These changes helped boost FDI flows to Mexico from US$12 billion during 1991–93 to roughly US$54 billion in the period 2000–02. The share of FDI flows in domestic gross fixed capital formation (investment) also increased from 6 percent in 1993 to 11 percent in 2002, mainly as a result of inflows from Mexico's NAFTA partners.

CAFTA-DR is likely to boost FDI flows to the Central American countries, as NAFTA did in the case of Mexico. Recent research suggests that NAFTA membership significantly affected the volume of FDI flows to Mexico. For example, Cuevas, Messmacher, and Werner (2002a) and Waldkirch (2003) show that NAFTA led to a significant increase in FDI flows to Mexico. The latter study argues that NAFTA's impact on FDI flows to Mexico was the result of increased vertical specialization as well as the agreement's effect on Mexico's commitment to liberalization and reform programs. As NAFTA did, CAFTA-DR could serve as a commitment device and encourage FDI flows while inducing a change in the nature of trade flows in favor of vertical trade. CAFTA-DR could also help attract foreign multinational corporations to the Central American countries, as Mexico's NAFTA experience proved (see Blomström and Kokko, 1997).[23]

CAFTA-DR could, however, encourage suboptimal policymaking in efforts to encourage FDI inflows. The individual Central American countries could be inclined to offer tax incentives to attract FDI flows and by doing so induce a "race to the bottom." To limit this risk, policy coordination might be warranted (see Section III on taxation and the fiscal implications of CAFTA-DR).

Implications for Economic Growth and Welfare

How would CAFTA-DR affect the long-run growth prospects of Central America? The theoretical impact of regional trade agreements on economic growth and welfare is somewhat ambiguous, since it depends on various factors, including changes in trade volume and terms of trade after the advent of such agreements.[24] However, various theoretical models emphasize the importance of trade openness

---

[23]Cuevas, Messmacher, and Werner (2002a) employ panel regressions and find that Mexico's participation in NAFTA led to roughly a 70 percent increase in FDI flows. Waldkirch (2003) concludes that NAFTA induced a 40 percent increase in the volume of FDI flows. Blomström and Kokko (1997) conclude that foreign multinationals increased their investment in Mexico in response to NAFTA as well as to the relaxation of various barriers on FDI flows since the mid-1980s.

[24]Baldwin and Venables (1995) provide a survey of theoretical studies on the growth and welfare implications of regional trade agreements.

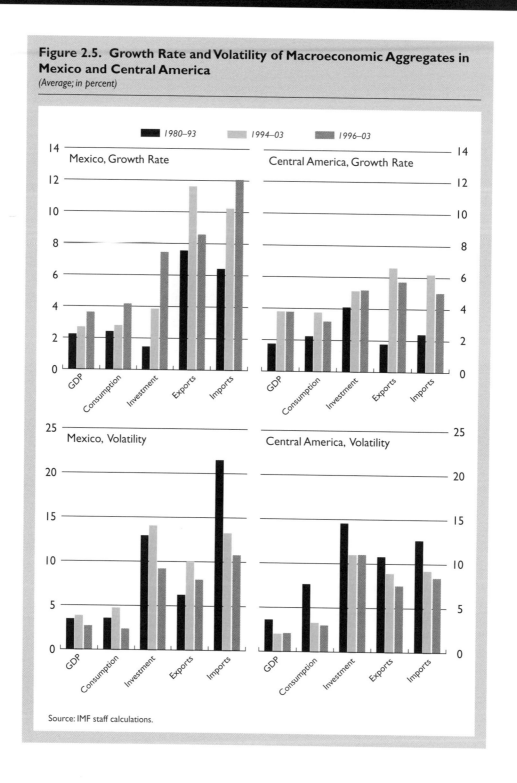

Figure 2.5. Growth Rate and Volatility of Macroeconomic Aggregates in Mexico and Central America
(Average; in percent)

Source: IMF staff calculations.

in promoting economic growth. Some of these models focus on static gains, including the gains derived from increased specialization. Others consider knowledge spillovers associated with international trade as an engine of growth (Grossman and Helpman, 1991).

Several empirical studies suggest that trade openness has a direct and positive effect on economic growth (Sachs and Warner, 1995; Frankel and Romer, 1999; and Dollar and Kraay, 2004). Some other studies focus on the positive effect of increased trade linkages on productivity (USITC, 2004) and on investment growth (Levine and Renelt, 1992; and Baldwin and Seghezza, 1996). Rodrik and Rodriguez (2000), however, present a critical review of some of these empirical studies.[25]

There are various direct and indirect channels through which increased financial flows can enhance growth in developing countries. While direct channels include augmentation of domestic savings, reduction in the cost of capital through better global allocation of risk, development of the domestic financial sector (Levine, 1996), and transfer of technological know-how, indirect channels are associated with promotion of specialization and inducement for better economic policies (Gourinchas and Jeanne, 2004).

However, recent empirical research has been unable to establish a clear link between financial integration and economic growth. Prasad and others (2003) review several empirical studies and conclude that the majority of the studies find financial integration has no effect or a mixed effect on economic growth. For example, Edison and others (2002) employ a regression model that controls for the possible reverse causality—that is, the possibility that any observed association between financial integration and growth could result from the mechanism that faster-growing economies are also more likely to liberalize their capital accounts. They conclude that there is no robust, significant effect of financial integration on economic growth. However, some other studies (Borenzstein, De Gregorio, and Lee, 1998) find that FDI flows (rather than other capital movements) tend to be positively associated with investment and output growth.

Mexico's growth performance improved after the inception of NAFTA. Compared with several other emerging market countries, the Mexican economy performed well since NAFTA's implementation and, in particular, after the 1995 crisis (Figure 2.5). Moreover, the average growth rate of investment was particularly impressive, as it rose almost eightfold during the period 1996–2003 (Table 2.9).

As pointed out in Section I, the average growth rate of the Central American countries increased notably during the period 1994–2003. In particular, the average growth rate of GDP more than doubled over this period, with all countries, except Honduras, recording significant increases in their growth rates (Figure 2.5). The average growth rate of investment also rose in the Central American countries, but it fell short of the increase in Mexico. Although El Salvador and Nicaragua were able to achieve much higher rates of investment growth, Costa Rica and Honduras witnessed a significant decline over the 1994–2003 period.

Mexico's experience under NAFTA suggests that CAFTA-DR could change the dynamics of economic growth in the Central American countries. The effects of exports and investment on growth in Mexico have changed after NAFTA's implementation, as their contributions to GDP growth have more than doubled following the introduction of the agreement (Table 2.10). For example, while the contribution of investment (exports) was about 0.4 (1.1) percentage points before NAFTA, it went up to 1.4 (2.6) percentage points during the period 1996–2003. A similar change in the roles of investment and exports took place in Central America over the period 1994–2003, although their contribution to growth is still lower in the Central American countries than in Mexico.

CAFTA-DR could generate various growth benefits to the Central American countries, as NAFTA did in the case of Mexico. Hilaire and Yang (2003) use a CGE model to examine the growth benefits of CAFTA-DR and conclude that GDP of the Central American countries could increase by as much as 1.5 percent as a result of the agreement.[26] This finding is in the range of the estimates produced by various studies using similar models to analyze the impact of NAFTA on the Mexican economy.[27] Hilaire and

---

[25]Berg and Krueger (2003), Baldwin (2003), and Winters (2004) provide extensive surveys of the literature on trade and growth. Winters (p. F4) concludes that "while there are serious methodological challenges and disagreements about the strength of the evidence, the most plausible conclusion is that liberalization generally induces a temporary (but possibly long-lived) increase in growth." Harrison and Tang (2004) argue that "while trade integration can strengthen an effective growth strategy, it cannot ensure its effectiveness. Other elements are needed, such as sound macroeconomic management, building trade-related infrastructure, and trade-related institutions, economy-wide investments in human capital and infrastructure, or building strong institutions." Brown, Kiyota, and Stern (2005) use a different CGE model and estimate that the GNP of Central American countries could increase by 4.4 percent after the inception of CAFTA-DR.

[26]Hilaire and Yang use the Global Trade Analysis Project (GTAP) model for their simulations, which assume that the agreement is signed by the United States and five Central American countries, including Costa Rica, El Salvador, Guatemala, Honduras, and Nicaragua. Their findings indicate that the welfare effect of CAFTA-DR on the United States is also positive, although it is much smaller than the positive effect on the Central American countries. The agreement also increases global welfare as the gains from expanded sales of textiles, clothing, and processed crops offset potential losses associated with trade diversion. Hilaire and Yang also conduct some alternative simulations involving the global removal of quotas in textiles and clothing alongside the CAFTA-DR agreement. These alternatives reduce the growth of the Central American countries' exports to the United States, but CAFTA-DR still leads to a 1.1 percent increase in regional GDP.

[27]Baldwin and Venables (1995) provide a summary of the studies using CGE models to evaluate the impact of NAFTA. Some recent empirical studies also establish a positive association between NAFTA membership and Mexico's growth performance (Arora and Vamvakidis, 2005; CBO, 2003).

Table 2.9. Dynamics of Economic Growth
(Average, in percent)

	Mexico	Emerging Markets	CAFTA-DR Average	Costa Rica	Dominican Republic	El Salvador	Guatemala	Honduras	Nicaragua
GDP									
1980–2003	2.45	3.45	2.66	3.84	3.91	1.72	2.47	2.87	1.16
1980–93	2.24	3.67	1.75	3.47	2.80	0.50	1.66	3.05	−0.96
1994–2003	2.73	3.17	3.84	4.31	5.36	3.30	3.54	2.65	3.91
1996–2003	3.63	2.45	3.79	4.31	5.57	2.65	3.30	2.96	3.93
Consumption									
1980–2003	2.60	3.40	2.92	4.23	3.49	2.88	3.22	3.76	1.74
1980–93	2.42	3.57	2.25	5.27	1.90	2.22	2.71	4.74	0.09
1994–2003	2.84	3.18	3.80	3.40	5.57	3.73	3.73	2.48	3.88
1996–2003	4.17	2.35	3.20	2.98	5.37	2.60	3.40	2.43	2.39
Investment									
1980–2003	2.52	3.27	4.57	6.78	5.61	3.95	5.37	4.02	4.26
1980–93	1.46	4.28	4.10	9.11	5.62	3.75	5.40	6.37	−0.21
1994–2003	3.91	1.94	5.18	4.91	5.60	4.21	5.34	0.95	10.07
1996–2003	7.46	−0.11	5.19	5.54	8.06	1.85	5.91	3.00	6.77

Sources: IMF, *World Economic Outlook*; and IMF staff calculations.

Table 2.10. Contributions to GDP Growth
(Average, in percent)

	Mexico	CAFTA-DR Average	Costa Rica	Dominican Republic	El Salvador	Guatemala	Honduras	Nicaragua
Investment								
1980–2003	0.39	0.75	1.23	1.01	0.61	0.71	0.70	0.76
1980–93	0.16	0.58	1.68	0.92	0.55	0.67	1.12	−0.40
1994–2003	0.69	0.98	0.87	1.12	0.70	0.74	0.14	2.28
1996–2003	1.37	1.03	0.97	1.64	0.25	0.83	0.69	1.79
Consumption								
1980–2003	1.74	2.21	2.90	2.69	2.55	2.73	2.60	1.08
1980–93	1.63	1.56	3.49	1.42	2.02	2.26	3.33	−0.77
1994–2003	1.87	3.06	2.42	4.35	3.24	3.19	1.64	3.49
1996–2003	2.78	2.56	2.11	4.17	2.25	2.92	1.63	2.25
Exports								
1980–2003	1.87	1.15	3.41	1.35	0.82	0.59	0.37	1.59
1980–93	1.09	0.39	3.73	0.83	−0.45	0.53	−0.27	0.22
1994–2003	2.88	2.15	3.16	2.02	2.47	0.65	1.20	3.38
1996–2003	2.63	1.94	3.29	1.76	2.51	0.45	1.01	2.64

Sources: IMF, *World Economic Outlook*; and IMF staff calculations.

Yang (2003) also find that if the agreement excludes agricultural sector liberalization, the growth effect associated with CAFTA-DR drops to 1.1 percent of GDP of the Central American countries.

CAFTA-DR's impact on economic growth could be larger than estimated by the static CGE models. As previously discussed, these models are unable to account for various dynamic effects associated with accumulation of capital, changes in specialization patterns, and stronger productivity spillovers. Though the growth impact associated with NAFTA is estimated to be about 2 percent in static models, it is more than 3 percent in dynamic models.[28] CAFTA-DR has extensive provisions involving services and investment flows. However, the static models, including the one employed by Hilaire and Yang (2003), do not incorporate the effects of such provisions, which could lead to potentially large changes in the flows of services and investment.[29]

Moreover, Mexico's experience under NAFTA suggests that CAFTA-DR could have a positive effect on productivity growth and institutional quality in Central America. Recent research shows that NAFTA contributed to total factor productivity in Mexico and accelerated economic convergence in the region. For example, Lopez-Cordova (2002), using plant-level data, finds that NAFTA raised total factor productivity by roughly 10 percent in Mexico over the sample period, partly in response to foreign capital inflows. Easterly, Fiess, and Lederman (2003) document that the speed of convergence of productivity among NAFTA partners accelerated after the implementation of NAFTA. Lopez-Cordova (2001) argues that the passage of NAFTA induced some institutional changes, among them a revamping of institutions in charge of competition policy, intellectual property protection, and standards.

Increased trade and financial integration associated with CAFTA-DR could reduce the adverse effects of macroeconomic instability (volatility) on economic growth. As documented by a growing literature, there is a negative relationship between volatility and growth (Ramey and Ramey, 1995). This implies that policies and exogenous shocks that affect volatility can also influence growth. Thus, even if volatility is considered intrinsically a second-order issue, its relationship with growth suggests that volatility could indirectly have first-order welfare implications. Highly volatile macroeconomic fluctuations have been a major impediment to sustained growth in Central America. Kose, Prasad, and Terrones (2005a, 2005b) document that increased trade and financial integration appear to diminish the negative impact of volatility on growth. Specifically, in regressions of growth on volatility and other con-

trol variables, they find that the estimated coefficients on interactions between volatility and trade integration are significantly positive. In other words, countries that are more open to trade appear to face a less severe tradeoff between growth and volatility. They also find a similar, although slightly less significant, result for the interaction of financial integration with volatility.[30]

The need to move forward with CAFTA-DR becomes more urgent given the rising competition from Asia, especially from China. Simulations based on the GTAP model suggest that the first round impact on exports and GDP could be sizable.[31] While the negative impact could be more moderate—given the proximity to the United States and deepening supply chain linkages—pressures are likely to rise. The recent decision by the United States to impose curbs on some categories of Chinese textile exports to the United States will give Central America some relief in the short term, allowing the region to implement CAFTA-DR.

The degree to which CAFTA-DR will lead to strong growth and improve the long-run growth potential of the region will depend critically on supporting policies. As Mexico's NAFTA experience shows, the Central American countries must undertake various structural reforms to sustain the potential benefits associated with CAFTA-DR. Although NAFTA has had a significant and favorable impact on exports and foreign direct investment flows, Mexico's growth performance could have been even stronger if structural reforms had been pursued more aggressively. The major lesson from Mexico's experience is that a trade agreement like CAFTA-DR should be used to accelerate, rather than postpone, needed structural reform.

In particular, the Central American countries need to employ policies to improve the quality of institutions, regulatory bodies, the rule of law, property rights, the flexibility of labor markets, and human capital infrastructure. Gruben (2005) argues that while the Central American countries have been able to liberalize their trade regimes during the past 10 years, they have lagged in undertaking the necessary

---

[28]Kouparitsas (1997) considers a dynamic general equilibrium model that captures the impact of NAFTA on investment flows in the region. He finds that the agreement increases Mexico's steady-state level of GDP by 3.3 percent, consumption by 2.5 percent, and investment by more than 5 percent.

[29]More importantly, CAFTA-DR could affect economic growth through its impact on the country risk premium of the Central American economies. This was the case in Mexico after the inception of NAFTA as documented by Manchester and McKibbin (1995).

[30]Kose, Prasad, and Terrones (2005a) document that during the 1990s, emerging markets had a similar level of output volatility, on average, to other developing economies but experienced much higher growth. Their findings indicate that the higher level of trade openness of emerging markets accounts for about half of the observed difference of about 2 percentage points in average growth rates between emerging markets and other developing economies. In other words, despite experiencing a similar level of volatility, emerging markets were able to post higher growth rates because of the greater degree of trade openness.

[31]The first-round static impact on GDP could range between 0.7 percent in the case of Guatemala and 4.7 percent in the case of Honduras.

structural reforms to improve various domestic policies, including those pertaining to financial systems,
labor markets, protection of property rights, transparency, regulatory frameworks, and importance of
the informal sector.[32] CAFTA-DR has the potential to
produce much larger benefits for the countries in the
region if the agreement is used effectively as an anchor to implement the necessary policy reforms (see
Salazar-Xirinachs and Granados, 2004).

There are some concerns about the potential effects of CAFTA-DR on fiscal balances in the region.
An immediate concern for the Central American
economies is the potential impact of CAFTA-DR on
their fiscal balances. Since a significant percentage
of the Central American economies' imports is
sourced from the United States, CAFTA-DR might
lead to a fall in customs revenue and deterioration of
the countries' fiscal positions. These issues are discussed in detail in Section III. Another concern is associated with the potential impact of the agreement
on poverty, which is discussed in the following.

Could CAFTA-DR Help Reduce Poverty in the Region?

Free trade agreements, like CAFTA-DR, could
have distributional implications involving various income groups. In particular, some argue that free trade
agreements could have an adverse impact on the poor-
est segments of the population since these agreements
could compress their employment opportunities and
wages (see Aisbett, 2005). Moreover, they claim that
these agreements could decrease government spending on the poor because of their potentially negative
effects on fiscal revenues. The following summarizes
the main issues about the potential impact of CAFTA-
DR on poverty in the region in light of recent empirical and theoretical studies.

Liberalization and Poverty: What Do We Know?

In theory, there are several channels through
which increased trade and financial flows could help
reduce poverty. As discussed earlier in the section,
some of these channels are related to growth-
enhancing effects of increased trade and financial

flows. For example, augmentation of domestic savings, reduction in the cost of capital, increase in productivity through transfer of technological know-
how, and stimulation of domestic financial sector
development could all provide direct growth benefits, which in turn help reduce poverty (see Agénor,
2002; Easterly, 2005, and Goldberg and Pavcnik,
2005). Trade liberalization could also translate into a
reduction in the prices of goods consumed by poor
households. Moreover, increased trade and financial
flows could help reduce macroeconomic volatility,
which also could have beneficial effects for the poor
(Aizenman and Pinto, 2005).

This is supported through some recent empirical
studies.[33] For example, research by Dollar and
Kraay (2002, 2003) suggests that increased trade
flows are associated with higher economic growth.[34]
Kraay (2004) provides strong evidence for the importance of economic growth in poverty reduction as
his analysis shows that most of the variation in
changes in poverty during the 1980s and 1990s is explained by growth in average income in developing
countries.[35] Agénor (2002) finds that there is a non-

---

[32]Gruben (2005) compares the extent of trade openness with an
index of market orientation that measures the degree of market
openness in eight nontrade domestic policy categories: fiscal policy and fiscal balance, government intervention in the economy,
monetary policy (with its inflationary implications), banking policy, flexibility of wages and prices, protection of property rights,
transparency and simplicity of regulation, and importance of the
informal sector versus the formal taxpaying sector.

[33]Since it is difficult to measure poverty and isolate the impact
of trade and financial flows on poverty from various other factors,
recent studies do not reach an unambiguous conclusion on this
issue. While Easterly (2005) documents that neither financial nor
trade flows have any significant impact on poverty, Harrison
(2005, p. 15) notes that "there is certainly no evidence in the aggregate data that trade reforms are bad for the poor." Winters,
McCulloch, and McKay (2004, p. 105) also argue that the empirical evidence often suggests that trade liberalization helps reduce
poverty in the long run and note that "it lends no support to the position that trade liberalization generally has an adverse impact."

[34]Although there has been an intensive debate about the potentially adverse impact of increased trade and financial flows associated with globalization on income inequality, there is no clear
empirical evidence that globalization has fostered a sharp rise in
worldwide inequality. Several recent studies focus on the impact
of globalization on income inequality across countries, but these
studies have yet to provide a conclusive answer. For example,
globalization could accentuate the already substantial inequality
of national incomes and, in particular, lead to stagnation of incomes and living standards in countries that do not participate in
this process. Consistent with this view, Quah (1997) has documented that there is evidence in cross-country data of a "twin
peaks" phenomenon whereby per capita incomes converge within
each of two groups of countries (advanced countries and globalizers) while average incomes continue to diverge across these two
groups of countries. In other words, advanced countries and globalizers converge in terms of per capita incomes and so do non-
globalizers, but these two groups diverge from each other in terms
of their average incomes. Sala-i-Martin (2002), on the other hand,
argues that a more careful analysis, using individuals rather than
countries as the units of analysis, shows that global inequality has
declined during the recent wave of globalization.

[35]Some researchers argue that there are severe data and measurement problems involving poverty series and suggest alternative
tests to analyze the impact of trade liberalization. For example, Wei
and Wu (2002) find that tariff reductions could lead to a significant
increase in life expectancy and reduction in infant mortality.

linear relationship between increased trade and financial flows and poverty. His empirical results indicate that while these flows could reduce poverty in countries that have a higher degree of integration with the global economy, they could have an adverse impact on the income levels of the poor in countries with a lower degree of integration.[36]

Mexico's experience during the 1990s also suggests that increased trade and financial flows could be beneficial to the poor. For example, while Hanson (2005) documents that poverty increased in Mexico during the 1990s, in part owing to the 1995 peso crisis, income in states that were more open to trade and financial flows increased relative to those that were less open. Moreover, the increase in poverty was only marginal in states that were more exposed to trade and financial flows while it was much higher in those with limited integration with the global economy. Some other country case studies, including those on China, India, and Poland, also suggest that trade liberalization could have poverty alleviating effects (Harrison, 2005).

Some studies emphasize the importance of complementary policies to help increase the benefits of trade and financial integration for the poor. In particular, policies encouraging labor mobility, improving access to credit and technical know-how, and establishing social safety nets seem to increase the benefits of increased integration for the poor. Trade liberalization could lead to contraction in some previously protected industries. Policies that could help workers move from such sectors to sectors that are expanding could diminish the adverse effects of trade liberalization on the poor in the short run while also contributing to poverty reduction in the long run.

Poverty in Central America and CAFTA-DR

Poverty, as pointed out in Section I, is a major problem in some Central American countries (except Costa Rica). The poverty rate is about 80 percent in Honduras, and about 50 percent in El Salvador, Guatemala, and Nicaragua. Heavy dependence on agriculture appears to accentuate the poverty problem in some Central American countries. For example, agricultural production accounts for roughly 25 percent of GDP in Guatemala and more than 30 percent in Nicaragua.

Some argue that CAFTA-DR could have a negative impact on the poor in the region. They note that by eliminating tariffs on agricultural goods, the agreement opens the small markets of Central American economies to relatively cheaper agricultural exports from the United States (see Oxfam, 2004). They suggest that severe dislocation problems could arise since workers in the agricultural sector, especially poor subsistence farmers, could lose their jobs. They also point out that this could further exacerbate the poverty problem in the region, with consequences for the dynamics of income distribution.

To provide the necessary relief for the vulnerable segments of the population, the CAFTA-DR agreement includes prolonged tariff phase-out and safeguard schedules to all countries with sensitive agricultural products.[37] For example, tariffs and quotas on various agricultural imports from the United States, including pork, beef, poultry, rice, and yellow corn, will be phased out over a 15-year period. Rice and dairy products are subject to longer transition periods (18 to 20 years). All agricultural trade would eventually become duty free except for sugar imported by the United States, fresh potatoes and onions imported by Costa Rica, and white corn imported by the other Central American countries.[38]

Moreover, CAFTA-DR could be beneficial to the poor in the region by improving growth prospects while contributing macroeconomic stability. Sustained economic growth appears to be highly correlated with poverty reduction, and CAFTA-DR has the potential to increase growth in the region. In addition, as discussed later in section, CAFTA-DR could reduce macroeconomic volatility, which has a significantly negative and causal impact on poverty (Laursen and Mahajan, 2005).

Complementary policies should be in place to maximize the benefits of CAFTA-DR for the poor. In particular, policies are needed to strengthen social safety nets and help poorer households take advantage of the benefits of CAFTA-DR. Since their dependence on agriculture varies, the Central American countries could utilize specific policies to ease

---

[36]Agénor (2002) uses a weighted average of trade and financial openness indicators as a measure of economic integration. The nonlinearity stems from the fact that trade and financial integration have a sizable impact on the quality of institutions only beyond a certain level of trade, and financial integration and institutions (including an efficient social safety net) play a major role in channeling the beneficial effects of globalization to the poor and shielding them from its costs.

[37]Tariffs on more than half of U.S. agricultural exports would be eliminated immediately but the rest are subject to phaseout periods of up to 20 years. For some agricultural products, changes in tariff schedules would be effective only after 7–12 years.

[38]Mason (2005) documents the effects of lifting tariffs on sensitive agricultural products on the poor in Nicaragua, Guatemala, and El Salvador using a net consumer-net producer approach, which helps isolate the first-order effects of such policy changes on welfare. His findings indicate that reduction of barriers could lead to welfare gains for a significant majority of households in these countries because of the reduction in prices, while producers of the sensitive agricultural products could experience welfare losses.

the transition process of workers in the agricultural sector to export-oriented manufacturing and services industries. In addition to providing the necessary infrastructure for labor mobility across sectors, improving access to credit, including microcredit, could also help in this transition.

CAFTA-DR's Potential Impact on Macroeconomic Volatility and the Co-Movement of Business Cycles

Increased trade and financial flows between the Central American economies and the United States as a result of CAFTA-DR could affect macroeconomic volatility and co-movement of business cycles in the region. Though the Central American economies have been successful in regaining macroeconomic stability over the past decade, they have continued to face substantial shocks. Against this background, the following analyzes how the nature of business cycle fluctuations in the region might change after the inception of CAFTA-DR.

Macroeconomic Volatility

The theoretical impact of increased trade and financial flows on output volatility depends on a number of factors, including the nature of financial flows, patterns of specialization, and sources of shocks. For example, increased trade openness, if associated with further *interindustry* specialization across countries and if *industry-specific* shocks are important in driving business cycles, could lead to an increase in output volatility. However, if increased trade is associated with increased *intra-industry* specialization across countries, which leads to a larger volume of intermediate inputs trade, then the volatility of output could decline. In addition, economic theory suggests that increased access to international financial markets should dampen the volatility of consumption while inducing an increase in investment volatility (Kose, Prasad, and Terrones, 2003a).

Recent empirical studies are unable to establish a clear link between stronger economic linkages and macroeconomic volatility. Although some of these studies find no significant relationship between the increased degree of economic interdependence and domestic macroeconomic volatility (Buch, Dopke, and Pierdzioch, 2005), others find that an increase in the degree of trade openness leads to higher output volatility, especially in developing countries (Easterly, Islam, and Stiglitz, 2001). Kose, Prasad, and Terrones (2003a) find that while trade openness increases the volatility of output, income, and consumption in emerging market economies, it reduces the relative volatility of consumption to output, implying that it improves the consumption risk–sharing possibilities. They also document that increased financial integration is associated with rising relative volatility of consumption, but only up to a certain threshold.

Macroeconomic volatility declined in Mexico after the inception of NAFTA. This can be seen in the uniform decline in the variance of several macroeconomic aggregates between the pre-NAFTA period (1980–93) and the post-crisis period (1996–2003) (Figure 2.5).[39] In particular, output volatility decreased by 20 percent and investment volatility fell by more than 40 percent in the latter period. Consistent with theoretical predictions, increased trade and financial linkages also led to a reduction in the volatility of consumption in Mexico. In addition, consumption became slightly less volatile than output during the 1996–2003 period. This, along with the increased cross-country consumption correlations (documented below), suggests that Mexico became better able to share macroeconomic risk with the United States through increased trade and financial linkages.

The decreased volatility of the Mexican economy during the past 10 years could be the result of several factors, including, in particular, NAFTA and the policy regime changes that Mexico enacted. However, the decrease in volatility could be the result of NAFTA's effect on intra-industry and vertical trade rather than the result of increased stability of domestic macroeconomic policies stemming from the implementation of sound monetary and fiscal policies over the period 1996–2001 (Cuevas, Messmacher, and Werner, 2002a). Both the theory reviewed earlier and the available evidence of the increased importance of regional and external shocks in driving the Mexican business cycles (Kose, Meredith, and Towe, 2005) suggest that this might be the case.

Reflecting in part the success of pursuing sound macroeconomic policies, the volatility of macroeconomic variables decreased in the Central America economies during the past 10 years (Figure 2.5). In particular, there was a significant decrease in the volatility of output fluctuations in El Salvador, Guatemala, and Nicaragua. Both consumption and investment volatility declined in Central America during the period 1996–2003. Although volatility of consumption in Nicaragua and the Dominican Republic declined from 18 percent to less than 7 percent, it was still high in these two countries relative to the rest of Central America. In all countries except

---

[39]Table 2.A1 in Appendix II presents the volatility of macroeconomic aggregates in detail. Volatility is measured as the standard deviation of the annual growth rate. Since only a limited number of annual date series are available, standard errors associated with volatility statistics are not reported.

Costa Rica, there was a moderation in the size of business cycle fluctuations in exports and imports.

Output volatility in Central America was lower than that of Mexico during the period 1994–2003. However, consumption and investment in those countries exhibited higher volatility than in Mexico over the same period. In addition, during the period 1996–2003, consumption fluctuations were more volatile than those of output in Central America, whereas the volatility of consumption was slightly below that of output in Mexico.

The NAFTA experience suggests that CAFTA-DR could help reduce output volatility in Central America. CAFTA-DR could further reduce volatility by accelerating the diversification of the export base and by fostering intra-industry and vertical trade linkages with the United States. After the inception of CAFTA-DR, shocks originating in the United States could play a more prominent role in Central America, as documented below. Given the stability of the U.S. economy, however, these shocks are expected to be relatively less volatile than shocks specific to Central America, which on balance would result in a more stable macroeconomic environment. Moreover, CAFTA-DR may have a positive effect on the quality of institutions and country risk premium, which in turn should further reduce volatility.

In the same vein, CAFTA-DR could play a major role in reducing consumption and investment volatility in Central America. NAFTA appears to have helped Mexico achieve relatively more stable consumption and investment dynamics through its impact on FDI flows. CAFTA-DR could be similarly instrumental in increasing the volume of FDI flows to the region, since it would signal a long-term commitment to implementing trade-promoting policies and thus help reduce the amplitude of investment fluctuations. In addition, CAFTA-DR could expand the scope of international risk-sharing opportunities, which in turn could help diminish the variation in consumption fluctuations.

CAFTA-DR could result in welfare gains in Central America by helping to expand the set of available financial instruments for international risk-sharing purposes. These instruments would allow domestic residents and firms to use international financial markets for consumption smoothing, resulting in significant welfare benefits. Recent studies document that the benefits from international risk sharing tend to be large when a country's consumption growth is volatile, positively correlated with domestic output growth, and not highly correlated with world consumption.

Some of the Central American economies face highly volatile consumption fluctuations, implying that the benefits to CAFTA-DR and consequent reductions in consumption volatility could be large.

Table 2.11. Potential Welfare Gains from International Risk Sharing
(In percent of consumption)

	Gains
Costa Rica	1.30
Dominican Republic	6.38
El Salvador	3.74
Guatemala	0.39
Honduras	1.21
Nicaragua	14.95
CAFTA-DR (average)	4.66
CAFTA-DR (median)	2.52

Source: IMF staff calculations.

Although these benefits would, on average, have the same effect as about a 5 percent permanent increase in the level of per capita consumption, they differ significantly across the Central American economies (Table 2.11).[40] The gains are generally inversely proportional to the volatility of consumption. To illustrate, Nicaragua, the most volatile Central American economy, stands to gain close to 15 percent, whereas the gain for the least volatile economy, Guatemala, is less than ½ percent.[41]

Sources of Business Cycles in Central America

Consistent with the high degree of openness to international trade of the countries in the region, both external and regional shocks play important roles in Central America, even though there are marked differences in their roles across countries. For example, in at least three countries, external

---

[40]A simple general equilibrium model is used to assess the extent of potential welfare gains from international risk sharing. The methodology is similar to the one employed in Van Wincoop (1999). In brief, the model compares two scenarios. The first scenario has no additional risk sharing relative to what is already implied by observed consumption behavior; in the second, there is perfect risk sharing so that each country consumes a constant fraction of total world consumption (see Prasad and others, 2003).

[41]There has been a substantial increase in the volume of remittance inflows to the region from Central Americans in the United States (see Taccone and Nogueira, 2004, and IMF, 2005). Although El Salvador and the Dominican Republic on average received the highest levels of remittances during the period 1990–2003, the growth of the remittances was quite significant in other countries, especially Nicaragua and Honduras. These flows could be instrumental in helping the Central American countries to mitigate the impact of various shocks and thereby lowering the volatility of consumption (Rapoport and Docquier, 2005, and IMF, 2005).

Table 2.12. Forecast Variance Decomposition of GDP Growth

	External Shocks	Domestic Shocks
Costa Rica	0.67	0.33
	0.31	*0.20*
Dominican Republic	0.10	0.90
	0.15	*0.33*
El Salvador	0.23	0.77
	0.23	*0.34*
Guatemala	0.55	0.45
	0.35	*0.28*
Honduras	0.42	0.58
	0.24	*0.27*
Nicaragua	0.18	0.82
	0.23	*0.35*
Average CAFTA-DR	0.36	0.64
Standard deviation	*0.24*	*0.32*
Average standard error	*0.25*	*0.29*
Mexico	0.33	0.67
	0.22	*0.26*

Sources: IMF, *World Economic Outlook*, and IMF staff calculations.

Notes: Data cover the period 1964–2003. Standard errors in italics.

shocks explain a larger share of GDP volatility than in Mexico, and they are particularly important in Costa Rica and Honduras. In Nicaragua and the Dominican Republic, domestic shocks are at least as important as regional shocks, whereas regional shocks are most important in El Salvador and Guatemala. The following subsections analyze these issues in detail by considering the roles of external, regional, and domestic shocks in accounting for macroeconomic fluctuations in Central America and Mexico.

Importance of External Shocks

Country-specific vector autoregressive systems (VARs) are estimated to assess the relative importance of external and domestic shocks in explaining business cycle variation in Central American economies. To capture the influence of external shocks, the following variables are included: the U.S. real GDP growth, a measure of the ex post U.S. real interest rate (the U.S. Federal Fund rate minus annual consumer price index inflation), and the ratio of oil to nonfuel commodity prices (a proxy for the terms of trade of

these economies). The domestic variables are the inflation rate, the ratio of the trade balance to GDP, and the real GDP growth rate.[42]

These VARs permit assessment of the relative importance of external and domestic shocks for growth variability. It is assumed that six shocks drive the business cycle dynamics of these economies: three external shocks and three domestic shocks. The identification strategy used in the VARs separates the influence of external shocks from those of domestic ones.[43]

External shocks play an important role in the Central American region, but there are differences across countries. While, on average, external shocks explain about the same share of growth variability as in Mexico (about 30 percent), in Costa Rica, Guatemala, and Honduras external shocks account for a much larger fraction of growth variability than in Mexico (Table 2.12). At the same time, in the Dominican Republic, El Salvador, and Nicaragua, domestic shocks explain a much larger share than in Mexico. In the countries in which external shocks play the largest role, the response to a U.S. supply shock is deeper and more persistent. In these countries GDP growth is affected significantly for several years (Figure 2.6).[44] By contrast, in those countries in which domestic shocks dominate, a U.S. supply shock has only a very short-lived effect. The great importance of external shocks for some countries of the Central American region is consistent with the relatively high degree of openness of these economies.[45] Conversely, in the Dominican Republic, El Salvador, and Nicaragua, the relatively high share of growth variance explained by domestic shocks, despite the sizable degree of openness, could reflect in part political instability and in part the resulting negative policy shocks.

---

[42]These VARs include six variables in addition to a constant and a linear trend. The data frequency is annual and the sample period is 1996–2003. The lag length is two for all VAR systems estimated. The estimation methodology follows Rebucci (1998). Since the sample contains only a small number of countries with a limited amount of annual data series, it is not possible to undertake a rigorous pooling exercise involving a panel VAR.

[43]To be more specific, a small open economy assumption justifies using the Cholesky decomposition of the reduced-form variance-covariance matrix to help separate the impact of external shocks from those of domestic ones. This decomposition also permits decomposition of the variability of growth in these two blocks of shocks without identifying individual shocks separately and without placing restrictions on their long-run dynamics.

[44]In these impulse responses, a positive supply shock is represented by a one-standard-deviation decrease in the U.S. real interest rate.

[45]These findings are also in line with those documented by Lederman, Perry, and Suescún (2002) and Hoffmaister and Hall (1999), as well as with the predictions of dynamic, small open economy models, including those of Mendoza (1995) and Kose (2002).

Figure 2.6. Impulse Responses of GDP

(Deviation from steady state in response to a one-standard-deviation increase in supply shock in the United States)

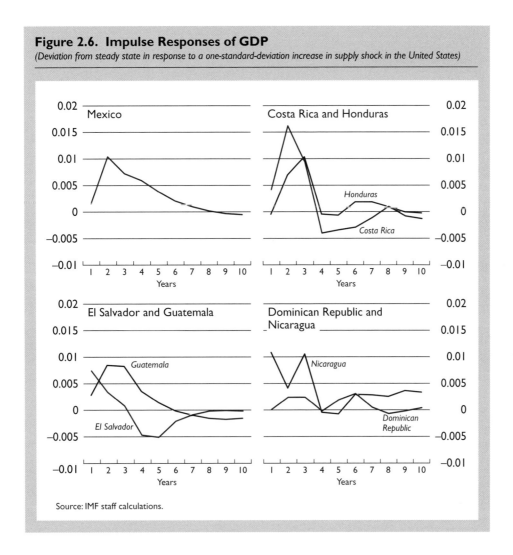

Source: IMF staff calculations.

Importance of Regional Shocks

A multicountry VAR system is employed to assess the relative importance of regional shocks. The multicountry VAR includes the United States and Mexico, and the six Central American economies considered before (Costa Rica, Dominican Republic, El Salvador, Guatemala, Honduras, and Nicaragua). By including the United States and Mexico, it is possible to control for external shocks. The VAR includes the real GDP growth series for each country to conserve the degree of freedom, a constant, and a linear trend. The VAR permits assessment of the relative importance of the North American, regional, and domestic shocks for growth variability.[46]

Regional shocks explain a relatively large share of growth variability, on average, in the Central America region, but there are still large cross-country differences. Regional shocks explain—on average—about 50 percent of growth variability (Table 2.13). The share of regional shocks is significantly larger for Guatemala and El Salvador and smallest for Honduras.

Co-Movement of Business Cycles with the United States

What impact could CAFTA-DR have on the co-movement of business cycles in Central America and

---

[46]As in the country-specific systems, a small open economy assumption motivates using the Cholesky decomposition of the reduced form residuals to identify different blocks of shocks. The Cholesky decomposition of a block recursive system is invariant to the order of variables within each block. So, by placing the U.S.

and Mexico GDP growth series in the first block and those of each Central America country in the last block, it is possible to assess the relative importance of the remaining block of Central American countries for the growth variability of the country placed last in the system. As a result, the relative importance of the domestic shock is also isolated by this identification strategy.

Table 2.13. Forecast Variance Decomposition of GDP Growth (Regional Shocks)

	NAFTA Shocks	Regional Shocks	Domestic Shocks
Costa Rica	0.26	0.58	0.16
	0.20	*0.26*	*0.10*
Dominican Republic	0.12	0.45	0.43
	0.17	*0.28*	*0.02*
El Salvador	0.26	0.63	0.11
	0.21	*0.31*	*0.08*
Guatemala	0.21	0.70	0.09
	0.19	*0.33*	*0.07*
Honduras	0.34	0.25	0.24
	0.24	*0.23*	*0.14*
Nicaragua	0.16	0.44	0.40
	0.18	*0.26*	*0.19*
Average CAFTA-DR	0.22	0.51	0.24
Standard deviation	*0.11*	*0.24*	*0.16*
Average standard error	*0.20*	*0.28*	*0.10*

Sources: IMF, *World Economic Outlook*, and IMF staff calculations.

Notes: Data cover the period 1964–2003. Standard errors in italics. NAFTA shocks include those from the United States and Mexico.

the United States? In theory, increased trade linkages have ambiguous effects on the co-movement of business cycles in Central America and the United States. Stronger trade linkages can result in more highly correlated business cycles, since they generate both demand- and supply-side spillovers across countries. Moreover, if stronger trade linkages are associated with increased intra-industry specialization across countries, and if industry-specific shocks are important in driving business cycles, then the co-movement of business cycles would be expected to increase. However, the degree of co-movement might diminish if increased trade is the result of a rise in interindustry trade and if industry-specific shocks are important in driving business cycles.

Increased financial flows also have an ambiguous theoretical effect on business cycle correlations. For example, stronger financial linkages could result in a higher degree of synchronization of output fluctuations by generating large demand-side effects. However, financial linkages could stimulate specialization of production through the reallocation of capital in a manner consistent with countries' comparative advantage. This type of specialization, which could result in more exposure to industry- or country-specific shocks, could lead to a decrease in the degree of output correlations while inducing stronger co-movement of consumption across countries (Kalemli-Ozcan, Sørensen, and Yosha, 2003).

Several recent empirical studies, however, suggest that both trade and financial linkages result in greater business cycle synchronicity. For example, using the results from cross-country or cross-region panel regressions, Frankel and Rose (1998), Clark and van Wincoop (2001), Calderón, Chong, and Stein (2002), and Kose and Yi (2005) show that pairs of countries that trade more with each other exhibit a higher degree of business cycle co-movement. Calderón (2003) documents that the impact of trade intensity on cross-country business cycle correlation is larger if the two countries have a free trade agreement. Kose, Prasad, and Terrones (2003b) report that countries that are more open to financial flows have business cycles more highly correlated with the G-7 aggregate. Imbs (2004) also finds that financial integration has a positive effect on the degree of co-movement of business cycle fluctuations in output and consumption.

NAFTA has been associated with an increased degree of co-movement of business cycles in Mexico and the United States.[47] This can be seen from the

---

[47]Co-movement is measured as the cross-country correlation of the annual growth rate of main macroeconomic aggregates (output, consumption, investment, exports, and imports). Since only a limited number of annual date series are available, standard errors associated with correlations are not reported. Table 2.A2 in Appendix II presents detailed co-movement statistics. A detailed description of the model is presented in Appendix I. Figure 2.A1 shows the structure of the model.

Figure 2.7. Co-Movement of Economic Variables in Mexico and the United States

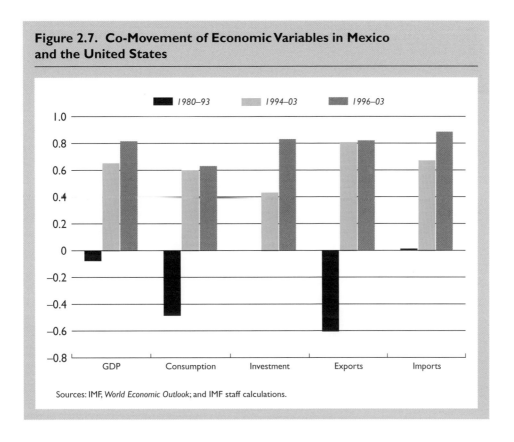

Sources: IMF, *World Economic Outlook*; and IMF staff calculations.

marked increase in cross-country correlations of the major macroeconomic aggregates, including output, consumption, and investment (Figure 2.7). In particular, the output correlation between Mexico and the United States rose from almost zero in the pre-NAFTA period to about 0.75 during the post-crisis period. There was a significant increase in consumption correlation, suggesting that Mexico was able to diversify its consumption risk more effectively after NAFTA. Cross-country correlations of exports and imports also increased significantly after the inception of NAFTA, possibly resulting from the increased intra-industry trade in the region.

The degree of co-movement of cyclical fluctuations in Central America and the United States on average rose during the past 10 years (Figure 2.8). While cross-country correlations of output in the United States and the Dominican Republic and Guatemala increased significantly in the 1994–2003 period, there was a considerable decrease in the correlations of El Salvador and Honduras with the United States. Output correlation between Costa Rica and the United States remained quite stable over the years. In all of the Central American countries, except Costa Rica, correlation of consumption with the United States rose in the 1996–2003 period. Although Honduran exports became less correlated

with U.S. exports, the other Central American countries exhibited increased co-movement of exports with those of the United States over the same period.

NAFTA's positive effect on business cycle synchronization between Mexico and the United States suggests that CAFTA-DR could have a similar effect on the Central American economies' business cycles. As discussed earlier in this section, CAFTA-DR could lead to a sizable increase in trade and financial linkages between Central America and the United States. The increased trade and financial flows could result in a higher degree of business cycle interdependence through stronger demand and supply channels. Moreover, CAFTA-DR could amplify the spillover of sector-specific shocks through its impact on the nature of trade flows.

CAFTA-DR could lead to an increase in the importance of external shocks in driving business cycles in Central America. Stronger trade linkages after the advent of NAFTA induced a similar change in Mexico's business cycles, as documented in Kose, Meredith, and Towe (2005). Using a dynamic factor model, they find that regional factors associated with the North American business cycle became more important in explaining macroeconomic fluctuations in Mexico over time. In particular, the proportion of output volatility explained by the North American

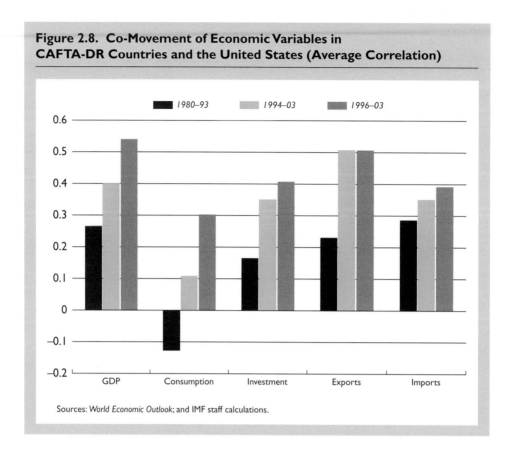

Figure 2.8. Co-Movement of Economic Variables in CAFTA-DR Countries and the United States (Average Correlation)

Sources: *World Economic Outlook*; and IMF staff calculations.

regional factor rose from less than 1 percent in the period 1980–93 to more than 19 percent in the NAFTA period, whereas the variance of investment accounted for by the regional factor increased almost tenfold. The increased role of the regional factors in the case of Mexico's business cycles was the result of stronger transmission channels associated with the impact of NAFTA on the regional trade flows. The results of the VARs reported in the previous section also suggest that the U.S. business cycle could become even more important for some countries of the Central American region following the inception of CAFTA-DR. The overall impact might vary significantly across countries, though, by also depending on other changes in policy regimes and institutions triggered by CAFTA-DR.

How Could CAFTA-DR Affect the Transmission of Business Cycles?

A multicountry dynamic stochastic general equilibrium (DSGE) model is employed to study the channels through which CAFTA-DR could affect the transmission of business cycles from the United States to Central America. The multicountry DSGE model is a natural setting for this purpose because it

accounts for the demand- and supply-side spillover channels that are critical in transmitting business cycles. The model, developed by Kose and Yi (2005), extends the two-country free trade, complete market model of Backus, Kehoe and Kydland (1994) by including three countries, trading frictions (tariffs and transportation costs), and international financial autarky, or economic self-sufficiency, and international financial autarky.[48]

The model economy includes a traded intermediate goods–producing sector and a nontraded final goods–producing sector. Perfectly competitive firms in the intermediate goods sector produce traded goods according to a Cobb-Douglas production function. When the intermediate goods are exported to other countries, they are subject to transportation costs, which are considered as a proxy for tariffs and other nontariff barriers, as well as actual transport costs. It is assumed that each country is completely specialized in the production of an intermediate good. Each country's output of intermediates is used as an input into final goods production. Final goods producers then combine domestic

---

[48]A detailed description of the model is presented in Appendix I.

and foreign intermediates. These assumptions imply that imports from the United States are used as intermediate inputs to produce final consumption and investment goods in Central America. In each country, households derive utility from consumption and leisure.

The model is calibrated to reflect some basic structural features of the CAFTA-DR members. Since the objective is to analyze the interdependence of business cycles in Central America and the United States, it is assumed that the three countries in the model are a representative Central American economy, the United States, and the rest of world, represented by an aggregate of the members of the European Union. The steady-state levels of trade flows among the three countries in the model are computed using the average trade flows during the past five years. It is assumed that the representative Central American economy is 2 percent of the world economy and that each of the other two countries constitutes 49 percent of the world economy. The elasticity of substitution between domestic and foreign goods is set at 1.05. The impact of CAFTA-DR is simulated by changing the level of transportation costs (trading frictions) between the representative Central American economy and the United States. The model is solved following the standard linearization approach in the international business cycle literature.

The results suggest that CAFTA-DR could magnify the impact of shocks originating in the United States on the Central America economies. To analyze the responses of macroeconomic aggregates in a representative Central American economy to shocks originating in the United States, the model computes the impulse responses of the Central American country's variables to a temporary productivity (supply) shock in the United States. The results indicate that the responses of the representative Central American country's output, consumption, and investment to the external shock increase after the inception of CAFTA-DR (Figure 2.9)

In addition, pre- and post-CAFTA-DR simulations illustrate the substantial increase in the Central American country's exports to the United States, which results from the lowering of tariffs and other trading frictions after the advent of the agreement. In other words, the reduction in trade barriers in the model results in greater intensity of trade flows between the Central American economy and the United States, which in turn leads to a higher degree of business cycle interdependence. An increase in the synchronization of business cycles between the Central American economies and the United States implies that the region is subject to more common shocks, which in turn would facilitate further macroeconomic policy coordination among the Central American countries.

Conclusions

This section analyzed the macroeconomic implications of CAFTA-DR for the Central American countries in light of Mexico's NAFTA experience. There are, of course, inherent difficulties associated with this analysis. First, isolating the effects of NAFTA on Mexico is itself a complicated task, given the significance of the other external and policy shocks that have occurred over the past decade. Second, Mexico differs from the Central American countries in several dimensions: it shares a common border with the United States, it has a much larger and more diverse economy, and its per capita GDP is much higher than the Central American countries, except Costa Rica. Hence, the analysis in this section and its findings are only tentative.

Nevertheless, Mexico's NAFTA experience provides some insights in evaluating the potential effects of CAFTA-DR. CAFTA-DR and NAFTA share several common characteristics, because both agreements envisage comprehensive tariff reductions, cover a broad spectrum of sectors, and include various provisions for dispute settlement. As in Mexico's case prior to NAFTA, Central America is already highly integrated with the United States as its trade linkages with the United States have grown rapidly over the past decade.

In addition to providing a growth stimulus, CAFTA-DR could constitute a turning point in the region's integration with the global economy. Estimates suggest that the region's GDP could grow by 1.5 percent as a result of the agreement. However, the full impact of the agreement on economic growth could be much larger because of the dynamic effects associated with the accumulation of capital, changes in specialization patterns, growth of trade associated with services, and stronger productivity spillovers. Mexico's NAFTA experience suggests that CAFTA-DR could significantly accelerate the pace of the region's integration with the global economy. Since Central America is faced with increased competition from abroad, and the textile sectors are faced with a phasing out of quotas under the Agreement on Textiles and Clothing, CAFTA-DR's successful implementation is paramount for the region to secure enhanced market access to its largest trading partner.

CAFTA-DR could also play a major role in reducing macroeconomic volatility in the region. Both Mexico's experience and ongoing specialization trends in the Central American economies suggest that shocks originating in the United States would play a more prominent role in driving macroeconomic fluctuations in the region after the advent of CAFTA-DR. Since these shocks are generally less volatile than shocks specific to the region, CAFTA-DR is expected to contribute to a more stable macroeconomic envi-

Figure 2.9. Impulse Responses
(1 percent increase in supply shock in the United States)

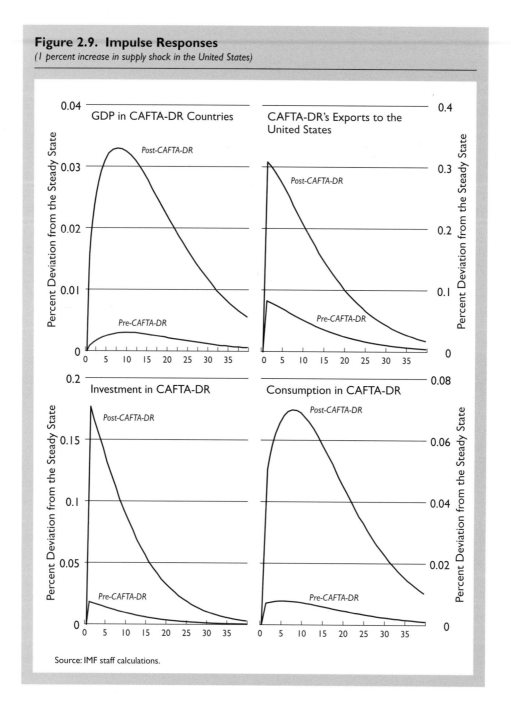

Source: IMF staff calculations.

ronment. Though the degree of co-movement of business cycles between the United States and Central America has on average increased substantially over the past 10 years, CAFTA-DR is likely to lead to further cyclical interdependence through increased trade and financial flows. Also, an increase in the importance of shocks from the United States implies that the Central American countries would be faced with more common shocks, which would further the regional coordination of macroeconomic policies.

For the growth and stability benefits of CAFTA-DR to be fully materialized, however, the agreement needs to be accompanied by structural reforms. A broad range of reforms are needed to secure the potential benefits associated with CAFTA-DR. In particular, most Central American countries need to strengthen their institutions, including regulatory bodies, the rule of law, property rights, labor market flexibility, and human capital. Institutional reform could enhance the credibility of the regulatory environment and improve trade-related institutions in the region. Although CAFTA-DR comes with a strong commitment from the United States to provide technical assistance in the implementation of this agreement, particularly in the areas of financial sector regulation, supervision, and sanitary and technical standards, the Central American economies themselves need to implement the necessary reforms to sustain the gains associated with the agreement.

Appendix I. The Model

This appendix briefly explains the main features of the model economy used in this section. The model extends the basic two-country, free trade, complete market Backus, Kehoe, and Kydland (1994) framework by having three countries, considering transportation costs, and allowing for international financial autarky (zero international asset markets). First, the preferences and technology formulations are described. Then the characteristics of the asset markets are explained. All variables denote own country per capita quantities.

Preferences

In each of the three countries, representative agents derive utility from consumption and leisure. Agents choose consumption and leisure to maximize the following utility function:

$$E_0\left(\sum_{t=0}^{\infty}\beta^t\frac{[c_{it}^{\mu}(1-n_{it})^{1-\mu}]^{1-\gamma}}{1-\gamma}\right), 0<\mu<1; 0<\beta<1; 0<\gamma,$$
$$i = 1, 2, 3 \qquad (1)$$

where c_{it} is consumption, n_{it} is the amount of labor supplied in country i in period t, μ is the share of consumption in intratemporal utility, and γ is the intertemporal elasticity of substitution. Each agent has a fixed time endowment normalized to 1.

Technology

There are two sectors in each country: a traded intermediate goods–producing sector and a nontraded final goods–producing sector. Each country is completely specialized in producing an intermediate good. Time subscripts were suppressed except where necessary.

Intermediate Goods Sector

Perfectly competitive firms in the intermediate goods sector produce traded goods according to a Cobb-Douglas production function:

$$y_i = z_i k_i^{\theta} n_i^{1-\theta}, \quad 0<\theta<1; i = 1, 2, 3 \qquad (2)$$

where y_i denotes (per capita) intermediate goods production in country i, z_i is the productivity shock, k_i is capital input, and θ denotes capital's share in output. Firms in this sector rent capital and hire labor in order to maximize profits, period by period:

$$\max_{k_i n_i} p_i y_i - r_i k_i - w_i n_i \qquad (3)$$

subject to $k_i, n_i \geq 0$; $i = 1, 2, 3$

where $w_i(r_i)$ is the wage (rental rate) and p_i is the factory gate or f.o.b. (freight on board) price of intermediate goods produced in country i.

The market-clearing condition in each period for the intermediate goods–producing firms in country i is

$$\sum_{j=1}^{3} \pi_j y_{ij} = \pi_i y_i, \qquad (4)$$

where π_i is the number of households in country i and determines country size, and y_{ij} denotes the quantity of intermediates produced in country i and shipped to each agent in country j.

The total number of households in the world is normalized to 1:

$$\sum_{i=1}^{3} \pi_i = 1. \qquad (5)$$

Transportation Costs

When the intermediate goods are exported to the other country, they are subject to transportation costs. These costs can be considered as a stand-in for tariffs and other nontariff barriers, as well as transport costs. Following Backus, Kehoe, and Kydland (1992) and Ravn and Mazzenga (1999), the costs are modeled as quadratic iceberg costs. This formulation of transport costs generalizes the standard Samuelson linear iceberg specification and takes into account that transportation costs become higher as the amount of traded goods gets larger. Specifically, if country i exports y_{ij} units to country j, $g_{ij}(y_{ij})^2$ units are lost in transit, where g_{ij} is the transport cost parameter for country i's exports to country j. That is, only

$$(1 - g_{ij}y_{ij})y_{ij} \equiv m_{ij} \qquad (6)$$

units are imported by country j, and $g_{ij}y_{ij}$ can be considered as the "iceberg" transportation cost, which is the fraction of the exported goods that are lost in transit. In the simulations, the transport costs are evaluated at the steady-state values of y_{ij}.

Final Goods Sector

Each country's output of intermediates is used as an input into final goods production. Final goods firms in each country produce their goods by combining domestic and foreign intermediates via an Armington aggregator. The Armington aggregator is widely used in international trade models because it allows imperfect substitutability between goods produced in different countries. To be more specific, the final goods production function in country j is given by

$$F(y_{1j}, y_{2j}, y_{3j}) = \left[\sum_{i=1}^{3} \omega_{ij} [(1 - g_{ij}y_{ij})y_{ij}]^{1-\alpha} \right]^{1/1-\alpha} \quad (8)$$

$$= \left[\sum_{i=1}^{3} \omega_{ij} m_{ij}^{1-\alpha} \right]^{1/(1-\alpha)}, \quad (9)$$

$$\omega_{1j}, \omega_{2j}, \omega_{3j} \geq 0; \quad \alpha \geq 0; \quad j = 1, 2, 3$$

where ω_{1j} denotes the Armington weight applied to the intermediate goods produced by country 1 and imported by country j (m_{1j}). It is assumed that $g_2 = 0$ and that $g_{ij} = g_{ji}$. In other words, there is no cost associated with intracountry trade; that is, $m_{22} = y_{22}$, and transport costs between two countries do not depend on the origin of the goods. $1/\alpha$ is the elasticity of substitution between the inputs.

Final goods–producing firms in each country j maximize profits, period by period:

$$\max_{m_{1j}, m_{2j}, m_{3j}} q_j \left[\sum_{i=1}^{3} \omega_{ij} m_{ij}^{1-\alpha} \right]^{1/(1-\alpha)} - p_{1j}m_{1j} - p_{2j}m_{2j} - p_{3j}m_{3j}, \quad (10)$$

where q_j is the price of the final goods produced by country j, and p_{ij} is the c.i.f. (cost, insurance, and freight) price of country i's good imported by country j. Note that $p_{jj} = p_j$.

As in Ravn and Mazzenga (1999), the first-order conditions from (10) are used to calculate the price of an imported good i relative to j's own good:

$$\frac{p_{ij}}{p_j} = \frac{\omega_{ij}}{\omega_j} \left(\frac{y_{jj}}{m_{ij}} \right)^{\alpha}. \quad (11)$$

Also, Ravn and Mazzenga show that, because $\partial F/\partial y_{ij} = (\partial F/\partial m_{ij})(1 - 2g_{ij}y_{ij})$:

$$p_i = (1 - 2g_{ij}y_{ij})p_{ij}. \quad (12)$$

Comparing (7) and (12), it is easy to see that the c.i.f. price multiplied by imports exceeds the f.o.b. price multiplied by exports:

$$p_{ij}m_{ij} - p_iy_{ij} = p_{ij}(1 - g_{ij}y_{ij})y_{ij} - p_iy_{ij}$$

$$= y_{ij}(1 - g_{ij}y_{ij}) - p_i) > 0. \quad (13)$$

In other words, if the transportation costs are considered as arising from transportation services provided to ship goods between countries, with the

quadratic costs arising because the transportation "technology" is decreasing returns to scale, then, in a perfect competition setting, there are positive profits. That is, the firms providing the transportation services pay the exporting country the factory gate or f.o.b. price of the good, and then receive the c.i.f. price from the final goods firm in the importing country. It is assumed that there is a single representative shipping firm that chooses y_{ij} to maximize the left-hand side of 13. Households in the importing country own these firms; the firms' profits are distributed as dividends to the households.

Capital is accumulated in the standard way:

$$k_{jt+1} = (1 - \delta)k_{jt} + x_{jt}, \quad j = 1, 2, 3 \quad (14)$$

where x_{it} is investment and δ is the rate of depreciation. Final goods are used for domestic consumption and investment in each country:

$$c_{jt} + x_{jt} = F(y_{1jt}, y_{2jt}, y_{3jt}). \quad j = 1, 2, 3 \quad (15)$$

Asset Markets

It is assumed that the form of the asset market structure is international financial autarky, under which there is no asset trade; hence, trade is balanced period by period. The following budget constraint must hold in each period:

$$q_{it}(c_{it} + x_{it}) - r_{it}k_{it} - w_{it}n_{it} - R_{it} = 0,$$

$$\forall t = 0, \ldots, \infty; \ i =, 1, 2, 3 \quad (16)$$

where R_{it} is profits that the transportation firms distribute as dividends to households. In the complete markets case, there is a single lifetime budget constraint:

$$E_0 = \left[\sum_{t=0}^{\infty} \sum_s (r_{ist}k_{ist} + w_{ist}n_{ist} + R_{ist}) = \sum_{t=0}^{\infty} \sum_s q_{ist}(c_{ist} + x_{ist}) \right], \quad (17)$$

where the subscript s indexes the state of nature.

Solution

Because analytical solutions do not exist, the model is solved following the standard linearization approach in the international business cycle literature. Under financial autarky, the optimization problems of the two types of firms, as well as of the households, are solved, along with the equilibrium conditions.

Appendix II. Volatility and Co-Movement of Macroeconomic Aggregates

Table 2.A1. Volatility of Macroeconomic Aggregates
(In percent)

	Mexico	CAFTA-DR Average	Costa Rica	Dominican Republic	El Salvador	Guatemala	Honduras	Nicaragua
GDP								
1980–2003	3.6	3.3	3.7	3.7	3.3	2.3	2.5	4.1
1980–93	3.5	3.6	4.4	4.0	3.7	2.7	2.6	4.3
1994–2003	3.9	2.1	2.7	2.9	1.6	1.1	2.5	1.6
1996–2003	2.7	2.1	3.1	3.3	1.0	1.1	2.3	1.8
Consumption								
1980–2003	4.1	6.2	3.2	6.2	6.6	1.6	5.1	14.3
1980–93	3.6	7.7	4.3	6.6	8.5	1.8	6.5	18.3
1994–2003	4.8	3.4	1.9	5.1	2.7	1.2	2.3	6.8
1996–2003	2.4	3.0	1.7	5.8	1.5	1.1	2.6	5.4
Investment								
1980–2003	13.2	13.0	10.6	14.6	8.6	10.6	14.1	19.5
1980–93	12.9	14.6	11.9	16.9	9.4	12.2	16.7	20.4
1994–2003	14.1	11.1	9.7	11.8	8.1	9.5	9.6	17.7
1996–2003	9.2	11.0	10.9	12.0	7.1	10.3	9.0	16.9
Exports								
1980–2003	8.2	10.5	8.6	9.3	13.1	6.5	10.7	14.9
1980–93	6.3	10.8	6.0	10.7	15.2	7.8	9.5	15.7
1994–2003	10.0	9.0	10.3	7.8	6.3	5.4	12.4	11.8
1996–2003	8.0	7.5	11.5	8.8	7.1	4.9	5.9	7.0
Imports								
1980–2003	18.1	11.5	9.3	10.4	12.5	11.4	8.9	16.6
1980–93	21.5	12.7	9.5	11.7	14.9	13.7	11.5	14.8
1994–2003	13.3	9.3	8.5	8.7	8.5	9.2	3.2	17.7
1996–2003	10.8	8.4	9.6	9.8	7.2	10.4	2.5	11.1

Sources: IMF, *World Economic Outlook*; and IMF staff calculations.

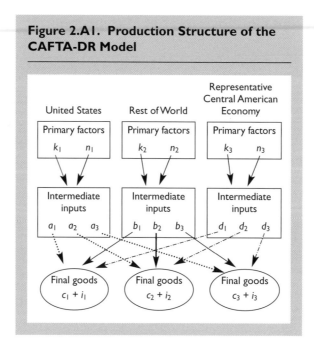

Figure 2.A1. Production Structure of the CAFTA-DR Model

Table 2.A2. Co-Movement of Macroeconomic Aggregates with U.S. Aggregates

	Mexico	CAFTA-DR Average	Costa Rica	Dominican Republic	El Salvador	Guatemala	Honduras	Nicaragua
GDP								
1980–2003	0.2	0.3	0.6	0.2	0.5	0.2	0.2	0.0
1980–93	−0.1	0.3	0.6	0.1	0.5	0.1	0.4	−0.2
1994–2003	0.7	0.4	0.6	0.5	0.3	0.6	−0.2	0.6
1996–2003	0.8	0.5	0.6	0.6	0.7	0.7	0.0	0.7
Consumption								
1980–2003	−0.1	−0.1	0.2	0.2	0.1	−0.3	−0.6	−0.1
1980–93	−0.5	−0.1	0.5	0.1	0.1	−0.6	−0.7	−0.1
1994–2003	0.6	0.1	0.1	0.3	0.0	0.1	0.0	0.2
1996–2003	0.6	0.3	0.2	0.3	0.7	0.4	0.0	0.2
Investment								
1980–2003	0.2	0.2	0.2	0.3	0.1	0.0	0.3	0.3
1980–93	0.0	0.2	0.7	0.2	0.1	−0.2	0.2	0.0
1994–2003	0.4	0.4	0.1	0.5	0.1	0.3	0.6	0.6
1996–2003	0.8	0.4	0.1	0.6	0.0	0.3	0.7	0.7
Exports								
1980–2003	0.1	0.3	0.3	0.5	0.1	0.4	0.4	0.2
1980–93	−0.6	0.2	0.2	0.4	0.0	0.0	0.7	0.1
1994–2003	0.8	0.5	0.2	0.7	0.6	0.9	0.1	0.5
1996–2003	0.8	0.5	0.3	0.8	0.6	0.9	0.0	0.5
Imports								
1980–2003	0.2	0.3	0.3	0.4	0.3	0.1	0.4	0.3
1980–93	0.0	0.3	0.8	0.1	0.2	0.0	0.5	0.1
1994–2003	0.7	0.4	0.4	0.8	0.3	0.3	−0.2	0.4
1996–2003	0.9	0.4	0.4	0.9	0.4	0.4	0.0	0.4

Source: IMF staff calculations.

References

Agénor, Pierre-Richard, 2002, "Does Globalization Hurt the Poor?" World Bank Institute, Policy Research Working Paper No. 2922 (Washington: World Bank).

Aisbett, Emma, 2005, "Why Are the Critics So Convinced that Globalization Is Bad for the Poor?" forthcoming in *Globalization and Poverty*, ed. by Ann Harrison (Cambridge, Massachusetts: National Bureau of Economic Research, forthcoming).

Aizenman, Joshua, and Brian Pinto, eds., 2005, *Managing Economic Volatility and Crises: A Practitioner's Guide* (forthcoming; Cambridge: Cambridge University Press).

Arora, Vivek, and Athanasios Vamvakidis, 2005, "How Much Do Trading Partners Matter for Economic Growth?" *IMF Staff Papers*, Vol. 52, No. 1, pp. 24–40.

Backus, David K., Patrick J. Kehoe, and Finn E. Kydland, 1992, "International Real Business Cycles," *Journal of Political Economy*, Vol. 100 (August), pp. 745–75.

———, 1994, "Dynamics of the Trade Balance and the Terms of Trade: The J-Curve?" *American Economic Review*, Vol. 84 (March), pp. 84–103.

Baldwin, Richard, 2003, "Openness and Growth: What's the Empirical Relationship?" NBER Working Paper No. 9578 (Cambridge, Massachusetts: National Bureau of Economic Research).

———, and Elena Seghezza, 1996, "Testing for Trade-Induced Investment-Led Growth," NBER Working Paper No. 5416 (Cambridge, Massachusetts: National Bureau of Economic Research).

Baldwin, Robert, and Anthony J. Venables, 1995, "Regional Economic Integration," in *Handbook of International Economics Vol. 3,* ed. by Gene M. Grossman and Kenneth Rogoff (Amsterdam: North-Holland), pp. 1597–1644.

Berg, Andrew, and Anne O. Krueger, 2003, "Trade, Growth, and Poverty: A Selective Survey," IMF Working Paper 03/30 (Washington: International Monetary Fund).

Birdsall, Nancy, 2003, "Chile FTA and Capital Flows: A Bad Precedent?" Have a View Series (Washington: Center for Global Development, January).

Blomström, Marcus, and Ari Kokko, 1997, "Regional Integration and Foreign Direct Investment," NBER Working Paper No. 6019 (Cambridge, Massachusetts: National Bureau of Economic Research).

Borensztein, Eduardo, Jose de Gregorio, and Jong Wha Lee, 1998, "How Does Foreign Direct Investment Affect Growth?" *Journal of International Economics*, Vol. 45 (June), pp. 115–135.

Brown, Drusilla, Kozo Kiyota, and Robert Stern, 2005, "Computational Analysis of the U.S. FTAs with Central America, Australia, and Morocco," with Drusilla K. Brown and Kozo Kiyota, *World Economy*, forthcoming.

Buch, Carolina M., Jorge Dopke, and Christian Pierdzioch, 2005, "Financial Openness and Business Cycle Volatility," *Journal of International Money and Finance*, forthcoming.

Calderón, César, 2003, "Do Free Trade Agreements Enhance the Transmission of Shocks Across Countries?" Working Papers Central Bank of Chile No. 213 (Santiago, Chile: Central Bank of Chile).

———, Alberto E. Chong, and Ernesto H. Stein, 2002, "Trade Intensity and Business Cycle Synchronization: Are Developing Countries Any Different?" Working Papers Central Bank of Chile No. 195 (Santiago, Chile: Central Bank of Chile).

Clark, Todd E., and Eric van Wincoop, 2001, "Borders and Business Cycles," *Journal of International Economics*, Vol. 55 (October), pp. 59–85.

CBO (Congressional Budget Office), 2003, "The Effects of NAFTA on U.S.-Mexican Trade and GDP" (Washington, May).

Cuevas, Alfredo, Miguel Messmacher, and Alejandro Werner, 2002a, "Changes in the Patterns of External Financing in Mexico Since the Approval of NAFTA," Central Bank of Mexico Working Paper (Mexico City), p. 17.

———, 2002b, "Macroeconomic Synchronization Between Mexico and Its NAFTA Partners," Central Bank of Mexico Working Paper (Mexico City).

Dollar, David, and Aart Kraay, 2002, "Growth Is Good for the Poor," *Journal of Economic Growth*, Vol. 7 (September), pp. 195–225.

———, 2003, "Institutions, Trade, and Growth," *Journal of Monetary Economics,* Vol. 50 (January), pp. 133–62.

Easterly, William, 2005, "Globalization, Poverty and All That: Factor Endowment versus Productivity Views," in *Globalization and Poverty,* ed. by Ann Harrison (Cambridge, Massachusetts: National Bureau of Economic Research, forthcoming).

———, Roumeen Islam, and Joseph E. Stiglitz, 2001, "Shaken and Stirred: Explaining Growth Volatility," in *Annual World Bank Conference on Development Economics*, ed. by Boris Pleskovic and Nicholas Stern (Washington: World Bank).

Easterly, William, Norbert Fiess, and Daniel Lederman, 2003, "NAFTA and Convergence in North America: High Expectations, Big Events, and Little Time," *Economia,* Vol. 4 (Fall).

Edison, Hali, Ross Levine, Luca Ricci, and Torsten Sløk, 2002, "International Financial Integration and Economic Growth," *Journal of International Money and Finance*, Vol. 21 (November), pp. 749–76.

Elliott, Kimberly A., 2004, "Trading Up: Labor Standards, Development, and CAFTA," *CGD Brief* (Washington: Center for Global Development, May 28).

———, 2005, "Big Sugar and the Political Economy of U.S. Agricultural Policy," *CGD Brief* (Washington: Center for Global Development, April).

Forbes, Kristin, 2004, "Capital Controls: Mud in the Wheels of Market Discipline," NBER Working Paper No. 10284 (Cambridge, Massachusetts: National Bureau of Economic Research).

Frankel, Jeffrey A., and Andrew K. Rose, 1998, "The Endogeneity of the Optimum Currency Area Criteria," *Economic Journal*, Vol. 108 (July), pp. 1009–25.

Frankel, Jeffrey A., and David Romer, 1999, "Does Trade Cause Growth?" *American Economic Review,* Vol. 89 (June), pp. 379–99.

Gil-Diaz, Francisco, and Agustin Carstens, 1996, "One Year of Solitude: Some Pilgrim Tales About Mexico's

1994–95 Crisis," *American Economic Review, Papers and Proceedings,* Vol. 86 (May), pp. 164–69.

Goldberg, Pinelopi, and Nina Pavcnik, 2005, The Effects of the Colombian Trade Liberalization on Urban Poverty, forthcoming in *Globalization and Poverty* (Cambridge, Massachusetts: National Bureau of Economic Research).

Gould, David M., 1998, "Has NAFTA Changed North American Trade?" *Economic Review*, Federal Reserve Bank of Dallas (First Quarter), pp. 12–23.

Gourinchas, Pierre Olivier, and Olivier Jeanne, 2004 "The Elusive Gains from International Financial Integration," IMF Working Paper 04/74 (Washington: International Monetary Fund).

Griswold, Daniel, and Daniel Ikenson, 2004, "The Case for CAFTA-DR: Consolidating Central America's Freedom Revolution," Trade Briefing Paper No. 21 (Washington: Cato Institute, Center for Trade Policy Studies).

Grossman, Gene M., and Elhahan Helpman, 1991, "Trade, Knowledge Spillovers, and Growth," *European Economic Review*, Vol. 35 (April), pp. 517–26.

Gruben, William, 2005, "Domestic Policy No Match for Trade Stance for Central American Countries," *Southwest Economy*, Federal Reserve Bank of Dallas Vol. 13–15 (March/April).

Hanson, Gordon H., 2002, "The Role of Maquiladoras in Mexico's Export Boom" (unpublished; San Diego, California: University of California at San Diego).

———, 2005, "Globalization, Labor Income and Poverty in Mexico," in *Globalization and Poverty*, ed. by Ann Harrison (Cambridge, Massachusetts: National Bureau of Economic Research, forthcoming).

Harrison, Ann, 2005, *Globalization and Poverty* (Cambridge, Massachusetts: National Bureau of Economic Research, forthcoming).

———, and Helena Tang, 2004, "Liberalization of Trade: Why So Much Controversy?" (unpublished; Berkeley, California: University of California at Berkeley).

Hilaire, Alvin D., and Yongzheng Yang, 2003, "The United States and the New Regionalism/Bilateralism," IMF Working Paper 03/206 (Washington: International Monetary Fund).

Hillberry, Russell H., and Christine A. McDaniel, 2002, "A Decomposition of North American Trade Growth Since NAFTA," *International Economic Review,* USITC Publication No. 3527 (May/June), pp. 1–5.

Hoffmaister, Alexander W., and Luis Hall, 1999, "Transmission of US and Mexico Shocks in Central America," Chapter 3 in *Fluctuations, Trends and Transmission of Shocks in Central America, Mexico, and USA*, ed. by Alexander Monge Naranjo, Alexander W. Hoffmaister, Luis J. Hall Urrea, and Edgar Robles Cordero, Regional Studies Committee, Latin America and the Caribbean Region (Washington: World Bank), pp. 57–86.

Hornbeck, John F., 2004, "The U.S.-Central America Free Trade Agreement (CAFTA): Challenges for Sub-Regional Integration," Congressional Research Service Report No: RL 31780 (Washington).

Imbs, Jean, 2004, "Real Effects of Financial Integration," *IMF Staff Papers*, Vol. 51 (Special Issue).

International Monetary Fund, 2005, "Workers' Remittances and Economic Development," *World Economic Outlook, April 2005* (Washington), pp. 69–84.

Jurenas, Remy, 2003, Agricultural Trade in a U.S.-Central American Free Trade Agreement (CAFTA), Congressional Research Service Report No. RL 32110 (Washington).

Kalemli-Ozcan, Sebnem, Bent Sørensen, and Ovid Yosha, 2003, "Risk Sharing and Industrial Specialization: Regional and International Evidence," *American Economic Review*, Vol. 93 (June), pp. 903–18.

Kehoe, Tim J., 2003, "An Evaluation of the Performance of Applied General Equilibrium Models of the Impact of NAFTA," Federal Reserve Bank of Minneapolis Research Department Staff Report No. 320 (Minneapolis, Minnesota).

———, and Kim J. Ruhl, 2003, "How Important Is the New Goods Margin in International Trade?" Federal Reserve Bank of Minneapolis Research Department Staff Report No. 324 (Minneapolis: Minnesota).

Kose, M. Ayhan, 2002, "Explaining Business Cycles in Small Open Economies: 'How Much Do World Prices Matter?'" *Journal of International Economics*, Vol. 56 (March), pp. 299–327.

———, and Kei-Mu Yi, 2005, "Can the Standard International Business Cycle Model Explain the Relation Between Trade and Comovement?" *Journal of International Economics*, forthcoming.

Kose, M. Ayhan, Guy Meredith, and Christopher Towe, 2005, "How Has NAFTA Affected the Mexican Economy? Review and Evidence," in *Monetary Policy and Macroeconomic Stabilization in Latin America*, ed. by Rolf J. Langhammer and Lucio Vinhas de Souza (Berlin: Springer-Verlag, forthcoming). Also published as IMF Working Paper 04/59 (Washington: International Monetary Fund).

Kose, M. Ayhan, Eswar S. Prasad, and Marco E. Terrones, 2003a, "Financial Integration and Macroeconomic Volatility," *IMF Staff Papers,* Vol. 50 (Special Issue), pp. 119–42.

———, 2003b, "How Does Globalization Affect the Synchronization of Business Cycles?" *American Economic Review, Papers and Proceedings*, Vol. 93 (May), pp. 57–62.

———, 2004, "Volatility and Comovement in a Globalized World Economy: An Empirical Exploration," in *Macroeconomic Policies in the World Economy*, ed. by Horst Siebert (Berlin: Springer-Verlag), pp. 89–122.

———, 2005a, "Has Globalization Changed the Relationship Between Growth and Volatility?" *Journal of International Economics*, forthcoming. Also published as "How Do Trade and Financial Integration Affect the Relationship Between Growth and Volatility?" IMF Working Paper 05/19 (Washington: International Monetary Fund).

———, 2005b, "Growth and Volatility in an Era of Globalization," *IMF Staff Papers,* forthcoming.

Kose, M. Ayhan, and Raymond Riezman, 2000, "Understanding the Welfare Implications of Preferential Trade Agreements," *Review of International Economics*, Vol. 8 (November), pp. 619–33.

Kouparitsas, Michael, 1997, "A Dynamic Macroeconomic Analysis of NAFTA," *Economic Perspectives: A Review from the Federal Reserve Bank of Chicago,* Vol. 21 (January/February), pp. 14–35.

Kowalczyk, Carsten, and Donald Davis, 1998, "Tariff Phase-Outs: Theory and Evidence from GATT and NAFTA," in *The Regionalization of the World Economy,* ed. by Jeffrey A. Frankel (Chicago, Illinois: University of Chicago Press), pp. 227–50.

Kraay, Aart, 2004, "When Is Growth Pro-Poor? Cross-Country Evidence," IMF Working Paper 04/47 (Washington: International Monetary Fund).

Krueger, Anne O., 1997, "Free Trade Agreements versus Customs Unions," *Journal of Development Economics,* Vol. 54 (October), pp. 169–87.

———, 1999, "Trade Creation and Trade Diversion under NAFTA," NBER Working Paper No. 7429 (Cambridge, Massachusetts: National Bureau of Economic Research).

———, 2000, "NAFTA's Effects: A Preliminary Assessment," *World Economy,* Vol. 23 (June), pp. 761–75.

Laursen, Thomas, and Sandeep Mahajan, 2005, "Volatility, Income Distribution and Poverty," in *Managing Economic Volatility and Crises: A Practitioner's Guide,* ed. by Joshua Aizenman and Brian Pinto (Cambridge: Cambridge University Press, forthcoming).

Lederman, Daniel, William F. Maloney, and Luis Servén, 2003, *Lessons from NAFTA for Latin America and the Caribbean Countries* (Washington: World Bank).

Lederman, Daniel, Guillermo Perry, and Rodrigo Suescún, 2002, "Trade Structure, Trade Policy, and Economic Policy Options in Central America," Policy Research Working Paper No. 3025 (Washington: World Bank).

Levine, Ross, 1996, "Foreign Banks, Financial Development, and Economic Growth," in *International Financial Markets: Harmonization versus Competition* (Washington: AEI Press), pp. 224–54.

———, and David Renelt, 1992, "A Sensitivity Analysis of Cross-Country Growth Regressions," *American Economic Review,* Vol. 82 (September), pp. 942–63.

Lopez-Cordova, J. Ernesto, 2001, "NAFTA and the Mexican Economy: Analytical Issues and Lessons for the FTAA," INTAL-ITD-STA Occasional Paper No. 9 (Washington: Inter-American Development Bank).

———, 2002, "NAFTA and Mexico's Manufacturing Productivity: An Empirical Investigation Using Micro-Level Data" (unpublished; Washington: Inter-American Development Bank).

Manchester, Joyce, and Warwick J. McKibbin, 1995, "The Global Macroeconomics of NAFTA," *Open Economies Review,* Vol. 6 (July), pp. 203–23.

Mason, Andrew D., 2005, "Policy Approaches to Managing the Economic Transition: Ensuring that the Poor Can Benefit from DR-CAFTA," in *DR-CAFTA: Challenges and Opportunities for Central America* (Washington: World Bank, forthcoming).

Mendoza, Enrique, 1995, "The Terms of Trade, the Real Exchange Rate and Economic Fluctuations," *International Economic Review,* Vol. 36 (February), pp. 101–37.

OECD (Organization for Economic Cooperation and Development), 2002, "Intra-industry and Intra-firm Trade and the Internationalization of Production," *OECD Economic Outlook,* Vol. 71, pp. 159–70.

OXFAM, 2004, "A Raw Deal for Rice under DR-CAFTA: How the Free Trade Agreement Threatens the Livelihoods of Central American Farmers," Oxfam Briefing Paper No. 68 (London: Oxfam).

Policy Research Initiative, 2003, "The North American Linkages Project: Focusing the Research Agenda," *Horizons,* Vol. 6, No. 2. Available via the Internet:http://policyresearch.gc.ca/page.asp?pagenm=v6n2_art_07.

Prasad, Eswar, Kenneth Rogoff, Shang-Jin Wei, and M. Ayhan Kose, 2003, *Effects of Financial Globalization on Developing Countries: Some Empirical Evidence,* IMF Occasional Paper No. 220 (Washington: International Monetary Fund).

Quah, Danny, 1997, "Empirics for Growth and Distribution: Stratification, Polarization, and Convergence Clubs," *Journal of Economic Growth,* Vol. 2 (March), pp. 27–59.

Ramey, Gary, and Valerie A. Ramey, 1995, "Cross-Country Evidence on the Link Between Volatility and Growth," *American Economic Review,* Vol. 85, No. 5 (December), pp. 1138–51.

Rapoport, Hillel, and Frédéric Docquier, 2005, "The Economics of Migrants' Remittances," in *Handbook on the Economics of Reciprocity, Giving and Altruism,* ed. by L.A. Gerard-Varet, S.C. Kolm, and J. Mercier-Ythier (Amsterdam: Elsevier North-Holland).

Ravn, Morten O., and Elisabetta Mazzenga, 1999, "Frictions in International Trade and Relative Price Movements" (unpublished; London: London Business School).

Rebucci, Alessandro, 1998, "External Shocks, Macroeconomic Policy, and Growth: A Panel VAR Approach," Global Economic Institutions Working Paper No. 40 (London: Centre for Economic Policy Research).

Rodrik, Dani, and Francisco Rodriguez, 2000, "Trade Policy and Economic Growth: A Skeptic's Guide to the Cross-National Evidence," in *NBER Macroeconomics Annual 2000,* ed. by Ben Bernanke and Kenneth Rogoff (Cambridge, Massachusetts: MIT Press), pp. 261–325.

Rogoff, Kenneth, 2002, "Rethinking Capital Controls: When Should We Keep an Open Mind?" *Finance and Development* (International Monetary Fund), Vol. 39, No. 4., pp. 55–6.

Romalis, John, 2002, "NAFTA's and CUSFTA's Impact on North American Trade" (unpublished; Chicago, Illinois: University of Chicago Graduate School of Business).

Sachs, Jeffrey, and Andrew Warner, 1995, "Economic Reform and the Process of Global Integration," *Brookings Papers on Economic Activity: 2,* pp. 523–64.

Sala-i-Martin, Xavier, 2002, "The Disturbing "Rise" of Global Income Inequality," NBER Working Paper No. 8904 (Cambridge, Massachusetts: National Bureau for Economic Research).

Salazar-Xirinachs, Jose M., and Jaime Granados, 2004, "The U.S.-Central America Free Trade Agreement: Opportunities and Challenges," in *Free Trade Agreements: U.S. Strategies and Priorities,* ed. by Jeffrey J.

Schott (Washington: Institute for International Economics), pp. 225–75.

Schiff, Maurice, and Yanling Wang, 2002, "Regional Integration and Technology Diffusion: The Case of NAFTA," World Bank Development Research Group, Policy Research Working Paper No. 3132 (Washington: World Bank).

Sobarzo, Horacio E., 1992, "A General Equilibrium Analysis of the Gains from Trade for Mexican Economy of a North American Free Trade Agreement," *World Economy*, Vol. 15 (January), pp. 83–100.

Taccone, Juan José, and Uziel Nogueira, eds., 2004, *Central American Report* No. 2, INTA (Institute for the Integration of Latin America and the Caribbean) (Washington: Inter-American Development Bank).

Tornell, Aaron, and Gerardo Esquivel, 1995, "The Political Economy of Mexico's Entry to NAFTA," NBER Working Paper No. 5322 (Washington: National Bureau of Economic Research).

Tornell, Aaron, Frank Westermann, and Lorenza Martinez, 2003, "Liberalization, Growth, and Financial Crises: Lessons from Mexico and the Developing World," *Brookings Papers on Economic Activity: 2*, pp. 1–112.

Torres, Alberto, and Oscar Vela, 2003, "Trade Integration and Synchronization Between the Business Cycles of Mexico and the United States," *North American Journal of Economics and Finance*, Vol. 14, pp. 319–42.

USITC (U.S. International Trade Commission), 1997, "The Impact of the North American Free Trade Agreement on the U.S. Economy and Industries: A Three-Year Review," *Investigation No. 332–81*, USITC Publication No. 3045 (Washington).

———, 2004, "U.S.-Central America-Dominican Republic Free Trade Agreement: Potential Economywide and Selected Sectoral Effects," USITC Publication No. 3717 (Washington).

USTR (Office of the United States Trade Representative), 2005a, "The Case for CAFTA," *CAFTA Facts* (CAFTA Policy Brief) (February).

———, 2005b, "The *Facts* About CAFTA's Labor Provisions," *CAFTA Facts* (CAFTA Policy Brief) (February).

———, 2005c, "Sugar: A Spoonful a Week," *CAFTA Facts* (CAFTA Policy Brief) (February).

Van Wincoop, Eric, 1999, "How Big Are Potential Welfare Gains from International Risk Sharing?" *Journal of International Economics*, Vol. 47 (February), pp. 109–35.

Waldkirch, Andreas, 2003, "The New Regionalism and Foreign Direct Investment: The Case of Mexico," *Journal of International Trade and Economic Development*, Vol. 12 (June), pp. 151–84.

Wei, Shang-Jin, and Yi Wu, 2002, "The Life-and-Death Implications of Globalization" (unpublished; Washington: International Monetary Fund).

Whalley, John, 1998, "Why Do Countries Seek Regional Trade Agreements?" in *The Regionalization of the World Economy*, ed. by Jeffrey A. Frenkel (Chicago: University of Chicago Press).

Winters, L. Alan, 2004, "Trade Liberalization and Economic Performance: An Overview," *Economic Journal*, Vol. 114 (February), pp. 4–21.

———, Neil McCulloch, and Andrew McKay, 2004, "Trade Liberalization and Poverty: The Evidence So Far," *Journal of Economic Literature*, Vol. 42 (March), pp. 72–115.

World Bank, 2000, *Trade Blocs* (Oxford: Oxford University Press).

III   Trade Liberalization and Tax Coordination

Chiara Bronchi and Dale Chua

The free trade agreements between the Central American countries, the Dominican Republic, and the United States (CAFTA-DR) are expected to have a significant impact in many areas of the region's economies, including public finances.[1] Given the importance of the United States as a major trading partner, and the continued reliance on trade taxes as a source of revenue, CAFTA-DR is likely to have a notable—albeit varying—impact on Central American budgets.

This section considers the revenue consequences of CAFTA-DR for each of the Central American countries.[2] It then provides estimates based on highly disaggregated customs data and on each country's calendar for trade liberalization. The revenue impact of CAFTA-DR was recently analyzed in Barreix, Villela, and Roca (2004) and in Paunovic and Martínez (2003), but with a lesser degree of custom data disaggregation than in this section.[3] Moreover, the trade liberalization schedule (agreed upon in 2004) was not known when these studies were completed. Using 2002 tariff data, Barreix, Villela, and Roca estimated a total revenue loss ranging from 1.6 percent of GDP for Nicaragua to 7.5 percent for Honduras. Assuming different liberalization calendars, Paunovic and Martínez found that in the first year of CAFTA-DR, revenue losses range from 0.1 to 0.3 percent of GDP in Costa Rica and from 0.23 to 0.69 percent of GDP in Honduras.

This section also considers possible compensating revenue measures and reviews the implications for tax policy and its coordination within the region. The first subsection provides background by summarizing the current tax systems in the region and outlining recent changes. The next subsection presents estimates of the near-term revenue cost of CAFTA-DR for each of the Central American countries. These estimates show that the impact is significant, although its size and timing vary across countries, depending on their reliance on trade taxes; trade patterns (particularly the importance of trade with the United States); and the respective calendars for transition to the new regime. This subsection also considers the possible long-term revenue effects of growth enhancement from CAFTA-DR. The following subsection discusses compensating revenue measures, and the final subsection before the conclusion considers the heightened need for tax coordination among the Central American countries as a result of CAFTA-DR.

Structure and Trend of Tax Revenues in Central America

Recent Evolution of the Tax System

The tax ratio—tax revenue relative to GDP—increased in nearly all Central American countries during the 1990s (Figure 3.1). For the region as a whole, the unweighted average rose from 11.0 to 13.1 percent between the periods 1990–94 and 1999–2003. These revenue increases were driven mainly by increased revenues from sales taxes (value-added tax—VAT) and excise taxes on particular commodities (Figure 3.2).

Though the trend has been the same in most countries, tax ratios vary significantly across the region, from about 9 percent in Panama to 16 percent in Honduras. This variation stems from differences in rates, coverage, and the effectiveness of tax administration. The measured ratios may in some cases be distorted by possible underestimates of GDP.[4] Nevertheless, they do point to real differences in the tax effort in the region.

---

[1]For a broad review of the economic impact of CAFTA-DR, see Section II. Trade within Central America is already largely liberalized. Key documents pertaining to Central America integration, including the Protocol to the General Treaty of Central American Economic Integration (Guatemala Protocol) of October 29, 1993, are available at www.sgsica.org, website of the General Secretariat, Central America Integration System.

[2]Costa Rica, El Salvador, Guatemala, Honduras, and Nicaragua.

[3]Barreix, Villela, and Roca (2004) estimate the tax revenue consequences of trade liberalization initiatives for the whole Western Hemisphere, including the Central American countries.

[4]In Nicaragua, for example, the tax ratio has fallen in recent years mainly as the result of a major upward revision of GDP in 2000.

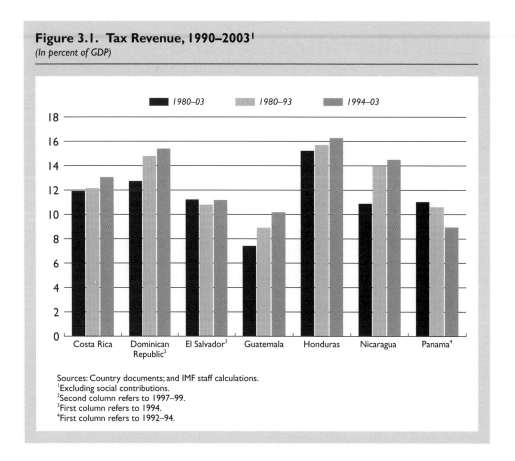

Figure 3.1. Tax Revenue, 1990–2003[1]
(In percent of GDP)

■ 1980–03   ■ 1980–93   ■ 1994–03

Sources: Country documents; and IMF staff calculations.
[1]Excluding social contributions.
[2]Second column refers to 1997–99.
[3]First column refers to 1994.
[4]First column refers to 1992–94.

All Central American countries have relatively modern tax systems that rely on diverse sources of revenue,[5] including a well-established and fairly broad-based VAT,[6] excises on a limited number of goods, taxes on individual and business incomes, and streamlined customs duties. Domestic taxes on goods and services are the broadest and largest source of tax revenue across the region. Taxes on income, profits, and capital gains are the second main source of tax revenues, and international trade taxes come third (Table 3.1).

The region has become less dependent on trade taxes over the past decade as the countries have eliminated taxes on intraregional trade and the common external tariff (CET) of the Central American Common Market has been reduced gradually. Export taxes have been eliminated (except in Costa Rica, where the authorities are phasing out a 1 percent tax on general exports and a specific tax on the export of

bananas), and the share of import duties in total tax revenue has declined on average from 23 percent in the early 1990s to 14 percent in the early 2000s. An exception is Nicaragua, where trade taxes have increased in importance over this period and now account for nearly 30 percent of total tax revenue.

The Central American countries have generally succeeded in increasing domestic tax revenues to replace customs revenue forgone as a consequence of trade liberalization (Figure 3.3). Though in the 1990s indirect taxes (VAT and excises) grew much faster than direct taxes (especially in 1995–99), in the early 2000s the trend was reversed, with direct taxes growing faster.

Tariff Policies

The Central American countries have been involved in a long process of trade integration, which has resulted in the adoption of a common trade nomenclature (1993) and a common external tariff (1997). Although the pace of liberalization and implementation of the common tariffs has been uneven across countries, a remarkable overhaul of tariff structures has taken place, bringing about a major re-

---

[5]See Stotsky and WoldeMariam (2002) for a recent description and assessment of the tax systems of Central American countries.

[6]Nicaragua was the first in the region to introduce a VAT (1975), and Costa Rica was the last (1992).

Figure 3.2. Central America: Composition of Tax Revenue, 1990–2003
(In percent of GDP)

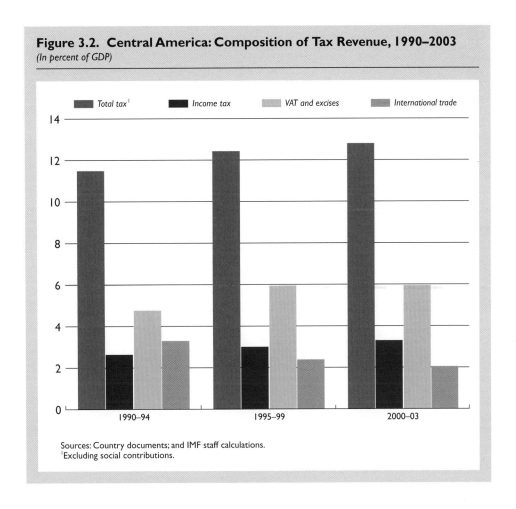

Sources: Country documents; and IMF staff calculations.
[1]Excluding social contributions.

duction in average collected tariffs. Table 3.2 shows that collected tariff rates[7] have declined in all countries of the region since the late 1980s. In Costa Rica, the collected tariff rate fell from an average of 11.2 percent in the period 1985–89 to 2.1 percent in 2003. All countries in the region now have collected tariff rates between 2.0 and 5.5 percent, which is relatively low by international standards.

The tariff structure reflects the participation of the Central American countries in the Central American Common Market (CACM).[8] Most-favored-nation (MFN) tariffs are defined by the Central American Customs System (CACS), with 6,256 eight-digit tariff lines.[9] About 92 percent of these lines are harmonized among the CACM members, establishing a common external tariff for these items. Those that

are not harmonized concern mainly sensitive items such as agricultural goods, textile, petroleum derivatives, metallic products, and pharmaceuticals.

The common external tariff is composed of four basic rates: zero for capital goods and raw materials not competing with those produced in Central America; 5 percent on raw materials competing with those produced in the region; 10 percent on intermediate goods not competing with those produced in Central America; and 15 percent on final consumer and other goods. For the complete liberalization of internal trade in goods, only 26 tariff lines need to be eliminated—although these apply to goods that are considered sensitive.

Customs Duty and Tax Revenue on Trade with the United States

Tax revenue on imports from the United States remains significant, although it varies among the Central American countries. In 2003, tariff revenues from these imports, together with the VAT and excise taxes, accounted for an average of 0.4 percent of

---

[7]Defined as the ratio of import tariff revenue to import values.
[8]The CACM includes Costa Rica, El Salvador, Guatemala, Honduras, and Nicaragua.
[9]The number of tariff lines varies across the region because some tariff lines have subcodes specific to each country. For example, in Honduras there are 6,310 lines, including the subcodes.

Table 3.1. Consolidated Central Government: Tax Structure for Selected Central American Countries, 2000–03
(In percent of tax revenues)[1]

| | Taxes on Income and Social Contributions | | | Taxes on Goods and Services | | | | Taxes on International Trade | | | | |
| | | | | | | Of which | | | | | Of which | |
	Total	Taxes on income, profits, and capital gains	Social contributions	Total	General taxes on goods and services; VAT	Excises	Other	Total	Customs and other import duties	Taxes on exports	Taxes on property	Other taxes
Costa Rica	26.3	23.2	...	64.6	36.5	11.8	16.2	6.8	6.3	1.7	2.5	1.0
Dominican Republic	31.6	26.6	5.0	44.8	24.7	20.2	...	25.7	19.7	0.0	1.7	1.1
El Salvador	29.0	29.0	...	60.3	52.0	8.3	...	9.8	9.8	...	...	0.9
Guatemala	28.0	26.1	1.9	60.3	44.8	12.3	3.2	12.0	11.9	0.0	0.1	1.9
Honduras	21.3	21.3	...	64.2	34.8	1.5	27.8	12.8	12.8	0.0	1.2	0.5
Nicaragua	37.1	19.4	17.7	51.5	24.0	27.4	0.1	24.4	24.4	0.0	–0.1	4.7
Panama	104.2	42.4	61.8	34.3	15.4	13.4	5.5	17.5	17.5	0.0	...	5.8
Unweighted average[2]	39.6	26.9	21.6	54.3	33.2	13.6	8.8	15.6	14.6	0.3	1.1	2.3

Sources: IMF, *Government Finance Statistics*; country documents; and IMF staff calculations.

[1]Total tax revenues exclude social security contributions.

[2]For each revenue classification, only countries for which data are available are included in the calculation.

Structure and Trend of Tax Revenues in Central America

Figure 3.3. Composition of Tax Revenue, 1990–2003
(In percent of tax revenue)

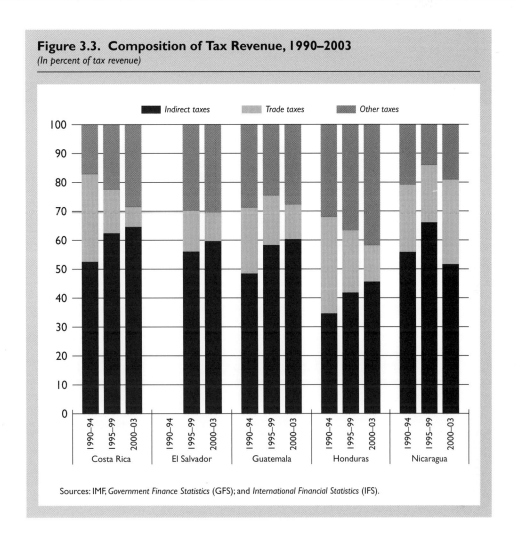

Sources: IMF, *Government Finance Statistics* (GFS); and *International Financial Statistics* (IFS).

Table 3.2. Average Collected Import Duty Rates
(In percent of total imports)

	1995	1996	1997	1998	1999	2000	Average		
							1985–89	1990–95	1996–2000
Costa Rica	7.2	4.1	4.2	3.2	2.3	2.1	11.2	9.5	3.2
Dominican Republic	12.5	11.9	12.9	12.1	13.1	14.2	16.0	17.6	12.8
El Salvador	6.4	5.4	4.1	3.9	3.8	3.0	5.5	6.4	4.0
Guatemala	9.1	8.5	7.0	6.2	5.8	4.9	9.2	8.6	6.5
Honduras	10.0	7.6	7.4	6.4	5.5	5.4	18.8	13.0	6.5
Nicaragua	4.7	3.8	4.1	5.9	2.9	3.1	n.a.	11.1	4.0
Panama	2.7	2.8	2.9	3.2	3.6	2.9	4.1	2.8	3.1
Unweighted average	7.5	6.3	6.1	5.8	5.3	5.1	10.8	9.9	5.7

Source: IMF, *Government Finance Statistics*.

Table 3.3. Customs Revenue on Imports from the United States, 2003

	Custom Duties	Import		Total Revenue from U.S. Imports	Revenue from Customs Duties on U.S. Imports
		VAT	Excises		
		(In percent of GDP)			(In percent of tax revenue)
Costa Rica	0.30	0.03	0.00	0.33	2.44
El Salvador	0.29	0.03	0.00	0.32	2.71
Guatemala	0.44	0.05	0.00	0.50	7.77
Honduras	0.57	0.03	0.01	0.61	5.21
Nicaragua	0.30	0.04	0.01	0.35	1.78
Unweighted average	0.38	0.04	0.00	0.42	3.98

Sources: National customs; and IMF staff calculations.

GDP in the region, which is equivalent to about 4 percent of total tax revenue. Again, there are quite marked differences across countries (Table 3.3). Tax revenue from U.S. imports ranges from a little less than 2 percent of total tax revenue in Nicaragua to nearly 8 percent in Guatemala.

Estimating the Loss of Tax Revenue from CAFTA-DR

Although CAFTA-DR was negotiated collectively, with all parties subject to the "same set of obligations and commitments," each Central American country negotiated its own schedule for market access on a bilateral basis with the United States. Annex 3.3 of each CAFTA-DR agreement defines the tariff elimination schedule for each custom line. Each traded good is classified into one of eight categories (labeled A through H), which define the period over which duties will be eliminated and the schedule of tariff reductions. Many goods will be zero rated immediately (Schedule A), and the tariffs for others will be phased out incrementally so that liberalization is reached in 5, 10, 15, or 20 years from the time the agreement takes effect. The phaseout periods differ for the various groups of products and within the same group of products; for example, in Honduras white and dark chicken meat is subject to different schedules.

The CAFTA-DR agreement is asymmetric. On the U.S. side, liberalization is immediate: from day one, 100 percent of nonagricultural and nontextile goods will enter the United States duty free. On the Central American side, each country has a different allocation of goods to the eight categories and, hence, a different time profile of tariff reduction.

When CAFTA-DR enters into force, for about 80 percent of nonagricultural and nontextile exports, all tariffs will be removed within 10 years (covering schedules A, B, and C). Tariffs on many product categories will be set to zero in the first year of the treaty, including information technology products, some agricultural and construction equipment, paper products, chemicals, and medical/scientific equipment under Schedule A. Tariffs on other goods are being removed linearly over 5 or 10 years, and others have lengthy periods of grace (of up to 20 years); some are to become duty free in a nonlinear way.

The entry into effect of CAFTA-DR, and trade liberalization more generally, will affect government revenue both directly and indirectly:

- The direct (or "static") revenue effect is that which arises at unchanged import volumes and prices (before customs duties). This includes not only the impact on tariff revenues themselves, but also the impact on the revenues from taxes imposed on tariff-inclusive import values (as is normal and recommended practice for VAT and ad valorem excises).[10] These effects—as well as the indirect effects discussed below—depend, in principle, on the nature of competition in the marketplace; except as specified below, competitive behavior and returns to scale are assumed constant, so that prices exclusive of tariffs remain unchanged by CAFTA-DR.[11]

---

[10]Note that revenue from many other taxes may also be directly affected; for instance, taxable corporate income will be increased as a result of reduced import costs. Such effects are ignored in the calculations reported here.

[11]Central American countries are small economies that cannot affect world market prices.

• Indirect effects result from changes in import volumes and/or tariff-exclusive prices induced by the reform. There are many potential effects of this kind. Tariff cuts would be expected—all things being equal—to increase the demand for imports, possibly to such an extent that revenue actually increases (though this seems improbable given the relatively low initial level of tariffs in Central America).[12] Trade liberalization may also spur economic growth—one of the underlying objectives of CAFTA-DR—which can help strengthen government finances, and tax revenue in particular; but this effect would tend to become evident only over time, and it may be prudent not to count on this effect to recover revenue losses (see Section II regarding CAFTA-DR's implications for growth).

A potential indirect effect of CAFTA-DR is the possibility of trade diversion, with imports from the United States replacing those from third countries that remain subject to the CET. Although this is a concern from a welfare perspective—to the extent that imports from third countries are cheaper than those from the United States, the former are socially preferable—the concern in this section is the additional erosion of tariff revenue that trade diversion causes. It is difficult to determine a priori the likely form or extent of such diversion. There are several possibilities. For instance, there may simply be no substitution between U.S. and third-country imports, even within the same tariff line, in which case there would be no trade diversion. Or, when substitution is perfect but competition is not, third-country exporters may seek to preserve their market position by cutting their pretariff price by enough to leave their tariff-inclusive price at the same level as the now tariff-free price of exports from the United States. In that case, one might expect the shares of third country and U.S. imports to remain unchanged—with the change in the overall volume reflecting the price elasticity of the demand for imports—and expect tariff revenues from third-country imports to fall to the extent that the unchanged MFN rate is charged on a lower tariff-exclusive price.

Quantifying the Impact

The quantitative analysis below considers several scenarios and aspects of the revenue implications of CAFTA-DR.[13]

• The immediate direct impact in the first year of implementation (taking account of the differing liberalization schedules of the Central American countries), assuming no change in the volume or composition of imports.

• Immediate effects, but allowing for impacts through third-country imports under the alternative assumptions that (1) third countries cut tariff-exclusive prices to offset tariff reductions on imports from the United States; (2) there is trade diversion of 20 percent (non-U.S. imports fall by one-fifth); and (3) diversion is 100 percent (as an illustrative scenario).

• The long-run effect, when there is trade diversion of 35 percent, and when tariffs on imports of U.S. goods are zero.

For the region as a whole, about two-fifths of imports from the United States will become duty free immediately, although the degree of front-loading varies widely across countries. Of all imports from the United States on which duty is currently payable, 43 percent will become duty free in the first year of the treaty. However, the degree to which imports from the United States are liberalized in the first year of the treaty varies substantially across countries (Table 3.4). Costa Rica will liberalize almost all of its imports from the United States, so that 97 percent of long-term revenue loss from CAFTA-DR—about 2.4 percent of all tax revenues—would come immediately (Table 3.5). Nicaragua, in contrast, liberalizes 17 percent of U.S. imports in the first year and front-loads only 13 percent of any long-term loss.

Revenue will decrease by an average of 0.2 percent of GDP, or 2 percent of total tax revenue, in the first year of CAFTA-DR. This impact reflects a direct loss of customs duties (0.15 percent of GDP) and indirect domestic taxes (0.02 percent of GDP); the effect on excise tax revenue is minimal. Once again, the extent of the revenue loss varies across countries. Costa Rica has the greatest degree of front-loading, although imports from the United States account for a relatively low share of all imports. Honduras has the second-largest loss in the first year; tax revenues fall by about 0.2 percent of GDP, representing one-third of the full long-term

---

[12]Ebrill, Stotsky, and Gropp (1999), for instance, conclude that the revenue-maximizing collected tariff rate is about 20 percent. Though one can question the validity of this notion for an individual tax (since many different tariff structures can yield the same collected rate), it is noteworthy that average collected rates in Central America are far below this level.

[13]The data and methodology used are described in the Appendix.

Table 3.4. Schedule A Imports, 2003[1]

	Total Imports from the United States (In percent of total imports) (A)	Schedule A Imports (In percent of total imports) (B)	Schedule A Imports (In percent of imports from the United States) (B/A)
Costa Rica	20.8	20.7	99.5
El Salvador	31.3	12.2	38.9
Guatemala	34.8	5.7	16.4
Honduras	...	...	...
Nicaragua	26.4	4.4	16.7
Unweighted average	28.3	10.7	42.9

Sources: National customs; and IMF staff calculations.
[1]Schedule A comprises imports from the United States that will be liberalized in the first year of CAFTA-DR.

Table 3.5. Revenue Impact of CAFTA-DR, First Year[1]

	Tariff Loss	Sales Tax Loss	Excise Loss	First-Year Revenue Loss		
	(In percent of GDP)			(In percent of GDP)	(In percent of tax revenue)	(In percent of total revenue loss)
Costa Rica	0.29	0.03	0.00	0.32	2.37	96.97
El Salvador	0.08	0.01	0.00	0.09	0.76	28.13
Guatemala	0.15	0.01	0.00	0.16	1.99	32.00
Honduras	0.21	0.01	0.00	0.22	1.35	25.88
Nicaragua	0.04	0.00	0.00	0.05	0.23	12.71
Unweighted average	0.15	0.01	0.00	0.17	1.34	39.14

Sources: National customs; and IMF staff calculations.
[1]Base year 2003.

revenue loss. Nicaragua has the lowest degree of front-loading (13 percent), and hence the lowest revenue loss (0.05 percent of GDP) in the first year.

These figures should be thought of as lower bounds on the likely revenue loss, as they do not allow for trade diversion.[14] To illustrate the possible impact of trade diversion, calculations were made for the cases of Honduras and Nicaragua—the only Central American countries for which the necessary line-by-line information on non-U.S. imports is available. The results, calculated under the three alternative assumptions described above, are summarized in Table 3.6. The *base case* assumes that there is no trade diversion, but that suppliers from outside the CAFTA-DR zone

lower the prices of goods competing with imports from the United States to offset their tariff disadvantage. The *intermediate case* assumes trade diversion of 20 percent in the first year of the trade agreement and 35 percent in the long term, and the *extreme case* assumes 100 percent of trade diversion for those goods that are already imported from the United States (meaning non-U.S. imports go to zero).[15]

With offsetting price cuts by third countries, the revenue losses in Honduras and Nicaragua are

---

[14]On the other hand, they overstate the revenue loss over the transition period to the extent that reduced (but nonzero) tariffs lead to increased imports from the United States.

[15]The diversion cases are presented for illustrative purposes. The process of trade diversion is likely to take longer than in the first year of the treaty. Krueger (1999, 2000) found that in the case of Mexico, NAFTA was not a trade-diverting agreement, since the categories in which Mexican exports to the United States registered the largest increase for the period 1990–96 overlapped with categories in which exports rose most rapidly, along with the rest of the world, suggesting that the impact of NAFTA on Mexico involved other trade dynamics.

Table 3.6. Honduras and Nicaragua: Revenue Impact of CAFTA-DR, First Year

	No Trade Diversion[1]	20 Percent Trade Diversion	100 Percent Trade Diversion
(In percent of GDP)			
Honduras	0.25	0.30	0.50
Nicaragua	0.06	0.08	0.20
(In percent of total tax revenues)			
Honduras	1.53	1.84	3.07
Nicaragua	0.20	0.42	0.99

Sources: National customs; and IMF staff calculations.
[1]Suppliers from outside the United States lower pre-tariff prices of goods competing with U.S. imports.

somewhat larger than when only direct effects arise. The loss in Honduras is estimated at 0.25 percent of GDP in the first year of the treaty, compared with a direct loss of 0.22 percent (0.06 percent of GDP versus 0.04 percent in Nicaragua). The impact in Honduras reflects the impact caused by the reduction in the c.i.f. price of goods competing with imports from the United States (0.03 percent of GDP), the direct loss of taxes in the form of customs duty, as before (0.22 percent of GDP), and the indirect impact on sales tax (0.01 percent of GDP). The impact on excise tax revenue is minimal. The impact is much smaller in Nicaragua, where the loss of customs duty is 0.05 percent, the loss from the sales tax and excises is negligible, and that from the reduction in the c.i.f. price of goods competing with imports from the United States is 0.01 percent of GDP.

The revenue loss could potentially double in Honduras and triple in Nicaragua if there were full trade diversion. With 20 percent diversion, the revenue loss in the first year would be 0.3 percent of GDP for Honduras, and about 0.08 percent of GDP for Nicaragua. With 100 percent diversion, the loss for Honduras would be 0.5 percent of GDP, and for Nicaragua it would be about 0.2 percent of GDP. The extent of the long-term revenue loss is highly sensitive to the extent of trade diversion. In the absence of trade diversion, the long-term total loss could amount to 0.4 percent of GDP for the region as a whole (Table 3.7). For Honduras, the loss would represent 0.6 percent of GDP, but it would rise to a total of 1.45 percent of GDP if all goods were subject to 100 percent trade diversion. Although for Nicaragua the loss without trade diversion would be 0.35 percent of GDP, it would reach 0.9 percent with 100 percent trade diversion.

Table 3.7. Summary Table: Revenue Loss of CAFTA-DR
(In percent of GDP)

	First Year					Long-Term		
	Only static effects	No trade diversion[1]	20 percent trade diversion	100 percent trade diversion	Total tax revenues	Only static effects	35 percent trade diversion	100 percent trade diversion
Costa Rica	0.32	...	...	...		0.33	...	...
El Salvador	0.09	...	...	...		0.32	...	...
Guatemala	0.16	...	...	...		0.50	...	...
Honduras	0.22	0.27	0.31	0.49	16.3	0.61	1.01	1.45
Nicaragua	0.05	0.06	0.08	0.20	19.9	0.35	0.51	0.88
Unweighted average	0.17	0.16	0.20	0.34		0.42	0.76	1.17

Sources: National customs; and IMF staff calculations.
[1]Suppliers from outside the United States lower pre-tariff prices of goods competing with U.S. imports.

Box 3.1. Revenue Effects of Growth Enhancement from CAFTA-DR

The improved growth performance expected to result from CAFTA-DR can be expected to increase tax revenues, offsetting to some degree the direct revenue losses. As private incomes rise, so do revenues from the income tax, VAT, excises, and other taxes (including remaining tariffs). Even in the absence of changes in the parameters of the tax system, revenue would be expected to increase as a consequence of expanded tax bases.

The magnitude of this indirect revenue recovery depends on (1) the extent to which CAFTA-DR spurs faster growth, and (2) the responsiveness of tax revenues to any increase in the level of income. Both of these quantities are subject to considerable uncertainty.

- On the first, Hilaire and Yang (2003) estimate that CAFTA-DR would increase the aggregate GDP of the Central American region by 1.5 percent in the long run. The modesty of this boost may reflect the high degree of trade integration that already exists between the Central American countries and the United States, or it might be that some dynamic links between CAFTA-DR and growth are not adequately captured. (Other studies point to stronger growth effects of trade liberalization (see, for example, Wacziarg and Welch, 2003), though they do not deal directly with CAFTA-DR.)

- On the second, time-series regressions can be used to estimate for each country the elasticity of tax revenue with respect to GDP. Using data for 1990–2003, this elasticity averages about 0.14 percent.[1] These estimates must be interpreted with caution. In particular, they do not distinguish increases in revenue from policy reform from the automatic effects of increased income levels, but indicate likely orders of magnitude.

These rough estimates imply that the indirect increase in revenue from improved GDP performance will not fully offset the direct revenue loss. Combining the Hilaire-Yang estimate of a 1.5 percent increase in GDP with the estimated revenue elasticities implies that revenue will, on this account, rise by an unweighted average of 0.22 percent for the region as a whole, ranging from 0.17 percent for Guatemala to 0.34 percent for Nicaragua. This compares with direct revenue losses estimated in the text of 3.1 percent under the long-term static scenario. Thus, indirect growth effects might offset about 7 percent of long-run direct revenue loss.

The extent of indirect revenue recovery will depend on the size of the boost to growth performance, about which there is considerable uncertainty. One way of assessing the potential revenue impact of enhanced growth is to ask instead: by how much would growth have to be increased by CAFTA-DR for the associated revenue increase (as implied by the income responsiveness estimated above) to offset the direct revenue loss estimated in the text? For the Central American countries as a whole, unweighted GDP would have to increase by an average of 21.9 percent to offset the direct revenue loss in the long run.[2] This corresponds to increased annual growth rates, over a 10-year period (roughly matching movement to the final phase of CAFTA-DR), of 2 percentage points, which seems on the high side, reinforcing the view that revenue recovery from CAFTA-DR is likely to require some positive policy response.

---

[1]Specifically, the estimated elasticities (all significantly different from zero at 1 percent) are Costa Rica, 0.13; El Salvador, 0.14; Guatemala, 0.11; Honduras, 0.17; and Nicaragua, 0.23.

[2]The required growth increase is calculated as (direct revenue loss, in percent of GDP) / [(estimated revenue elasticity)×(tax revenue, in percent of GDP)].

CAFTA-DR is expected to strengthen growth, which should partially offset the direct revenue losses from tariff reduction. The size of the indirect revenue increase will depend on the effect of CAFTA-DR on growth as well as the responsiveness of the tax revenue to GDP. However, the indirect growth effect of CAFTA-DR on revenue is rather small, based on the CAFTA-DR-induced GDP growth estimated by Hilaire-Yang (2003) and estimates of revenue elasticities to GDP for the Central American countries (see Box 3.1). The growth dividend would be larger if dynamic growth effects not considered in Hilaire-Yang, are taken into account (see Section II).

Dealing with the Revenue Impact of CAFTA-DR

The discussion in the previous subsection leads to the conclusion that countries will need to take tax measures to maintain revenue-to-GDP ratios. For the region as a whole, tax measures on the order of 0.17 to 0.2 percent of GDP are needed to maintain the revenue ratio in the first year of CAFTA-DR. In the long term, the need to compensate for revenue losses may total 0.4 to 1.2 percent of GDP. These resources can be obtained by broadening tax bases (consumption and income) and strengthening tax administration.

Economic principles and experience elsewhere both suggest that indirect taxes have a key role to play in responding to revenue shortfalls due to trade liberalization. One simple strategy for dealing with a tariff reduction on a final consumption good, for instance, is to impose an equal increase in the tax on domestic consumption. For a small open economy—one that can have no impact on commodity prices in world markets—this will leave the price faced by consumers unchanged. It will also preserve the efficiency gain from the tariff cut, since the change in the consumption tax does not offset the effect of the reform in bringing the prices faced by domestic producers closer to those in world markets. The government's total tax revenue, however, will go up, since these revenues are now collected on all consumption, domestically produced as well as imported. That increase in government revenues could, in turn, be used to smooth the transition cost of those sectors that stand to lose from trade liberalization—for example, by temporary targeted subsidies—or to reduce consumption taxes to ensure that consumers also end up directly better off as a consequence of the reform. Although there are several qualifications to this argument,[16] it suggests a coherent and simple strategy for securing the efficiency benefits of trade liberalization without jeopardizing revenue and, moreover, without significantly affecting the distribution of the tax burden.

Unless the base of the VAT is broadened, Central American countries would have to increase the statutory VAT rate by at least 1 percentage point to compensate for the revenue loss from the CAFTA-DR.[17] In general, base-broadening measures are preferable to rate increases because they help improve the structure of the VAT and facilitate its administration: there would be fewer exceptions to the rule and less room for misreporting and abuse. Though rate increases are likely to result in increased revenues, they may also have unintended effects on taxpayers' compliance. For illustrative purposes, Figure 3.4

shows by how much the VAT statutory rate[18] in each country would have to increase—given the present tax base—to offset the direct revenue loss from CAFTA-DR. In the first year of liberalization, the VAT rate adjustment required is close to 1 percentage point for Costa Rica, and in the remaining countries it is quite small. However, the VAT rate increase that would be needed to compensate for the full application of the CAFTA-DR is almost 2 percentage points for Nicaragua, and over 1 percentage point for Guatemala and Honduras. These estimates indicate that, everything else being equal, the standard VAT rate that is needed to compensate tariff losses is slightly over 13 percent for Guatemala, 15 percent for Nicaragua, and close to 14 percent for the remaining countries.[19]

Although the VATs of the region are reasonably well structured, with fairly broad bases and low rates, there is scope for improving their design and administration in order to enhance collection and compliance. VAT revenue productivity,[20] a rough efficiency measure that offers some standardization of measurement across countries, is fairly low. Table 3.8 shows that it has not improved over the past 14 years, and that in some countries, such as Honduras and Nicaragua, it has actually worsened. Low and declining productivity often reflects base erosion through legislative changes or reduced tax compliance. Indeed, the VAT base in these countries is punctured by an excessive number of zero-rated and/or exempt items. For example, in Costa Rica, the VAT base excludes many services and does not allow full credit for the VAT paid on purchases of inputs—refunds are granted only when the inputs are effectively used in the production process. There appears to be substantial scope for reducing exemptions as part of a strategy to strengthen Central America's revenue effort, including a plan to offset the impact of CAFTA-DR. Moreover, the rate of VAT evasion is considered high in several Central American economies. Recent estimates point to as much as 40 percent evasion, suggesting that VAT collections could be significantly higher if administrative practices, such as audits, were improved (Stotsky and WoldeMariam, 2002).

[16]See Keen and Ligthart (2004). One qualification deserves particular comment. Strictly, the argument requires that, in order to leave all consumer prices unchanged, the rate structure of the new domestic consumption tax mimic in full the tariff structure that is being replaced. Since most countries apply multiple tariff rates, the reform strategy requires that there also be multiple rates of domestic consumption taxation. But such multiple rates can create their own problems. Nevertheless, the point remains valid that there are likely to be more welfare gains made by combining the shift away from trade taxes with a movement toward a more uniform consumption tax system.

[17]Part of the adjustment could also come from increasing excises on excisable goods on which tariffs on U.S. imports are reduced.

[18]The increase of the statutory VAT rate required to offset the revenue loss is estimated as follows: [VAT revenues and tariff loss in percent of GDP]/(VAT revenues in percent of GDP) minus (statutory VAT rate)].

[19]This is needed to compensate for the loss in revenue under the static long-term scenario (Table 3.7). It is assumed here that there is no behavioral response to the increase in the VAT rate.

[20]This is defined as the ratio of VAT revenues to the product of the standard rate of VAT and final consumption: for a uniform VAT levied on all consumption and with full compliance, the ratio would be one. See Ebrill and others (2001) for further discussion of the VAT productivity notion and its limitations.

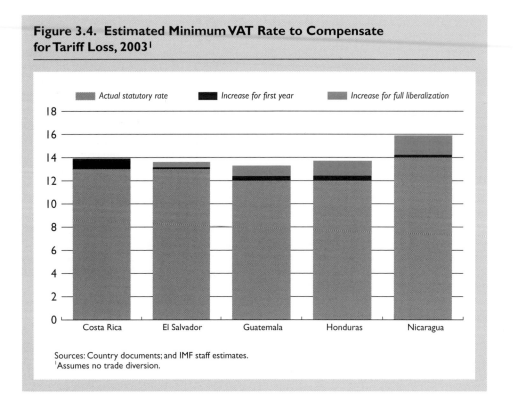

Figure 3.4. Estimated Minimum VAT Rate to Compensate for Tariff Loss, 2003[1]

Sources: Country documents; and IMF staff estimates.
[1]Assumes no trade diversion.

Improving VAT compliance will require both management and technical improvements in tax administration, supported by strong political backing for necessary audit and enforcement activities. Tax administrations in the region tend to have poor management control of taxpayers in general, and VAT payers in particular. The VAT registration thresholds are low, implying that there are many more VAT-registered taxpayers than the tax administration can effectively control. Compliance is poor—even with basic return filing and payment requirements (this is also the case for the large taxpayers)—and the VAT crediting and refund systems are weak. In addition, the effectiveness of the VAT audit is weak; available information is not used effectively to detect noncompliant VAT payers, and when it is used, follow-up actions to enforce payment of undeclared VAT are not rigorous.

The income tax may also have a role to play in recovering revenue—in particular, the base of the cor-

Table 3.8. VAT Productivities[1]

	1994	1997	2001	2003
Costa Rica	0.75	0.53	0.69	0.71
Dominican Republic	0.51	0.43	0.41	0.38
El Salvador	0.51	0.43	0.48	0.54
Guatemala	0.39	0.43	0.53	0.42
Honduras	0.55	0.65	0.58	0.53
Nicaragua	0.45	0.45	0.47	0.19
Panama	0.50	0.43	0.36	0.41
Unweighted average	0.52	0.48	0.50	0.45

Sources: IMF, *World Economic Outlook*; country documents; International Bureau of Fiscal Documentation, *Taxation in Latin America, Taxation and Investment in the Caribbean*; PricewaterhouseCoopers, *Corporate Taxes 2003–2004, Worldwide Summaries*; and IMF staff estimates.
[1]Revenue productivity = total VAT revenue as percentage of final domestic consumption divided by the VAT standard rate.

porate income tax should be broadened and tax incentives reassessed. There are signs that other countries that have succeeded in replacing revenues lost from trade tax reform have done so in part by strengthening the personal income tax.[21] In Central America there is also clear scope for revenue enhancement through the corporate income tax. Each of these countries offers special tax regimes to exporters and nonresident corporations. Special regimes, such as the free trade zones and industrial processing zones arrangements, narrow the corporate income tax base by making the offshore processing sector exempt from the payment of any tax other than labor contributions. The regimes create incentives for tax arbitrage by transferring earnings from taxed enterprises to exempt enterprises. Indeed, the use of transfer pricing and financial arrangements may enable other enterprises located onshore to shift taxable profits to offshore processing enterprises with which they are associated in order to reduce their tax burden.[22] Tax incentives should be phased out, since they are an inefficient way to attract additional investment, shift the tax burden onto other bases, create avoidance opportunities, distort economic decisions, discriminate against different types of investment, and complicate tax administration. Some tax incentives may also be in violation of World Trade Organization (WTO) rules.[23] A preferred manner of providing incentives to investment is through generous depreciation allowances and loss carry-forward provisions. If tax incentives are used, they should be narrowly targeted to specific sectors or disadvantaged regions. In all cases, tax incentives should be subject to tax expenditure analysis so that the cost of these incentives is transparent.

---

[21]See IMF (2005), on dealing with the revenue consequences of trade reform.

[22]The offshore processing sector in the region has been growing over the past 10 years, for various reasons, including the existence of preferential fiscal regimes and preferential access to the U.S. market under arrangements such as the agreement on textiles and clothing under the Caribbean Basin agreement. There is evidence in one country in the region that the ratio of earnings to sales for enterprises operating under special arrangements is about double that of those enterprises not operating under special regimes.

[23]The existence of export-related tax concession regimes contravenes WTO principles. The Agreement on Subsidies and Countervailing Measures (ASCM) prohibits subsidies that require recipients to meet certain export targets; also, the jurisprudence related to the ASCM has defined tax exemptions as subsidies. However, the least-developed countries—in particular those with an annual per capita income of less than US$1,000, measured using a certain methodology—have received a waiver that has allowed them to maintain those subsidy systems. Such waivers, according to the WTO legislation, should be temporary.

CAFTA-DR and Issues of Tax Coordination

CAFTA-DR strengthens the case for tax coordination within the region. The theoretical case for tax coordination—not necessarily for full harmonization, in the sense of complete uniformity of taxation—comes from mobility of the tax base across countries (whether capital, goods, services, or labor). In the absence of any tax coordination, countries in Central America may be induced to lower the tax rates in order to attract the mobile taxable base. This harmful competition can lead to effective tax rates being set too low.[24] The largely free trade within these countries already implies significant base mobility between them (discussed further below), but a free trade agreement with the United States would intensify this in two main ways.

- Firms (including from the United States and third countries) that wish to sell in the United States will find Central America a more attractive location after U.S. tariffs are eliminated. Each Central American country will then have an incentive to compete with the others in offering more attractive terms to attract such enterprises.

- U.S. companies wishing to sell in Central America will no longer have an incentive to locate there in order to jump over tariff barriers; so each Central American country also has an incentive to offer better terms than its neighbors in order to retain or attract such companies.

In particular, coordination may be needed to avoid or limit further reduction in corporate tax revenues. Central American countries already offer quite extensive breaks in the form of tax holidays and free trade zones, and—in line with worldwide trends—statutory corporate tax rates in the region have fallen significantly. A continuation of these pressures can be expected irrespective of CAFTA-DR, but for the reasons discussed above CAFTA-DR is likely to intensify them.

Corporate tax coordination could take a variety of forms. The most intense would be the adoption of a single Central America–wide corporate tax, with revenues allocated across the countries by some revenue-sharing formula. Requiring somewhat less, but still very extensive, coordination would be a system of formula apportionment (along the lines of state-level corporate taxes in Canada and the United States), with countries agreeing on a common base

---

[24]Some argue that tax competition should be welcomed as imposing constraints on wasteful governments, but in Central American countries stronger revenue mobilization is an acknowledged priority.

but being allowed to set different rates, with taxable profits then allocated across them by some formula.[25] Or there might be agreement on a minimum rate of corporate income tax (as proposed in the early 1990s by the Ruding Committee for the European Union; see Ruding, 1990) though this may do little unless some agreement is also reached on the tax base. Or a code of conduct might be imposed to eliminate harmful practices in business taxation.

A nonbinding code of conduct, a relatively loose form of corporate tax coordination, may be a useful first step. A code of conduct on business taxation was adopted by the European Union in 1997 and has been largely successful.[26] It was specifically aimed at measures that unduly affect the location of business activity in the European Union by being targeted at nonresidents, providing them with a more favorable tax treatment than that which is generally available in the member state concerned. This also helped European Union members to identify many existing national provisions that violated European Union state aid rules. Although Central American countries do not have such counterparts, the European experience suggests that it would be advisable to adopt a strategy toward corporate tax coordination sooner in the integration process rather than later.

There may also be a case for coordination of taxes on capital income and/or enhanced information sharing, to prevent residents of one Central American country from avoiding or evading taxes by locating their savings in another. But there may be only limited scope for this in the case of Central America, because of the availability of the option to save in third countries outside the region.[27]

Excises are the other main candidate for coordination. The concern here is that cross-border shopping and smuggling driven by differences in tax rates will lead governments to respond by setting lower excise rates than they otherwise would. A problem can exist even if no cross-border smuggling is actually observed; countries may defensively and spontaneously

set rates too low. Table 3.9 shows that excise tax rates differ significantly across the Central American countries and that excise tax levels are fairly low by regional standards—both of which suggest that there might indeed be a case for harmonization efforts.

Agreement on minimum excise rates is a natural way to deal with this problem. This has been the strategy in the European Union. Individual countries can be allowed to keep a certain flexibility in setting excise tax rates for meeting immediate budgetary needs or to respond to revenue shortfalls due to trade liberalization.

A strong case can also be made for VAT rate and base coordination. Differences in VAT rates and exemptions can cause problems. When the difference in the rates that countries apply to some commodity is large relative to the cost of transporting it, cross-border shopping and smuggling can become an issue. These erode revenue directly, and moreover can lead to mutually harmful tax competition as countries seek to protect their tax bases by setting lower tax rates than they otherwise would. As noted, this is often more of a problem with excises, but big cross-border differences in VAT rates can lead to significant cross-border shopping, as on the Danish-German border, where the rate differential is considerable (25 percent against 16 percent). Differences in VAT-exempted items can also cause trade distortions, with the VAT in effect akin to an import subsidy.[28]

Agreement on a minimum standard VAT rate would be a desirable element of VAT coordination. Standard VAT rates in Central America countries fall in a narrow range (12–14 percent), except Panama (5 percent). For most countries this tight range should, generally speaking, limit—but not eliminate—cross-border shopping/smuggling of high-value, easily transported goods. Agreeing on a minimum standard rate of VAT, a strategy adopted in the European Union, would protect against downward pressures on rates created by cross-border shopping/smuggling while allowing each country flexibility in setting it depending on budgetary needs. To be meaningful, adoption of a minimum rate would need to be combined with agreement on the bundle of commodities to which that standard rate applies.

---

[25]The European Union is currently considering schemes of this form. See, for instance, Sørensen (2004).

[26]The Code of Conduct for Business Taxation and Fiscal State Aid was set out by the ECOFIN council of December 1, 1997, in Brussels. It is not a legally binding instrument, but clearly it does have political force. By adopting this code, member states have undertaken to roll back existing tax measures that constitute harmful tax competition and refrain from introducing any such measures in the future.

[27]To ensure the taxation of interest payments earned by European Union citizens in third countries, the recently adopted EU Savings Directive ensures taxation either by exchanging information with third countries or by having member or third countries become collecting agents of European Union member countries. Switzerland, for example, retains only 35 percent of the withholding tax revenue it collects and acts as a collecting agent for the European Union.

---

[28]Suppose, for instance, that one Central American country (country A) exempts some good used as an intermediate input while another (country B) taxes it fully under the VAT. Then exporters from country B actually have a competitive advantage in country A's internal market, since the uninterrupted chain of VAT means that the zero-rating of exports removes all input VAT throughout the production chain, whereas producers in country A will implicitly bear an unrecovered burden of the tax paid on purchases by their exempt suppliers. Addressing this potential problem in Central America would require undertaking a systematic comparative study of exemptions as a first step toward harmonizing the VAT base.

Table 3.9. Excise Tax Summary

	Costa Rica 2003[1]	Dominican Republic 5/8/2002	El Salvador 2003	Guatemala 2003	Honduras 2004[2]	Nicaragua 11/20/2002	Panama 5/31/2003
Alcoholic/nonalcoholic beverages:	(percent)	(percent)				(percent)	
Beer	40	25	All alcoholic beverages 20 percent plus specific tax US$0.00751/degree of alcohol	US$0.13/liter	US$0.1692/liter	36	US$1.325/liter
Wine	40	35		For wine, whisky, rum, vodka and distilled alcohol US$0.515–2.47/liter	For wine, whisky, rum, vodka and distilled alcohol US$0.192–2.695/liter	37	US$0.05/liter
Whisky	50	45				37	Spirits:
Rum	...	35				36	US$0.35/degree of
Vodka	...	45				37	alcohol content/liter
Distilled alcohol	...	...				42	
Soft drinks	US$0.0198/unit of consumption	US$0.0028/bottle	10 percent	US$0.022/liter	US$0.0213/liter	9	5–6 percent[3]
Taxes on petroleum and natural gas:		Prices (US$/gallon)[4]	Prices (US$/gallon)	Prices (US$/gallon)[4]			Prices (US$/gallon)
Gasoline (regular)	...	2.0213	0.3591	0.4722	15 percent over c.i.f. import value[8,9]	...	0.60
Gasoline (premium)	...	2.3269	0.3591	0.4787		...	...
Diesel	...	1.3387	0.3591	0.1682		...	0.25
Fuel oil	...	0.9614	...	0.0712 (Bunker)[5,6]		...	0.15
Taxes on tobacco:	(percent)	(percent)	(percent)	(percent)	(percent)	(percent)	
Cigarettes	100	50	39	100	47.5	39	32.5 percent of the consumer sales price
Cigars	...	25	...	...	...	39	

Sources: IMF, International Financial Statistics; country document tax summary tables; International Bureau of Fiscal Documentation; and United States Department of Commerce—National Data Bank.
[1]Soft drinks and gaseous concentrates: US$0.0198 per unit of consumption; other bottled beverages, including water: US$0.01721 per unit of consumption; water containers of 18 liters or more: US$0.00685 per unit of consumption.
[2]Rate is as of 9/3/1999.
[3]Domestically produced or imported carbonated beverages: (5 percent); and syrups or concentrate used in the production of carbonated beverage: (6 percent).
[4]Prices in effect on May 8, 2002. Resolution 112–00 allows for prices to be adjusted periodically for, inter alia, changes in the consumer price index, world oil prices, and the official exchange rate, but in practice, adjustments have been infrequent.
[5]Rates are for 2000.
[6]Additional products and specific rates per gallon are provided as follows: Aircraft gasoline: US$ 0.2587; gas oil: US$0.1682; liquid petroleum gas, crude oil used as fuel and other fuel derived from petroleum asphalt are: US$0.0647.
[7]Data for 2002.
[8]Ad valorem tax on imported oil derivatives (gasoline, diesel, kerosene, jet fuel, bunker, propane and butane). Honduras imports 100 percent of its oil derivatives.

Box 3.2. Current Status of Customs Administration in Central America

Selected indicators of customs administration in Central America are as follows.

- Regarding the harmonization of customs documentation, since 1994 there has been a common form for customs transit. In addition, four countries have a common Internet technology system.

- There is a common control system for interregional transit and a common transit system.

- A number of common border posts have been established, but only between some countries.[1]

---

[1] In a true customs union, the final objective would be to abolish customs posts between the member countries and to establish modern customs posts and controls at the entry points to the region: ports, international airports, and the borders. However, in the transition period it may be useful to retain the posts to keep collecting duties and indirect taxes on imports.

- Although there is a common standard system for the valuation of goods (the WTO agreement), each country interprets the agreement differently. To date, no customs service in the region is fully compliant with the agreement. However, a group of regional customs officials is preparing a common regulation to establish a standard system of goods valuation.

- Common terms and conditions for duty suspension and refund procedures have not been established. A group of regional customs officials has been assigned the task of preparing such common procedures.

- A mechanism for coordinated cooperation and information exchange between customs services has been in place at least since the early 1990s. However, the system is not being used as designed, partly because of a lack of training.

- Joint customs and trade training programs are not yet in place.

The case for coordinating taxes on labor income is weak, since labor tends to be less mobile than goods or capital. Special arrangements may be needed for border workers, who live in one Central American country and work in another. Differences in the tax treatment of higher paid workers, who may be more mobile within Central America, may require some study, but there are no signs that this has emerged as a significant concern.

On tax administration, coordination efforts are needed to continue modernizing the tax administrations in the Central American countries. The focus should be on (1) exchange of tax-related information between countries, especially regarding the indirect taxes (which will require the adoption of a standard taxpayer identification numbering system in each country and maintenance of an updated taxpayer register), and (2) establishing joint auditing capacity to effectively identify and prosecute tax fraud.

Efforts have begun to establish a customs union, but progress has been slow. Although there is now uniformity in parts of customs administration (for example, harmonized customs documentation and transit procedures), and some countries have even taken steps to establish common customs border posts in order to facilitate border control,[29] there are other areas where considerable work remains to be done to move toward common customs administra-

---

[29]As a result of such initiatives, for example, between Nicaragua and Honduras, customs border controls now take 17 to 20 minutes, whereas previously these controls required one day.

tion procedures (Box 3.2). There are also large differences in health and sanitary standards, as well as in migration policies, with respect to imports. Some countries will be required to improve their standards in these areas before all the Central American countries will agree to joining such a union.

Conclusions

The revenue challenges from CAFTA-DR are significant for all Central American countries, although they vary markedly in timing and extent. Nicaragua, for instance, appears well placed to cope with these pressures: less than 2 percent of revenue comes from imports from the United States, and the related tariff reductions are back-loaded. Even for Nicaragua, however, trade diversion could lead to losses of up to 0.2 percent of GDP, or 1 percent of tax revenue, in the first year of implementation. The challenges appear greatest in Costa Rica, with a prospective revenue loss in the first year of about 2.4 percent of tax revenue even in the absence of trade diversion.

Dealing with the revenue losses from CAFTA-DR will require strengthening domestic tax systems, especially the VAT. Increased indirect taxation is the natural way to recoup trade tax revenue losses, as it largely preserves the preexisting distribution of the tax burden. Widening the base of the VAT through policy measures and better tax administration would limit the extent to which the standard VAT rate needs to be increased.

CAFTA-DR will also raise the benefits that can be gained from increased tax cooperation among Central American countries. This does not necessarily mean full harmonization, but it does mean looser forms of coordination, such as a code of conduct on business taxation and a common external tariff system. Experience in the European Union and elsewhere suggests that it is wise to address such issues early in the integration process.

Appendix. Data and Methodology for the Calculation of Revenue Losses

Data

The General Directorates of Customs of Costa Rica, El Salvador, Guatemala, Honduras, and Nicaragua provided most of the data required for calculating the fiscal cost of tariff reduction. These include figures by tariff line of imports (c.i.f. values),[30] tariff rates, sales and excise taxes, and customs duty collected, by type of tax, for 2003.

For Costa Rica, El Salvador, and Guatemala, the database covers only information on imports from the United States. The databases for Honduras and Nicaragua identify imports registered at customs from the United States, the other Central American countries, and the rest of the world in aggregate.

The tariff elimination schedule for Costa Rica, El Salvador, Guatemala, and Nicaragua is based on Annex 3.3 of the CAFTA-DR, which is available via the Internet at www.ustr.gov/Trade_Agreements/.

For Honduras, the tariff elimination schedule was supplied by the Ministry of Industry and Trade. The data include both the tariff elimination schedule and the tariff rate, by tariff line, and by precision subcode.

Methodology for Estimating Direct Revenue Impact

The estimation of direct fiscal cost includes assessing the impact of tariff exemption on the collection of taxes on foreign trade, as well as its impact on the collection of indirect taxes (sales and excise taxes). This does not allow for any behavioral response, but consideration is given to two scenarios regarding the possible impact of trade diversion for Honduras and Nicaragua.

The simplest case is that of the collection of revenue from tariffs on foreign trade. The base for estimating the impact is the total collection of revenue in the form of customs duty for 2003, grouped in accordance with the tariff elimination schedule.

The base for estimating the impact on the collection of excise taxes is the revenue from customs duty multiplied by the actual rate of the excise tax. This is done for each import line where customs duties are collected.[31]

In the case of the sales tax, the base for estimating the impact on the collection is revenue from customs duty multiplied by the actual rate of the sales tax. This is done for each import line where customs duties are collected.[32] For each of the three taxes, an estimate is made of the total aggregate impact, based on the rates of import duty corresponding to each tariff elimination schedule. The fiscal cost is estimated as being directly proportional to the decline in tariffs. Consequently, we assume that exemption rates do not change with tariff elimination.

Methodology for Estimating Losses from Trade Diversion

A base case was considered in which the proportion of imports from the United States remained unchanged. However, for countries' products to be able to compete with products from the United States, the prices of imports from third countries must be reduced. The case assumes that the price reduction of goods competing with the United States from third countries is directly proportional to the ratio between the revenue loss, described above, and the value of the imports plus the revenue yielded by the above-mentioned taxes. In other words, the price reduction is equivalent to the reduction in the cost of taxing goods from the United States.

For this case, the loss is estimated on the basis of the customs duty collected from the rest of the world for the pertinent goods,[33] grouped by tariff elimination schedule. The fiscal cost is calculated as being directly proportional to the reduction in import duty.

To analyze the impact of possible trade diversion from other countries, the extreme case was considered, with total imports of the pertinent goods coming from the United States. The methodology used to estimate the cost includes assessing the impact on the three taxes and is similar to the methodology described for estimating the direct static impact.

---

[30]Classified in accordance with the Central American Customs System (eight-digit) and precision subcode (two-digit, primarily for tax purposes).

[31]The actual excise tax rate is calculated as the ratio of revenue from the excise tax to the sum of the value of imports plus import duty.

[32]The actual sales tax rate also applies to excise taxes, and is therefore defined as the ratio of the revenue collected from sales tax to the sum of the value of imports, plus import duty collected, plus excise tax collected.

[33]Only the impact on the tariff lines for which there are currently exports from the United States is taken into consideration.

Total trade diversion is truly an extreme case; it is mentioned in this study for illustrative purposes only. Two intermediate cases with 20 percent and 35 percent of trade diversion are considered in this study.

Methodology for Estimating Revenue Elasticity to GDP

Revenue elasticity to GDP for each Central American country is estimated using a suppressed constant log linear model: log (*Revenue*) = *b* log (*GDP*) + error. Both tax revenue and GDP are expressed in local currency. The estimated coefficient *b* gives the revenue elasticity. Annual time-series data from 1990 to 2003 are used.

References

Barreix, Alberto, Luiz Villela, and Jerónimo Roca, 2004, *Fiscal Impact of Trade Liberalization in the Americas*, Periodic Note (Washington: Inter-American Development Bank, January).

Ebrill, Liam, Michael Keen, Jean-Paul Bodin, and Victoria Summers, 2001, *The Modern VAT* (Washington: International Monetary Fund).

Ebrill, Liam, Janet Stotsky, and Reint Gropp, 1999, *Revenue Implications of Trade Liberalization*, IMF Occasional Paper No. 180 (Washington: International Monetary Fund).

Hilaire, Alvin, and Yongzheng Yang, 2003, The United States and the New Regionalism/Bilateralism, IMF Working Paper 03/206 (Washington: International Monetary Fund).

International Monetary Fund, 2005, "Dealing with the Revenue Consequences of Trade Reform" (Washington: February 15). Available via the Internet: www.imf.org/ external/np/pp/eng/2005/021505.htm.

Keen, Michael, and Jenny E. Ligthart, 2004, "Information Sharing and International Taxation" (Washington and Tilburg, The Netherlands; International Monetary Fund and Tilburg University, November). Available on the Internet: http://center.kub.nl/staff/ligthart/primer.pdf.

Krueger, Anne O., 1999, "Trade Creation and Trade Diversion under NAFTA," NBER Working Paper No. 7429 (Cambridge, Massachusetts: National Bureau of Economic Research).

———, 2000, "NAFTA's Effects: A Preliminary Assessments," *World Economy*, Vol. 23 (June), pp. 761–75.

Paunovic, Igor, and José Octavio Martínez, 2003, *El Impacto Fiscal del CAFTA-DR en los Países Centroamericanos* (Mexico City: CEPAL/ECLAC).

Ruding, Onno S., 1990, *Report of the Committee of Independent Experts on Company Taxation* (Brussels: Commission of the European Communities).

Sørensen, Peter Birch, 2004, "Company Tax Reform in the European Union," *International Tax and Public Finance*, Vol. 11, pp. 91–115.

Stotsky, Janet, and Asegedech WoldeMariam, 2002, "Central American Tax Reform: Trends and Possibilities," IMF Working Paper 02/227 (Washington: International Monetary Fund).

Wacziarg, Romain, and Karen Horn Welch, 2003, "Trade Liberalization and Growth: New Evidence," NBER Working Paper No. 10152 (Cambridge, Massachusetts: National Bureau of Economic Research).

IV   Fiscal Sustainability: A Value-at-Risk Approach

Ricardo Adrogué

Recurring debt problems and high public debt have brought the issue of fiscal sustainability to the foreground in several Central American countries. Although public debt-to-GDP ratios have started to come down in recent years, they still exceed 50 percent in most of the region's countries, making the debt a source of vulnerability that deserves close attention. Over the past three decades, the region experienced a number of debt write-downs, and high debt levels have constrained implementation of effective policy responses in the case of adverse shocks (see Offerdal, 2004).

There has been no regional study on public debt sustainability in Central America. So far, sustainability assessments have been country specific, aimed at ensuring attainment of fiscal viability for the country in question. As a consequence, the results of existing sustainability assessments are less suited for comparisons across the region.

Although substantial progress has been made in recent years, the methodology of debt and fiscal sustainability assessments are still at an early stage of development.[1] Projections of debt dynamics, which are intrinsically uncertain and highly variable, are typically stable and deterministic with only a limited number of possible outcomes being explored. As stated by the International Monetary Fund (2002, p. 6), ". . . assessments of sustainability are probabilistic, since one can normally envisage some states of the world under which a country's debt would be sustainable and others on which it would not. Standard frameworks currently used do not supply these probabilities explicitly; rather, they trace the implications of alternative scenarios and leave the user to determine the respective probabilities."

To assess the degree of vulnerability posed by current debt levels in Central America, this study summarizes recent sustainability assessments and proposes a complementary probabilistic framework to evaluate sustainability. The traditional debt sustainability framework is taken one step further by estimating explicitly the probabilities of alternative scenarios using a common set of assumptions.[2] A Value-at-Risk (VaR) approach is utilized to calculate the probability distribution of the debt-to-GDP ratios of several Central American countries, the latter used as proxy for the degree of fiscal vulnerability. This VaR approach is in line with the stochastic simulation method suggested in IMF (2003). The approach is not, however, without drawbacks since the VaR approach is based entirely on historical data. This caveat applies, in particular, in the case of a regime change, like the one in El Salvador, which officially dollarized in 2001. Also, data limitations and potential problems of endogeneity make the results tentative. This is why the VaR approach should be seen as a complement to, and not a substitute for, the traditional debt sustainability approach. Nevertheless, the VaR framework allows a more explicit comparison of vulnerabilities across countries and ranks countries along a common vulnerability index. It offers additional information over traditional sustainability assessments by probabilistically computing the relative contribution of the different risk factors to the country's overall vulnerability.[3]

Analytical Issues and the Traditional Sustainability Approach

The IMF defines debt sustainability, as "a situation in which a borrower is expected to be able to continue servicing its debt without an unrealistically large future correction to the balance of income and expenditure."[4] The assessment of sustainability, as high-

---

[1]This refers to forward-looking assessments of fiscal sustainability, as opposed to the empirical tests of sustainability done by Corsetti and Roubini (1991), Hakkio and Rush (1991), Hamilton and Flavin (1986), Kremers (1989), Roberts (1991), Trehan and Walsh (1988), Wilcox (1989), and others, who concentrate on historical OECD country experiences.

[2]As it will become clear, the extension of the current framework comes at a cost, i.e., the probabilities are calculated using solely historical information. It should be noted, however, that this is not a limitation of the VaR technique, but rather the desire to perform cross-country comparisons with the greatest possible objectivity.

[3]While the traditional debt sustainability analysis includes stress tests, it does not explicitly calculate their corresponding probabilities.

[4]IMF (2002, p. 4, para. 7).

lighted in the definition, is intrinsically probabilistic and based on an expectation and judgment about what constitutes an unrealistically large future correction. Consequently, there is only a limited degree of objectivity in any analysis of sustainability. While experience has shown that unrealistically large adjustments are generally easier to determine ex post than ex ante, current sustainability analyses can be improved with respect to the expectational aspect of the definition.

The risk of default is proxied by the probability distribution of the debt-to-GDP ratio. Despite being a poor indicator of solvency, the debt-to-GDP ratio is the measure typically used to assess sustainability and is the focus of traditional sustainability assessments.[5] Comparability of analysis, then, calls for the use of the same indicator in the present study.

The traditional approach to assess fiscal sustainability is based on the following steps.

- In order to establish a baseline/"current-policy scenario," projections are made based on forecast of key variables from the real, external, monetary, and fiscal sectors, assuming policy continuity.[6] Although historical trends are commonly used as a basis for the projections, these are not mechanically followed. Instead, judgment is used to assess the most likely course of events going forward.

- These baseline/"current-policy" scenario projections are used to predict the path of the public sector debt-to GDP ratio. A resulting debt ratio judged to be uncomfortably high or vulnerable typically prompts the creation of an alternative adjustment scenario, that is, an "active policy" scenario.[7] In this case, adjusting the primary fiscal balance is the policy tool used to meet the targeted debt ratio.

- The robustness of the results is then analyzed by assuming alternative paths for the macroeconomic variables used in the exercise.

Table 4.1 summarizes the results of the most recent sustainability assessments done for the countries in the region:[8]

- In all countries, baseline/"current-policy" scenarios have assumed an improvement in the primary fiscal balance. The projected fiscal effort is largest for the Dominican Republic (3.8 percent of GDP), followed by Honduras (3.0 percent of GDP), Nicaragua (2.8 percent of GDP), El Salvador (1.7 percent of GDP), Guatemala (1.1 percent of GDP), Costa Rica (1 percent of GDP), and Panama (0.4 percent of GDP).

- As a result of the fiscal effort, debt ratios are projected to fall in all but one of the countries (El Salvador).[9] However, not all fiscal efforts produce equivalent reductions in the debt ratio.[10] A 1 percentage point of GDP improvement in the primary balance is forecast to reduce the debt-to-GDP ratio by 2½ percentage points in the Dominican Republic and by more than 5 percentage points in Guatemala.

- The standard sustainability assessments reveal that a shock in the form of a currency depreciation represents the largest risk. The risk of currency depreciation (a one-off 30 percent permanent drop in the value of the local currency) ranked first in six out of the seven countries in the region (second in the seventh, i.e., Guatemala).

The traditional approach used to assess fiscal sustainability in Central America has, however, a number of caveats when used for cross-country comparisons:

- Using the primary fiscal balance as a summary indicator for debt sustainability gives a spurious sense of consistency across debt sustainability exercises. As stated before, the underlying macroeconomic assumptions vary across the Central American countries, making the primary fiscal balance calculated for one country not comparable to that calculated for another. Hence, debt sustainability outcomes derived from independent sustainability calculations may not be strictly comparable.

- The stress tests performed in the traditional approach are somewhat arbitrary. Several metrics are used in the definition of the shocks in the

---

[5]The literature has found only a weak relationship between debt-to-GDP ratios and events of default, making this ratio a poor indicator of solvency. See Pattillo, Poirson, and Ricci (2002) and Reinhart, Rogoff, and Savastano (2003).

[6]The concept of "policy continuity" is defined in slightly different ways across scenarios, which therefore may not be fully comparable. Often the IMF staff also projects a "weak" or "low" scenario assuming a weaker policy effort than in the baseline/ "current-policy" scenario to illustrate the risks of policy slippage. The variables that are most commonly projected are output growth, inflation, interest rates, fiscal revenues, noninterest expenditures, and interest payments. Detailed projections for these variables can be found in the respective country staff reports.

[7]It is commonly assumed that the macroeconomic environment is dependent on whether the debt dynamics are deemed sustainable or not, thus reinforcing the benefits associated with the proposed fiscal adjustment of the alternative scenario.

---

[8]For each country, the ratio of the 2003 public debt to GDP is reported in Column 2.

[9]It should be noted, however, that El Salvador's debt ratio, albeit increasing, is projected to remain below 50 percent until 2008.

[10]Debt dynamics are also affected by the projected paths for the real interest rate, the growth rate, the exchange rate, and the size of the debt ratio itself, all of which differ across countries.

Table 4.1. Results from Traditional Debt Sustainability Analysis

	Debt/GDP (t)	Average Historical Primary Balance	Projected Primary Balance	Debt/GDP (t + 5)	Stress Tests[1]
Costa Rica					
Baseline/"current-policy"[2]	54.5	0.4	1.4	50.2	Depreciation
Passive			0.0	62.0	Growth
Active			2.3	43.3	Contingent losses
					Interest rate
					Primary balance
Dominican Republic					
Baseline/"current-policy"[2]	54.3	−1.6	2.2	44.8	Depreciation
Passive			0.8	61.4	Primary balance
					Contingent losses
					Growth
					Interest rate
El Salvador					
Baseline/"current-policy"	46.1	−2.0	−0.3	47.2	Depreciation
Reinforced			0.5	43.7	Contingent losses
					Growth
					Interest rate
					Primary balance
Guatemala					
Baseline/"current-policy"	20.1	−0.7	0.4	14.3	Contingent losses
					Depreciation
					Primary balance
					Growth
					Interest rate
Honduras[3,4]					
Baseline/"current-policy"	64.1	−3.1	−0.1	52.2	Depreciation
					Primary balance
					GDP growth
Nicaragua					
Baseline/"current-policy"	160.0	−1.1	1.7	149.1	Depreciation
					Privatization
					Primary balance
					Growth
Panama					
Baseline/"current-policy"[5]	63.3	1.7	2.1	55.6	Depreciation
Low-scenario			0.6	67.2	Growth
					Contingent losses
					Interest rate
					Primary balance

Sources: IMF staff reports and debt sustainability assessments.

[1] Ranked from highest to lowest debt ratio at end of 2008.

[2] Assumes implementation of some fiscal-enhancing measures.

[3] Based on a 15 percent real exchange rate depreciation.

[4] Public external debt ratio reported instead of total public debt ratio.

[5] Described as active scenario in IMF staff report.

stress tests making comparability across countries and among shocks challenging.[11] Is a 30 percent real depreciation comparable with a two-standard deviation interest rate shock? Is the combination of two or three types of shocks in the form of one standard deviation of the parameters in question comparable to shocks of other parameters measured as two-standard deviations? Is the likelihood of a 30 percent currency depreciation the same for Guatemala as for Costa Rica? Is

[11] While some stress tests are defined in terms of standard deviations (making them comparable across countries and among risks), others are not.

a 10 percentage point increase in the debt-to-GDP ratio a good characterization of the expected realization of contingent liabilities across all countries? These limitations raise doubts about the information conveyed by the ranking of risks resulting from the stress tests.

- While the primary fiscal balance has been the most reliable tool when addressing issues of debt dynamics, other policy tools are ignored in standard debt sustainability assessments. In particular, the traditional approach does not easily lend itself to the analysis of the pros and cons of changes to the structure of the public debt.[12]

- The policy recommendations that can be distilled from the traditional approach are limited to the primary balance. Thus, countries with no obvious problems in their debt dynamics find little use for the traditional debt sustainability assessment. To complement the traditional analysis and to address the caveats discussed above, the following uses the VaR to assess fiscal sustainability in Central America.

Modeling the Debt-to-GDP Ratio Using VaR[13]

The VaR methodology was originally developed to calculate the market risk of a financial portfolio, that is, the probability distribution of returns of a given portfolio due to changes in market prices. More recently, Barnhill and Kopits (2003) have extended VaR to the analysis of fiscal accounts of sovereign countries. Their specific application of VaR assumes that a government's balance sheet is available. The objective of the approach developed in this section is to compute the probability distribution of the ratio of public sector debt to GDP at some future year using VaR. The advantage of this approach—as opposed to the one proposed by Barnhill and Kopits—is its direct comparability with current sustainability analyses. However, unlike the approach used by Barnhill and Kopits, this exercise does not explicitly provide information about the probability of default.[14]

The traditional approach projects the future path of the debt-to-GDP ratio based on subjective macroeconomic forecasts of key variables.[15] The technique proposed here, on the other hand, is strictly rooted on historical data and does not allow for judgment when projecting future outcomes. At the same time, the historical information is used more effectively than in the traditional approach because the correlation matrix of the risk factors is included in the calculation of the future path of the debt-to-GDP ratio. The departure from the traditional approach due to the application of VaR can be summarized as follows.

- *The set of primary risks.* While primary risks are roughly the same as those considered in the traditional approach (GDP growth, inflation, primary fiscal spending, the domestic short-term interest rate, the exchange rate, the medium-term foreign interest rate, and the sovereign spread), future projections for these variables are strictly derived from their historical performance, making the results comparable across countries.

- *The probability distribution and correlation matrix of the risk factors.* The traditional approach, as any deterministic approach, ignores probabilities. In this framework, the probability distributions and the interrelationship among risk factors are explicitly included.[16] The explicit formulation of the probability distributions and the interrelationship among risk factors reduces the arbitrariness in the rankings produced by the conventional stress tests.

- *The treatment of contingent claims.* The traditional approach requires the user to identify the size and timing of future implicit or contingent liabilities. Seeking uniformity of treatment while recognizing intrinsic differences across countries, the approach proposed here uses a stylized fact reported in the literature on crises—that is, the fact that foreign exchange crises have typically been associated with financial sector crises, the latter being among the

---

[12]As explained below, debt-service projections in the traditional approach are typically (though not always) based on historical debt-service information by type of debt. Debt service, however, is dependent on the debt structure that evolves over time and might be quite different from the historical composition of the debt.

[13]Owing to data limitations, only contemporaneous correlations among risk factors have been considered.

[14]Contrary to Barnhill and Kopits (2003), this paper uses VaR to estimate the probability distribution of the debt ratio instead of the probability distribution of the fiscal portfolio (balance sheet). The number of assumptions involved in constructing a "synthetic" balance sheet from expected future flows is significantly larger than the one proposed here.

[15]Using subjectivity in projecting the paths of key macroeconomic aggregates should not be regarded as inferior to the historical method proposed here. On the contrary, as long as subjective projections represent best assessments using all available data, they could be regarded as superior.

[16]Normal probability distributions are assumed for GDP growth, inflation, and real primary fiscal spending with mean and variance calculated from the last 10 years of data; log-normal distributions are assumed for interest rates and spreads; and a frequency table calculated from the last 50 years of real exchange rate data is used as proxy for the probability distribution of the real exchange rate. Additionally, the interrelationship among risk factors is appraised from the correlation matrix of risks.

most common sources of contingent liabilities of the public sector.[17]

- *The composition of debt.* Instead of using the series of interest payments to project future interest payments, which is the default mechanism used in the traditional approach that depends on the history of the debt structure, this approach uses the actual composition of the debt at present combined with alternative simulation of interest rates (domestic and foreign plus spread) to produce a forecast of future interest payments.[18] The stock of public debt is classified into two main categories: foreign currency debt (assumed to be fully denominated in U.S. dollars) and domestic currency debt. Each of these is then subdivided into short-term (with a remaining maturity of less than one year) and medium- to long-term debt. The stock of inflation-indexed domestic debt completes the stylized description of the debt composition, which is assumed to remain constant throughout the simulation exercise. This formulation allows for a more complete study of the consequences of alternative debt structures.

In every VaR analysis, the debt-to-GDP ratios are calculated assuming no "portfolio" change in reaction to the realization of the risks. This represents the passive scenario, that is, it is assumed that no policy adjustment takes place. Moreover, the correlation matrix of risks is also assumed to be invariant.[19]

Based on the assumptions outlined above, alternative debt paths are simulated and the probability distribution of the debt ratio is computed from 10,000 simulations. As a result, different measures of vulnerability can be calculated from the computed distributions.

- The VaR of the debt-to-GDP ratio for a common confidence interval across countries.

- The probability that a certain debt-to-GDP ratio will be surpassed.[20]

- The expected increase or decrease in the debt-to-GDP ratio from current levels.

- The relative contribution of the risks to the debt dynamics for each country.[21]

- In addition, a possible extension of the current framework for the analysis of policy options is exemplified by the simulation of an alternative debt structure.

The following table summarizes the first three vulnerability measures. A comparison between columns two and three in Table 4.2 highlights an important vulnerability of the Central American countries, namely, the expected increase in debt-to-GDP ratio under current trends. The expected increase in the debt ratio differs among the other countries. El Salvador's debt ratio deteriorates the most, followed by Guatemala, the Dominican Republic, and Costa Rica. The need for policy action to prevent an escalation of the debt ratios is consistent with the recommendations obtained from the traditional approach (Figure 4.1).

Relying purely on historical data negatively biases the results against the more active reformers. The effect of recent reforms, while probably important for debt sustainability, have not been incorporated into the vulnerability measures calculated above. This bias appears to be particularly relevant for El Salvador, which has been one of the most active reformers in recent years.[22]

The need for policy action, however, should be associated with the risk profile of the debt. The worse the risk profile the greater the urgency to act. The VaR (column three of Table 4.2) explicitly measures such risk by calculating the highest debt-to-GDP ratio by 2008 with a 95 percent confidence level. Based on this measure, Panama is the country in need of most urgent action. Its VaR (95.2) is the highest of the five Central American countries considered. That is, there is a 95 percent probability that Panama's debt-to-GDP ratio will not exceed 95.2 percent by 2008. The other countries do not follow very far behind though. The VaR for El Salvador is 94.8 percent of GDP, Costa Rica's is 94 percent, and the Dominican Republic comes in fourth at 81½ percent. The only country with a reasonably low

[17]As shown in Kaminsky and Reinhart (1996), balance of payments crises, most of which involve a large depreciation of the domestic currency, tend to overlap with banking crises that is a common type of contingent liabilities. Contingent liabilities associated with unfunded pension schemes are not considered in this exercise.

[18]Notwithstanding this, knowledgeable users can make the necessary adjustments to the traditional framework to produce a more realistic path for debt-service payments.

[19]Ideally, the exercise would use contingent correlation matrices, since the correlations among macroeconomic variables tend to vary between noncrisis and crisis periods (see Forbes and Rigobon, 2000). Because of data limitations, the exercise assumes that the correlation matrices of risk are constant.

[20]Reinhart, Rogoff, and Savastano (2003) have estimated threshold levels for ratios of external debt to GDP. However, no similar study exists on thresholds of public debt to GDP.

[21]Though not a stress test of the results per se, it is a better approximation to the relative risk exposure of the different countries than the traditional stress tests.

[22]In particular, the results presented for El Salvador reflect a history of very volatile real exchange rates (the variable used a 50-year time span), and the fiscal cost of reconstruction in the late 1990s (a 10-year time span was used for this variable). It ignores the effects of the ambitious tax reform approved only a few months ago.

Table 4.2. Main Vulnerability Measures

	Debt/GDP	E(D)[1]	VaR[2]	> 60 percent[3]
Costa Rica	54.5	65.5	94.1	60.1
Dominican Republic	54.3	64.5	81.5	66.9
El Salvador	46.1	64.1	94.8	54.3
Guatemala	20.1	36.7	50.6	0.5
Panama	63.3	70.4	95.2	76.2

Source: IMF staff calculations.
[1]Expected debt-to-GDP ratio by end-2008.
[2]Debt-to-GDP ratio four years out measured at 5 percent confidence level.
[3]Probability, in percent, that the debt-to-GDP ratio will surpass 60 percent by 2008.

Figure 4.1. Distribution of the Ratio of Public Debt to GDP in 2008

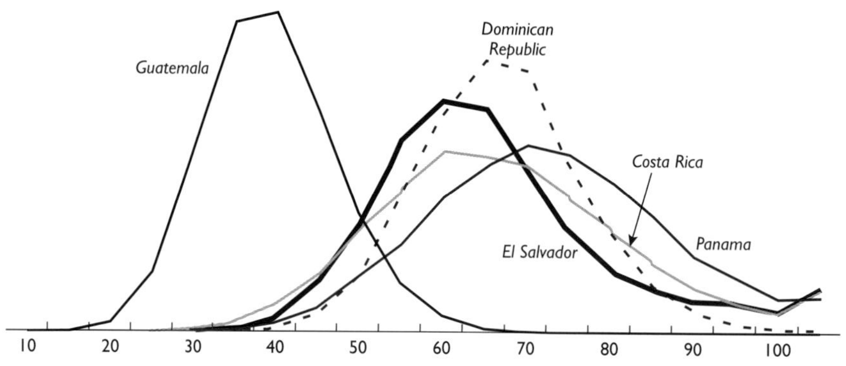

Source: IMF staff calculations.

VaR figure is Guatemala, which is slightly above 50 percent.[23]

Using the projected change to the primary fiscal balance of the traditional approach as an indicator of urgency of adjustment leads to different conclusions than the ones just discussed. Table 4.3 ranks the seven countries reported in Table 4.1 according to the projected fiscal effort measured for the baseline/"current-policy" scenario as the difference between column four and column three of that table. The Dominican Republic comes in first with an ef-

fort of 3.8 percent of GDP, followed by Honduras, Nicaragua, El Salvador, Guatemala, Costa Rica, and Panama.[24] The disparity of objectives and assumptions across traditional debt sustainability assessments makes the projected primary balance adjustments difficult to interpret across countries.

An alternative way to examine the results is to consider the probability that a certain debt threshold will be surpassed (a third alternative measure of vulnerability). Although the economic literature does not provide conclusive evidence on what that

---

[23]These VaRs result from the interaction of the seven risk factors reported above. For an analysis of the relative importance of the different risks please refer to Table 4.4.

[24]It turns out that the order presented in the previous paragraph, using VaR, is almost the opposite of the one in Table 4.1.

threshold is for the overall public debt, most of it seems to agree on a positive and nonlinear relationship between debt levels and the cost of borrowing. Work done by Pattillo, Poirson, and Ricci (2002) and Reinhart Rogoff, and Savastano (2003) suggests there is a level for the external debt/GDP ratio that, once surpassed, results in the cost of borrowing becoming prohibitive. They find that external debt ratios on the order of 30–40 percent have historically been associated with worsening growth conditions (Pattillo) and defaults (Reinhart). The 60 percent of GDP assumed in Table 4.2 appears to be a reasonable threshold for the public sector debt ratio for Central American countries; it is higher than most actual levels and fairly uncommon among emerging countries. The probability this level will be surpassed by 2008 is greatest in Panama (76 percent), followed by the Dominican Republic (67 percent), Costa Rica (60 percent), and El Salvador (54 percent). On the other end of the spectrum, Guatemala is the only country with less than a 50 percent probability of surpassing 60 percent of GDP by 2008.

Surpassing the 60 percent debt-to-GDP threshold is not necessarily associated with an imminent financial crisis. For example, Panama's public debt has been above 60 percent of GDP since the year 2000, yet it has not experienced a financial crisis despite the international and regional turbulence during the past four years. Its sovereign spread has remained stable throughout the period showing no clear positive relationship with its rising debt-to-GDP ratio. Notwithstanding the Panamanian experience, debt ratios above 60 percent of GDP are likely to be associated with increases in vulnerability.

The main drivers behind the expected increase in the debt ratios shown above are presented in Table 4.4.[25] GDP growth, for example, is expected to explain 10 percent of the debt dynamics for the Dominican Republic and 16 percent for Costa Rica, while the real exchange rate explains 32 percent of the change in the debt ratio for Costa Rica and only 15 percent for the Dominican Republic. The fact that the numbers reported in Table 4.4 are positive does not imply that all variables contribute positively to the debt ratio. GDP growth and inflation tend to reduce it. Table 4.4, then, only reports the relative contribution, positive or negative, that is expected from each variable on the change in the debt-to-GDP ratio.

Table 4.3. Projected Change in Primary Balance
(In percent of GDP)

	Change
Dominican Republic	3.8
Honduras	3.0
Nicaragua	2.8
El Salvador	1.7
Guatemala	1.1
Costa Rica	1.0
Panama	0.4

Sources: IMF staff reports and debt sustainability assessments.

While it is hardly surprising that primary spending is the largest contributor to debt buildup, there are noticeable differences among the relative contributions of the risk factors across countries. Most notably, the expected increase in the public sector debt for El Salvador has more to do with the real exchange rate than primary spending.[26] The contribution of real primary spending to debt accumulation varies across the remaining four countries. In Costa Rica, primary spending is expected to explain almost 40 percent of the debt buildup, whereas in Panama it is responsible for almost two-thirds of the increase in the debt ratio. This variation reflects the fact that in some countries, the debt has developed dynamics of its own, with more than 50 percent of the expected increase in the debt ratio explained by variables that are not under the direct control of the authorities. This compares to the results of the stress tests of the standard sustainability analysis where currency depreciation appears to be the largest risk factor to the debt dynamics of the Central American countries, with Guatemala being the notable exception (see Table 4.1).[27]

The second-largest risk to the debt dynamics according to this framework is a real exchange rate depreciation. Costa Rica, Guatemala, and the Dominican Republic all have this risk as the second largest,

---

[25]The table reports the partial R^2 of regressing the change in the debt-to-GDP ratio between 2003 and 2008 on the seven risk factors used in the simulation. Only the risk factors with contributions consistently above 5 percent are reported in Table 4.4. In particular, the contributions of the interest rate and inflation to the expected change in the debt ratio are quite low, both in this analysis and the traditional approach, and were thus excluded for presentational purposes.

[26]This apparent anomaly can be explained by El Salvador's rather volatile real exchange rate history. If El Salvador's real exchange rate becomes more stable as a consequence of official dollarization (2001), the relative contribution of this variable to the debt buildup will fall.

[27]Traditional debt sustainability analysis concludes that depreciation and contingent losses are the two main sources of risk to the debt dynamics of El Salvador. Both risks are combined in this section under the heading of the real exchange rate risk which, as shown in Table 4.4, is the largest contributor to the expected increase in the debt ratio for El Salvador.

Table 4.4. Relative Contribution by Risk Factor
(In percent)

	Costa Rica	Dominican Republic	El Salvador	Guatemala	Panama
Growth	16	10	1	1	15
Real primary spending	39	54	18	52	63
Real exchange rate	32	15	64	32	0

Source: Based on simulated data using current debt structures.

although the relative contribution to the debt dynamics is twice as large for the first two (32 percent) than for the latter (15 percent). The following subsection concludes, on a preliminary basis, that altering the composition of the public sector debt in favor of domestic currency debt would reduce the vulnerabilities of both Costa Rica and Guatemala, but increase it in the Dominican Republic.

Growth is a prominent factor affecting debt dynamics for Costa Rica, Panama, and Dominican Republic, contributing 16, 15, and 10 percent, respectively. For the other two countries the growth impact is insignificant, reflecting a relatively larger correlation between GDP growth and the other risk factors in these countries.

Assessment of Policy Options

The VaR framework can also be used for a stylized analysis of different policy options. In the following, a change in the debt composition is presented as an example: foreign currency liabilities tend to dominate emerging market debt structures, further limiting the capacity that these countries have to formulate policy responses.[28] Using the framework developed in this paper, the potential benefits of an alternative debt structure with a larger fraction of domestic currency debt are evaluated for the three nonofficially dollarized economies in Central America. The simulation of an alternative debt structure reveals a three-dimensional indifference curve among currency denomination, real interest rate, and maturity. Thus, the simulation of the alternative debt structures keeps the maturity and interest rates profiles of each currency-denominated debt unaltered, changing only the proportion of domestic currency debt vis-à-vis the external debt. Conse-

quently, the alternative debt structure simulated in each one of the three countries is of shorter average maturity and subject to higher (and generally more volatile) real interest rates. In all three cases it has been assumed that foreign currency denominated debt falls to 30 percent of total debt, from 60 percent in Costa Rica, 73 percent in Dominican Republic, and 76 percent in Guatemala.[29]

As shown in Table 4.5 greater reliance on domestic currency debt appears to be a viable complement to fiscal adjustment for Costa Rica and Guatemala.[30] Reducing the composition of foreign currency debt to 30 percent of total debt decreases the 2008 debt-to-GDP ratio by more than 4 points in Guatemala's case, and by 2½ points in the case of Costa Rica. The risk profile would also improve in both cases. In contrast, Dominican Republic's current debt structure appears to serve that country better than one with greater reliance on domestic debt. Increasing the share of domestic currency debt to 70 percent of total debt would increase the debt-to-GDP ratio by almost 8 points by 2008, and worsen the risk profile from 81.5 percent to 88.5 percent.

Conclusions

The analysis presented in this section complements traditional sustainability assessments by providing a sense of the probability distribution of the debt-to-GDP ratio using VaR techniques. The pro-

---

[28]See Hausmann and Panizza (2003) for an in-depth analysis of the issue.

[29]It should be noted that increasing the share of domestic currency debt could negatively affect the incentives to repay, particularly in the context of flexible exchange rates, as inflation becomes an effective way to reduce the real value of such debt. Also, increasing the share of domestic currency debt could potentially increase the contingent liabilities of the public sector if private agents dollarized their portfolios further as a consequence of the government actions.

[30]For the estimation of the VaR, the period 1991–2003 is used. In the case of the Dominican Republic the crisis-free period 1993–2001 was used instead, entailing lower exchange rate volatility.

Table 4.5. Effect of Increased Reliance on Domestic Currency Debt
(In percent of GDP)

	Debt/GDP (2008)		VaR (at 5 percent)	
	Original	New	Original	New
Costa Rica	65.5	63.0	94.1	88.5
Dominican Republic	64.5	72.2	81.5	88.5
Guatemala	36.7	32.5	50.6	43.7

Source: IMF staff estimates.

posed framework confirms the main finding of the traditional approach, namely, that policy actions are required in all of the Central American countries, with the exception of Guatemala, to make their ratios of public debt to GDP sustainable. Nevertheless, the traditional approach provides a somewhat different characterization of the risk profiles of the debts, and the sensitivity of the debt ratios to the different risks appears to not be appropriately captured by conventional stress tests. Both of these shortcomings can be addressed using the VaR technique discussed in this section. This analysis reveals that the factors that contribute to the risks differ across countries. While government spending is a key factor in almost all countries, some countries are particularly vulnerable to changes in the real exchange rate, while others depend critically on the growth performance. Therefore, despite many commonalities, the emphasis and type of policy response may have to differ across countries.

Appendix. Value-at-Risk Methodology

The VaR methodology was originally developed to calculate the market risk of a financial portfolio—that is, the probability distribution of returns of a given portfolio due to changes in market prices. It was created to provide a numerical estimate of the potential loss in the value of the portfolio over a given time period. More recently, it has been extended to assess the risk characteristics of financial institutions around the world, and to the measurement and management of credit risk, liquidity risk, operational risk, and the analysis of natural disasters, among others. It is also used as a source of information and as a risk management tool, primarily by financial institutions and regulators, but increasingly by nonfinancial companies. VaR can be extended, in principle, to the analysis of any type of risk or combination of risks and to any type of institution. The VaR provides an estimate of "the worst

possible loss over a target horizon with a given level of confidence.[31]

The technique, as originally developed, computes the potential loss from the variance of the portfolio returns, based on some assumption about the probability distribution of returns and a given confidence level. The technique, in its original form, consists of estimating the distribution of portfolio values based on the portfolio composition and a set of market risks.

The VaR methodology does not provide much structure on how to estimate the relationship between the actual realization of an outcome and the set of underlying risk factors; it provides a way to calculate the probability distribution function of the final outcome. To implement VaR, the underlying risk factors of the portfolio need to be identified, as do the interrelationships (covariance matrix) among those risk factors. This is done by decomposing the assets and liabilities of a given portfolio into a set of primitive securities, each exposed to a small number of risk factors. The function that describes the relationship between primitive securities and underlying risk factors is referred to as mapping in the VaR terminology. There are many ways in which this mapping can be done.

The probabilistic distribution of outcomes can be computed analytically or through simulation using as inputs the mapping matrix, the probability distribution of the underlying risks, and the covariance matrix of risks. The VaR is then computed from the probability distribution for a given confidence level.

The most general VaR formulation assumes normally distributed returns and uses the following expression to compute the VaR for a specific confidence level:

$$VaR = \alpha \sigma_P W, \qquad (1)$$

[31]Definition provided by Jorion (2001), p. 22.

where W is the initial value of the portfolio, α is the standard normal deviate for a given confidence level, and σ_P is the standard deviation of portfolio returns, calculated as

$$\sigma_P^2 = w'\Sigma w, \qquad (2)$$

where w is the vector of weights for the various securities in the portfolio and Σ is the variance-covariance matrix of returns. This approach, also known as delta-normal approach, has important drawbacks in its application to the fiscal accounts: it assumes normal distribution of fiscal outcomes and it requires the decomposition of the assets and liabilities into a set of primitive securities—that is, securities exposed to only one risk factor each.

In contrast to the delta-normal approach, simulation methods, also known as full-valuation methods, are better suited to the analysis of fiscal risks. These methods are less restrictive about underlying probabilistic functions and allow for the direct estimation of portfolio values from simulated financial and economic environments. Under the full-valuation methods, the portfolio valuations obtained from a large number of simulations are sorted from worst to best, and the VaR is the nth observation of the sorted results, where n is the confidence level defined in percent times the number of simulations that were carried out.[32]

References

Barnhill, Theodore M., Jr., and George Kopits, 2003, "Assessing Fiscal Sustainability Under Uncertainty," IMF Working Paper 03/79 (Washington: International Monetary Fund).

Corsetti, Giancarlo, and Nouriel Roubini, 1991, "Fiscal Deficits, Public Debt and Government Solvency: Evidence from OECD Countries," *Journal of the Japanese and International Economics*, Vol. 5 (December), pp. 354–80.

Eichengreen, Barry, Ricardo Hausmann, and Ugo Panizza, 2003, "Currency Mismatches, Debt Intolerance and Original Sin: Why They Are Not the Same and Why It Matters," NBER Working Paper No. 10036 (Cambridge, Massachusetts: National Bureau of Economic Research).

Forbes, Kristin, and Roberto Rigobon, 2000, "Contagion in Latin America: Definitions, Measurement, and Policy Implications" NBER Working Paper No. 7885 (Cambridge, Massachusetts: National Bureau of Economic Research).

Hakkio, Craig S., and Mark Rush, 1991, "Is the Budget Deficit 'Too Large'?" *Economic Inquiry*, Vol. 29 (July), pp. 429–45.

Hamilton, James D., and Marjorie A. Flavin, 1986, "On the Limitations of Government Borrowing: A Framework for Empirical Testing," *American Economic Review*, Vol. 76 (September), pp. 809–19.

Hausmann, Ricardo, and Ugo Panizza, 2003, "The Determinants of 'Original Sin:' An Empirical Investigation," *Journal of International Money and Finance,* Vol. 22 (December), pp. 957–90.

International Monetary Fund, 2002, "Assessing Sustainability" (Washington, May 28). Available via the Internet: www.imf.org/external/np/pdr/sus/2002/eng/052802.pdf.

———, 2003, "Sustainability Assessments—Review of Application and Methodological Refinements," (Washington, June 10). Available via the Internet: www.imf.org/external/np/pdr/sustain/2003/061003.htm.

Jorion, Philippe, 2001, *Value at Risk: The New Benchmark for Managing Risk* (New York: McGraw-Hill).

Kaminsky, Graciela L., and Carmen M. Reinhart, 1999, "The Twin Crises: The Causes of Banking and Balance of Payments Problems," *American Economic Review,* Vol. 89 (June), pp. 473–500.

Kremers, Jeroen J.M., 1989, "U.S. Federal Indebtedness and the Conduct of Fiscal Policy," *Journal of Monetary Economics*, Vol. 23 (March), pp. 219–38.

Offerdal, Erik, 2004, "Fiscal Sustainability," in *The Macroeconomy of Central America*, ed. by Robert Rennhack and Erik Offerdal (New York: Palgrave Macmillan), pp.1–40.

Pattillo, Catherine, Hélène Poirson, and Luca Antonio Ricci, 2002, "External Debt and Growth," IMF Working Paper 02/69 (Washington: International Monetary Fund).

Reinhart, Carmen M., Kenneth S. Rogoff, and Miguel A. Savastano, 2003, "Debt Intolerance," NBER Working Paper No. 9908 (Cambridge, Massachusetts: National Bureau of Economic Research).

Roberts, William, 1991, "Implications of Expected Present Value Budget Balance: Application to Postwar U.S. Data," in *Rational Expectations Econometrics*, ed. by Lars Peter Hansen and Thomas J. Sargent (Boulder, Colorado: Westview Press).

Trehan, Bharat, and Carl. E. Walsh, 1988, "Common Trends, The Government's Budget Constraint, and Revenue Smoothing," *Journal of Economic Dynamics and Control*, Vol. 12 (June/September), pp. 425–44.

Wilcox, David W., 1989, "Sustainability of Government Deficits: Implications of the Present-Value Borrowing Constraints," *Journal of Money, Credit and Banking,* Vol. 21 (August), pp. 291–306.

---

[32]For example, the VaR at a 99 percent confidence level in an exercise of 10,000 simulations is given by the 100th observation of the sorted portfolio returns (1 percent x 10,000).

V   Regional Integration and Exchange Rate Arrangements

Jun Il Kim and Laura Papi

The Central American–Dominican Republic Free Trade Agreement (CAFTA-DR) with the United States, combined with increasing integration among the Central American countries, provides an opportunity to reflect on the long-run options for exchange rate regimes in Central America.[1] Although the macroeconomic conditions of the Central American countries present similarities and have improved significantly in recent years, their exchange rate regimes cover the whole spectrum: floating regimes in the Dominican Republic and Guatemala, and crawling pegs in Costa Rica, Honduras, and Nicaragua, and full dollarization in the cases of Panama and El Salvador. Looking forward, CAFTA-DR, together with other regional integration mechanisms such as the customs union, is expected to boost trade and financial flows with the United States and also within the region and increase the synchronization of business cycles.[2] These developments could affect some important factors in the choice of exchange rate arrangements.

This section examines the long-run options of exchange rate regimes available to the Central American countries. It does not address specific short-run considerations that affect the choice of exchange rate regimes in the near future, but focuses on evaluating the exchange rate arrangement options in the long run—that is, over a period of, say, a decade or longer. The analysis employs a uniform methodology across countries and offers a regional perspective. It takes a long-run view by using an approach derived from the literature on optimum currency areas to evaluate the relative suitability of these countries for different exchange rate arrangements. As a measure of comparison, the suitability of the Central American countries for a common currency (pegged to the U.S. dollar, or full dollarization) is compared to that of the European

countries participating in the European Monetary Union (EMU).[3]

The key conclusions are that even after taking into account the expected impact of further CAFTA-DR-related integration with the United States, Central America would still be less suitable for a common currency (independently floating or dollar-peg/officially dollarized) than Western Europe was in the 1970s. While increased synchronization of business cycles, reduced inflation differentials, and rising trade flows with the United States have made the region relatively more suitable for dollarization/a dollar peg during the decade ending in 2003, there is still a large distance before a common currency would be a realistic option for the region. To ensure that policymakers have, in the long run, the option to choose among the full range of possible exchange rates regimes, it is important to maintain strong macroeconomic frameworks and continue progress with structural reforms and institution building, especially in the financial sector. For countries that are officially dollarized, the focus should be on policies to ensure the sustainability of dollarization regimes, including through sound macroeconomic frameworks, appropriate wage policy, and structural reforms to maintain competitiveness.

Issues Concerning Exchange Rate Regimes in Developing Countries

Despite intense debate over several decades, no consensus has been reached on the most desirable exchange rate regime. Though pegged regimes and certain intermediate regimes, such as crawling pegs and bands, were preferred in the 1980s and early 1990s for their anti-inflation credentials, they fell out of favor following the emerging market crises of the 1990s. This led to the emergence of the "bipolar view," which favors either hard pegs or freely floating arrangements and considers intermediate regimes

---

[1]The countries considered are Costa Rica, the Dominican Republic, El Salvador, Guatemala, Honduras, Nicaragua, and Panama. These countries are henceforth referred to as the Central American countries.

[2]See Section II on the macroeconomic implications of CAFTA-DR.

[3]This comparison should be interpreted with caution, as strong political will toward greater integration was one of the key ingredients behind the success of EMU, which might not be present in Central America.

difficult to sustain. This approach was partly based on the concept of the "impossible trinity" (Fischer, 2001; IMF, 2003; and Obstfeld and Rogoff, 1995). The bipolar view, in turn, came into question following the collapse of Argentina's currency board. Also, some have argued that the impossible trinity does not prevent a country from choosing an intermediate solution between floating and monetary union (Frankel, 1999, 2004). In this vein, Reinhart and Reinhart (2003), among others, have noted that intermediate regimes are not at all dead, with many developing countries suffering from "fear of floating" (Calvo and Reinhart, 2002).

Empirical studies that compare alternative exchange rate regimes' macroeconomic performance and crisis vulnerability have also failed to reach consensus. For example, while Ghosh, Gulde, and Wolf (2003) find that countries with pegged regimes experience lower inflation with a growth performance that is no worse than that of countries with floating regimes, Levy-Yeyati and Sturzenegger (2001) argue that this lower inflation comes at the cost of lower growth.

The classification of exchange rate regimes is also subject to controversy. Although it is now generally recognized that de facto classifications are preferable to de jure ones, there are competing methodologies for classifying de facto exchange rate regimes. The IMF, in its *Annual Report on Exchange Arrangements and Exchange Restrictions (AREAER)*, has since 1999 employed a de facto classification based on quantitative and qualitative information, which also includes the authorities' stated policy intentions (see IMF, 2003). Other de facto classifications can be found in Reinhart and Rogoff (2004) and Levy-Yeyati and Sturzenegger (2005). Differences in the methodology employed to classify regimes may account for the different findings of various empirical studies.

Rogoff and others (2004) move away from advocating an exchange rate regime that is best for all countries and instead group countries according to the degree of integration with global financial markets. They view the degree of capital markets integration as the key factor on the basis of which exchange rate regimes can be recommended. They conclude that the benefits of flexible exchange rate regimes increase as countries become more integrated with global capital markets and develop sound financial systems. In developing economies, however, pegs are found to yield lower inflation without an apparent cost in terms of growth, suggesting the presence of a credibility effect. In emerging markets, fixed or limited-flexibility exchange rate regimes incur crises more frequently, but do not have better inflation or growth performance.

Authors that argue that no single exchange rate regime is right for all countries or at all times focus on the *relative* suitability of countries for different regimes (Frankel, 1999). The criteria used in the choice of the exchange rate regime result both from the theoretical models that compare fixed versus floating arrangements and the literature on optimum currency areas (e.g., Mundell, 1961, and Alesina and Barro, 2002).

The relative suitability of each country for a given exchange rate regime has been linked to macroeconomic and structural variables, such as international trade and the synchronization of business cycles. Countries that trade more among each other, are smaller in size, experience similar shocks, have more highly correlated business cycles and prices, and enjoy higher factor mobility and fiscal flexibility are more likely to benefit from a pegged exchange rate regime, including a currency union. This is because the main advantages of fixed exchange rate regimes and currency unions are the promotion of trade and financial flows, whereas the drawbacks are related to the inability to use the exchange rate as a tool to offset shocks. An additional benefit of pegging the exchange rate is that some countries could "import" policy credibility (Alesina and Barro, 2002). Hence, countries that lack policy discipline (manifested, for example, in high inflation) could benefit most from pegging their exchange rate or joining a currency union where the anchor country has an established record of low inflation and stability. This would result in lower risk premiums and interest rates, while forgoing seignorage.[4]

In addition, a body of the literature has found that currency unions increase trade beyond the levels associated with fixed exchange rate regimes (Frankel and Rose, 2002; Rose, 2000; and Tenreyro and Barro, 2003). Alesina, Barro, and Tenreyro (2002) find that currency unions also increase the co-movement of prices. If this is so, currency unions may create virtuous circles, in that participation in the currency union actually increases the participating countries' suitability for such a union. Conflicting results, however, have been obtained as to whether currency unions promote trade specialization and increase co-movements in output.

Besides these long-term factors, short-term and operational considerations affect the feasibility of adopting a certain exchange rate arrangement. A low level of reserves, low tolerance for high interest rates, fiscal dominance, or a weak banking system would make a pegged exchange rate regime highly vulnerable. More generally, a crisis situation might make a floating arrangement the only viable option. On the other hand, an underdeveloped financial system, the difficulty of adopting an alternative nominal anchor, or large currency mismatches might cause "fear of floating" and make moving toward flexibility inadvisable in the short run, because the conditions for the devel-

---

[4]Seignorage would still accrue in the case of a peg or a currency board, but not under full dollarization.

Table 5.1. Exchange Rate Regimes
(End of year)

	1990	1995	2000	2001	2002	2003
Costa Rica	5	5	5	5	5	5
Dominican Republic	3	7	7	7	7	8[1]
El Salvador	7	3	3	1	1	1
Guatemala	7	7	7	7	7	8
Honduras	3	5	6	6	6	6
Nicaragua	5	5	5	5	5	5
Panama	1	1	1	1	1	1

Sources: Bubula and Ötker Robe, 2002; and IMF, *Annual Report on Exchange Arrangements and Exchange Restrictions.*
Note: 1 = No separate legal tender; 2 = currency board; 3 = conventional fixed peg; 4 = pegged within a horizontal band; 5 = crawling peg; 6 = crawling band; 7 = managed floating; 8 = independently floating.
[1]The Dominican Republic was classified as freely floating starting on January 31, 2004.

opment of a reasonably deep and competitive foreign exchange market would be absent or macroeconomic stability might be compromised. Short-term macroeconomic objectives might also argue for the adoption of a regime that is not appropriate from a longer-run perspective; for example, exchange-rate-based stabilizations to reduce high inflation have been adopted by countries better suited for a floating regime. If an exchange rate regime is adopted on the basis of short-term considerations, issues of exiting to a more appropriate long-term choice arise.

Finally, some have de-emphasized the importance of choosing the optimal exchange rate regime and focused instead on the underlying institutions and policies needed to ensure a country's satisfactory macroeconomic performance. Calvo and Mishkin (2003) have questioned the applicability of the standard theory of exchange rate regimes to emerging markets. They underscore that some characteristics of emerging markets, such as weak fiscal and monetary discipline, high currency substitution, and vulnerability to sudden stops in capital flows, make the application of standard theory problematic in emerging economies. They also question the ability of exchange rate regimes to generate desirable institutional traits, and hence conclude that focusing on developing solid institutions is more important than the choice of exchange rate regime in ensuring successful macroeconomic performance.

The literature on exchange rate regimes in Central America reflects the divided debate on exchange rate arrangements. Although Corbo (2002) and Dornbusch (2001) favor dollarization, others emphasize its risks (including political costs) and the costly requirements of such a strategy (Collins, 1996; Palerm, 2002; and Rodlauer, 2004). Garcia-Lopez, Larrain, and Tavares

(2001) favor a currency union among Central American countries, but not full dollarization. Rennhack, Offerdal, and Mercer-Blackman (2004) conclude that for Honduras, Nicaragua, and Costa Rica, a flexible exchange rate regime would be more consistent with their structural characteristics; however, in general they find that the relative suitability for a peg corresponds to the actual regimes of Central American countries. Finally, Papaioannou (2003) finds that although structural characteristics of the Central American countries can partly explain their choice of regime, specific institutional and political conditions are more important determinants.

Current Exchange Rate Arrangements

The classification of Central American countries' exchange rate arrangements is sensitive to the measure used. The IMF classification suggests a range of arrangements.[5] These range from dollarization in El Salvador and Panama to the floating regimes of the Dominican Republic and Guatemala. Costa Rica and Nicaragua have a crawling peg, and Honduras has a crawling band (Table 5.1). In recent years, the salient changes in regimes have been El Salvador's dollarization in 2001 and Guatemala's shift from managed to independently floating in 2003; the Dominican

[5]The IMF uses a de facto classification that combines quantitative and qualitative information, including the authorities' stated exchange rate policy (IMF, *Annual Report on Exchange Arrangements and Exchange Restrictions*, various years). Although the IMF changed from a de jure to a de facto classification in 1999, the data for previous years were obtained from Bubula and Ötker-Robe (2002), who constructed the back series using the same de facto methodology used since 1999.

Box 5.1. History of Exchange Rate Regimes in Central America

The exchange rate regimes of all the Central American countries were dollar pegs before diverging in the 1980s, when most of the pegs had to be abandoned for different reasons, including external shocks, civil conflict, and inconsistent domestic policies. The notable exception is Panama, which has been fully dollarized since 1904.

All the countries, with the exception of El Salvador and Panama, then had "freely falling" exchange rate regimes according to Reinhart and Rogoff (2004). According to their classification, Costa Rica abandoned the peg in 1981, El Salvador in 1983, Guatemala in 1984, Honduras in 1990, and Nicaragua in 1979. The Dominican Republic had a very narrow de facto crawling band until 1982. Some of the countries then went through several different regimes, at times involving multiple currency practices, before converging to their current arrangements.

After the freely falling exchange rate period, Costa Rica followed a real exchange rate rule based on the inflation differential with the United States. The rule was modified to take into account targeted rather than actual inflation in 1996. Today the rate of crawl of the colón is adjusted on the basis of the inflation differential between Costa Rica and its main trading partners.

The Dominican Republic adopted a managed floating exchange rate regime in 1992, after a period with a freely falling exchange rate, but then moved to a de facto crawling band, which lasted until 2003. At that time, a severe currency crisis brought the country back to a freely falling regime according to the natural classification, which would still apply today given the high inflation rate. According to the IMF classification, the Dominican Republic had a managed floating regime

from 1991 to 2003 before moving to an independently floating arrangement in January 2004.

After abandoning the peg in 1983, El Salvador had a managed floating regime until 1990, when it moved to a de facto peg. However, in the early 1990s after the cessation of civil conflict, the exchange rate came under appreciating pressures which were resisted using sterilized intervention. Dollarization was adopted in 2001.

Guatemala oscillated between freely falling and managed floats in the years following the abandonment of the crawling band (1984). In 1991, the system converged to a de facto crawling peg, which is still the present regime according to the natural classification. In the IMF classification, however, Guatemala had a managed float in the 1990s and early 2000s, until it moved to an independent float in 2003.

After a brief spell in the freely falling category, Honduras had a de facto crawling band from 1991 to 1998 before converging to a de facto crawling peg according to the natural classification. In the IMF classification, however, Honduras adopted a float in 1992–94. It then moved to a crawling peg and finally a crawling band in 1996. The rate of crawl is determined by the projected inflation differential with its main trading partners and the exchange rate of its main trading partners vis-à-vis the U.S. dollar. The band was widened from 1 to 7 percent in 1998, but movement within the band has been limited.

Nicaragua spent a long period with a freely falling regime owing to hyperinflation. In 1991 the exchange rate was pegged and since 1993 it has been a crawling peg. The rate of depreciation is now preannounced by the central bank.

Republic's exchange rate system was reclassified from a managed to an independent float in January 2004 (see Box 5.1 for a history of exchange rate regimes in Central America).

The natural classification of Reinhart and Rogoff (2004)[6] generates a less diverse result. According to this classification, the Dominican Republic and Guatemala also had a de facto crawling band and a de facto crawling peg, respectively, in 2001, the last year for which these data are available (Table 5.2). This contrasts with the IMF classification, which categorized both countries as managed floaters in that year.

Updating the Reinhart and Rogoff classification for the countries under consideration for 2002 and 2003 reveals that the Dominican Republic would have shifted to the freely falling category in 2003, after having experienced a deep currency crisis and annual inflation of over 40 percent. Another remaining important difference between the IMF and the natural classification concerns Guatemala, which has a free float under the IMF categorization but a de facto crawling peg under Reinhart and Rogoff's category.[7]

Long-Run Options for Exchange Rate Regimes in Central America

With increased integration, stronger institutions, and sustained robust macroeconomic frameworks, Central American countries may want to reevaluate

---

[6]Reinhart and Rogoff (2004) use a purely de facto classification, which is based mainly on time-series data on exchange rate variability. The exchange rate data from the parallel market are used whenever there is a discrepancy with the official exchange rate. A new category that is identified in this study is that of freely falling, which is characterized either by annual inflation exceeding 40 percent or, in the six months following a currency crisis, by a shift from a pegged to a floating regime (the crises are themselves identified on the basis of whether the depreciation exceeds a certain threshold).

[7]Honduras is classified as a crawling band under the IMF's classification and a de facto crawling peg under Reinhart and Rogoff's.

Table 5.2. Exchange Rate Regimes, Natural Classification

(End of year)

	1990	1995	2000	2001	2002[1]	2003[1]
Costa Rica	10	8	8	8	8	8
Dominican Republic	14	8	8	8	8	14
El Salvador	4	4	4	2	1	1
Guatemala	14	7	7	7	7	7
Honduras	14	10	7	7	7	7
Nicaragua	14	7	7	7	7	7
Panama	1	1	1	1	1	1

Sources: Reinhart and Rogoff (2004); and IMF staff estimates.

Note: 1 = No separate legal tender; 2 = pre-announced peg or currency board; 3 = pre-announced horizontal band < 2 percent; 4 = de facto peg; 5 = pre-announced crawling peg; 6 = pre-announced crawling band < 2 percent; 7 = de facto crawling peg; 8 = de facto crawling band < 2 percent; 9 = pre-announced crawling band > 2 percent; 10 = de facto crawling band < 5 percent; 11 = moving band < 2 percent; 12 = managed floating; 13 = freely floating; 14 = freely falling.

[1]The classification for 2002 and 2003 has been updated by IMF staff using the Reinhart and Rogoff (2003) methodology.

their options for long-run exchange rate regimes. Although operational considerations, institutional constraints, or short-term objectives might, as noted, dictate a different exchange rate regime choice in the short term, it is useful to know what the most suitable long-term regime would be in order to consider future plans.

Several long-run options for the exchange rate regimes of Central America can be considered. Besides the status quo, these options are increased flexibility, possibly with inflation targeting; a common currency area among the Central American countries, either pegged to the U.S. dollar or freely floating versus the U.S. dollar; or full dollarization.

Increased Flexibility

Adjustment to shocks would be one of the main benefits of increased exchange rate flexibility for Central America.[8] Exchange rate flexibility can help counter shocks to the current account (such as terms-of-trade shocks) as well as reduce the vulnerability to capital flow reversals. Improving short-term competitiveness could be another argument in favor of flexible regimes, but this objective might also be achieved with a one-time devaluation in cases where this is feasible. The more integrated the country is with international capital markets, the more difficult

it is to sustain a pegged regime after a step devaluation, because expectations that it might be followed by additional devaluations would typically heighten the risk of large capital outflows.

A flexible exchange rate regime should increase monetary policy independence. The degree of monetary independence is likely to be greater the less integrated the country is with international capital markets; furthermore, monetary independence is likely to be strengthened over time, as policy credibility becomes established.

Increased exchange rate flexibility requires an alternative nominal anchor. The possible choices would be either monetary targeting or inflation targeting. The latter has been the preferred choice of several emerging markets recently that are moving toward greater exchange rate flexibility, given the frequent instability of monetary aggregates. Because adopting a fully fledged inflation targeting requires time,[9] immediately after the abandonment of a peg, countries have adopted monetary targets as interim arrangements.[10]

Freely Floating Currency Area

A currency area that is freely floating against the dollar would have the ability to use exchange rate movements to adjust to real shocks affecting Central America; however, it would lack the credibility benefits stemming from anchoring to the United States. The choice of floating freely would be more

---

[8]Broda (2001) finds empirical support for the argument that flexible exchange rates can insulate economies better against terms-of-trade shocks. For a comprehensive analysis of the operational issues involved in moving from a pegged to a floating exchange rate regime, see IMF (2004).

[9]See, for example, Truman (2003) and Schaechter, Stone, and Zelmer (2000).

[10]This paragraph draws from IMF (2004).

appropriate the stronger the co-movements in output among the Central American countries and the weaker the region's co-movements in output with the United States. The credibility benefits of a Central American currency area are likely to be limited, as no Central American country is sufficiently dominant economically to act as an anchor country.[11] Furthermore, the credibility of a common Central American currency independently floating against the dollar would depend on the standards that are set by the Central American countries, such as their anti-inflation credentials, the fiscal discipline pursued in the region, and their record in maintaining them.

Common Currency Area Pegged to the U.S. Dollar

The benefits and costs of a Central American currency pegged to the U.S. dollar would be the mirror image of the option of a common currency that floats freely versus the dollar. A Central American currency pegged to the dollar would have the benefit of importing monetary credibility—which should entail lower inflation and interest rates—and reducing transaction costs, but at the cost of forgoing an instrument to deal with external shocks that affect Central America differently from the United States. Furthermore, a peg to the dollar would require a strong fiscal policy, which renounces monetary financing of the fiscal deficit and maintains fiscal discipline to stem expectations of a future devaluation. Similarly, the central bank's function is more constrained, particularly under a currency board arrangement (or, of course, under full dollarization), calling for a healthy banking system and alternative arrangements to deal with banks' liquidity problems. With a pegged exchange rate regime, policies aimed at increasing the flexibility of factor markets—in particular, labor markets—would be important as alternative ways to counter real shocks.

Pegged exchange rate regimes can also take intermediate forms, such as crawling pegs or bands. Beyond the general considerations that apply to pegged regimes, as reviewed above, the advantage of a crawling peg is the prevention of large misalignments in competitiveness due to the adjustments of the nominal exchange rate with inflation differentials.[12] However, this might have the cost of reducing the anti-inflation properties of the pegged regime. A band (or crawling band) would have the advantage of introducing some exchange rate flexibility and

some degree of monetary policy independence; this choice has been made by some countries exiting pegged regimes. However, the authorities might face tensions between the exchange rate and inflation objectives at the edges of the band.

Full Dollarization

Full dollarization[13] would have benefits and costs similar to pegging a common Central American currency to the U.S. dollar, but it would be perceived as a more irrevocable commitment. Additional benefits in terms of increased trade with the United States might accrue with dollarization, although the evidence for this is not clear.[14] The lack of seigniorage would represent the main cost of dollarization compared with a regional currency union pegged to the dollar.[15]

The choice of exchange rate regimes for the Central American countries is likely to be interdependent. Exchange rate movements of one country have spillover effects on other countries in the region, both because of their effect on bilateral trade (and hence output and inflation) and because some of them compete in third markets. For example, the costs of dollarization are likely to be reduced with an increase in the number of countries that have already dollarized.

In the following subsection, the analysis of the various options proceeds first by considering the individual factors for the exchange rate regime choice, and then by aggregating these determinants into a summary measure, an index.

Choosing Among the Long-Run Options: Key Factors

This subsection evaluates the relative suitability of Central American countries for different exchange rate arrangements. It adopts a long-term perspective, applying a consistent methodology across countries and using a common database. The analysis examines the recent and likely future developments in some of the key variables that affect the choice of the exchange rate regime. In addition, Central America is compared with the European countries partici-

---

[11]Alesina, Barro, and Tenreyro (2002) point out that anchor countries tend to be large relative to their clients.

[12]The rate of crawl is determined differently in each country. Some countries preannounce the rate of crawl and determine it in a forward-looking way with projected inflation; others accommodate inflation differentials.

[13]In the rest of the paper, dollarization refers to full dollarization unless otherwise noted.

[14]Empirical studies of this issue (for example, Rose, 2000) have focused on the impact of currency unions, supporting that currency unions promote trade well beyond fixed exchange rate arrangements. However, it should be noted that these studies deal mainly with advanced economies, and in the East Caribbean Currency Area convergence and trade have not increased homogenously either among the participating countries or with the United States in recent years.

[15]Dollarization might also reduce the need for open market operations aimed at sterilizing foreign inflows.

pating in EMU to assess the region's absolute suitability for dollarization.

The factors that are examined in this subsection have been identified mainly by the optimum currency area and fixed versus floating exchange rate regime literature. These factors include international trade and other cross-border flows, size of the economy, synchronization of business cycles, terms-of-trade shocks, degree of informal dollarization, inflation, factor mobility, fiscal flexibility, and seigniorage. These variables are examined in turn below.

Openness of the Economy

The effect of the extent of bilateral trade on the desirability of a currency union is ambiguous.[16] On the one hand, the more countries trade with each other, the greater the benefits of a currency union, because the larger the reduction in transaction costs. Similarly, the deeper the financial interaction between countries, the greater the benefits of a currency union. On the other hand, in more open economies, external shocks have a larger impact on output and consumption, and hence the exchange rate is more useful as an adjustment tool (see, for example, Ricci, 1997). Thus, the effect of trade on the desirability of a currency area is ambiguous.[17] Which effect will prevail will depend partly on the extent to which nominal exchange rate changes translate into real exchange rate changes. If prices and wages adjust quickly with the exchange rate, the exchange rate is not an effective adjustment tool and the first effect (reduced transaction costs) might dominate. Typically, the literature on optimum currency areas emphasizes the first effect.

The United States is the dominant trading partner for the Central American countries and trade with the United States is more important than intraregional trade. On average, the United States received 60 percent of Central American exports and supplied 42 percent of imports over the past five years (Table 5.3).[18]

On the other hand, other countries in the region received an average of 17 percent of exports and supplied 11 percent of imports over the same period. In addition, the extent to which these countries trade with the other Central American countries varies greatly, from less than 5 percent of trade for the Dominican Republic to about 30 percent for Nicaragua.[19] In most cases, the share of trade with the United States rose over the past decade and, as shown in Section II, this trend is projected to intensify as a result of CAFTA-DR.[20] Trade among the seven Central American countries did not show a clearly rising trend.

On average, the Central American countries are about as open as the European economies were in the 1980s, but they trade less among themselves. If, however, the percentage of trade with the United States is added to the trade among the Central American countries, the Central American countries have more internal trade than the European countries did in the 1970s and 1980s.

The United States is the main creditor of most of the Central American countries. Bank for International Settlements (BIS) data were used to gauge the extent of financial transactions of the Central American countries with the United States and among themselves (Table 5.4).[21] These data indicate that, with the exception of the Dominican Republic and Nicaragua, the United States is the single largest creditor country of Central America.[22] When taken as a group, European banks also have large exposures, in some cases larger than American banks. For most Central American countries, except Nicaragua and Costa Rica, American, European, and Japanese banks account for over two-thirds of BIS reporting banks, leaving a relatively small residual share to be explained. The share of financial transactions among Central American countries is not very high.

---

[16]Other current account transactions, for example remittances, would also be relevant in this discussion. However, consistent data on the geographical composition of these flows are not available, and hence the analysis focuses on trade flows, implicitly assuming that the geographical composition of other current account transactions broadly reflects that of trade flows.

[17]The trade channel could be less relevant for large countries. For example, Mexico, Canada, and the United Kingdom have joined free trade agreements but chosen not to fix their exchange rates. Transaction costs may have been relatively low for these countries, with their relatively well-developed financial markets in which exchange rate risk can be hedged more easily. Indeed, Frankel and Rose (2002) present evidence of a positive and large impact of a currency union on bilateral trade, but with the qualification that their result may not be applicable to large countries.

[18]See Section II for a detailed analysis of trade flows of the Central American countries. Trade data suffer from breaks in the series and other data problems. In spite of this, the overall qualitative results showing that the United States is the main trading partner and

trade with the United States is significantly more important than regional trade with the rest of Central America are deemed robust.

[19]Although trade among the Central American countries is not homogenously high, the countries that export similar commodities may compete in the U.S. market. COMTRADE data confirm that the United States is the leading market for most of the Central American exports, especially for the traditional ones.

[20]Other free trade agreements and other world trade developments might take place—such as competition from other emerging markets and developing economies—that would affect the geographical composition of Central America's trade. Were such changes to lead to a significantly different geographical composition of the region's trade, they would affect the conclusions regarding exchange rate arrangements.

[21]Of course, these are partial data and capture only financial exposures of BIS reporting banks, not those of nonbank corporations or official creditors. Furthermore, they do not include foreign direct investment. Nevertheless, they do provide an indication of the geographic distribution of international financial transactions.

[22]For the Dominican Republic and Nicaragua, Spanish and German banks, respectively, are the largest creditors.

Table 5.3. Trade Structure and Openness
(In percent of totals, period averages unless otherwise indicated)

	Costa Rica			Dominican Republic			El Salvador			Guatemala		
	1990–94	1995–99	1999–2003	1990–94	1995–99	1999–2003	1990–94	1995–99	1999–2003	1990–94	1995–99	1999–2003
Regional distribution of exports												
United States	76.1	64.7	61.8	59.9	80.2	86.2	57.4	49.6	65.2	61.5	61.5	62.9
Other Central American countries[1]	14.8	13.4	12.1	0.4	0.6	0.9	37.3	49.6	33.1	31.6	24.3	17.1
Rest of the world	9.1	21.8	26.1	39.6	19.2	12.9	5.3	0.8	1.7	7.0	14.2	20.0
Regional distribution of imports												
United States	52.8	44.0	40.3	41.7	59.8	57.6	43.0	40.3	47.4	43.3	40.9	34.7
Other Central American countries[1]	9.4	8.1	5.9	1.3	1.8	2.3	18.3	22.9	19.6	10.5	10.8	11.0
Rest of the world	37.8	47.9	53.8	57.1	38.4	40.2	38.6	36.8	33.0	46.1	48.3	54.4
Openness[2]												
Goods	59.1	71.6	73.0	61.7	74.8	72.3	27.4	52.2	58.2	35.7	37.5	40.3
Goods and services	76.6	88.9	91.8	85.4	99.4	95.1	37.0	60.8	73.3	43.3	43.3	46.6

	Honduras			Nicaragua			Panama		
	1990–94	1995–99	1999–2003	1990–94	1995–99	1999–2003	1990–94	1995–99	1999–2003
Regional distribution of exports									
United States	55.8	65.1	68.5	27.9	39.2	37.6	39.1	32.2	39.9
Other Central American countries[1]	8.0	13.6	6.5	20.6	23.6	32.4	13.3	15.1	15.8
Rest of the world	36.2	21.4	25.0	51.5	37.1	30.0	47.6	52.7	44.2
Regional distribution of imports									
United States	42.5	48.3	54.9	22.2	32.8	27.7	36.7	39.5	28.7
Other Central American countries[1]	11.7	14.4	8.4	26.0	33.8	26.9	5.0	6.0	5.8
Rest of the world	45.8	37.3	36.7	51.8	33.4	45.3	58.4	54.5	65.5
Openness[2]									
Goods	61.4	73.4	65.8	48.3	44.8	56.8	32.0	32.5	29.1
Goods and services	76.4	97.3	83.5	52.0	58.8	73.7	75.0	62.8	56.8

Sources: IMF, World Economic Outlook; Direction of Trade Statistics; and IMF staff estimates.

Note: In some cases, partner countries' data were used and adjustments made to obviate some data problems in the original series. Because of these problems, the data should be interpreted with caution.

[1]The Central American countries are Costa Rica, Dominican Republic, El Salvador, Guatemala, Honduras, Nicaragua, and Panama.

[2]Sum of exports and imports in percent of GDP.

Table 5.4. Consolidated Claims of BIS Reporting Banks on Central American Countries
(By nationality of reporting banks; in millions of U.S. dollars)

		Creditor Banks			
	Total Claims	United States	European banks	Japan	Other
Costa Rica	2,988	496	656	24	1,812
Percent of total claims	100.0	16.6	22.0	0.8	60.6
Dominican Republic	2,947	500	1,416	0	1,031
Percent of total claims	100.0	17.0	48.0	0.0	35.0
El Salvador	2,322	905	718	0	699
Percent of total claims	100.0	39.0	30.9	0.0	30.1
Guatemala	1,962	797	547	0	618
Percent of total claims	100.0	40.6	27.9	0.0	31.5
Honduras	761	216	391	0	154
Percent of total claims	100.0	28.4	51.4	0.0	20.2
Nicaragua	342	51	101	0	190
Percent of total claims	100.0	14.9	29.5	0.0	55.6

Sources: Bank for International Settlements, *Quarterly Review;* and IMF staff calculations.

Size of the Economy

The smaller the economy, the greater the benefits of a currency union. This is because smaller economies are typically also more open.

The Central American countries are relatively small. Their average GDP was US$13.7 billion in 2003. Comparing them with the European countries 10 years and 20 years before EMU reveals that the Central American countries are significantly smaller, with Luxembourg the only European economy of the same order of magnitude. This is all the more true for the size of the Central American countries in relation to the United States, their potential anchor country, compared with the European countries in relation to Germany.[23]

Co-Movements of Business Cycles

The higher the co-movements of business cycles, the lower the costs of forgoing exchange rate flexibility. In fact, when the co-movements in business cycles are high, the appropriate policies of the anchor country (or the union) would also be appropriate for economic stabilization in the other countries.

As discussed in Section II, the synchronization of business cycles vis-à-vis the United States and partly within the region has risen in recent years and is expected to increase further with CAFTA-DR. Table 5.A1 in the Appendix complements the correlation analysis by also taking into account the size of output fluctuations in Central America relative to that in the United States and European countries.[24] The reason for focusing on this measure is that besides capturing the co-movements between the output growth of two countries, as correlation does, the table also reflects the magnitude of the variability of the individual growth rates of the two countries. This is important because if, for example, the output of the anchor country is much less variable than that of the client country, despite moving together, the anchor country's response to the shocks will be largely irrelevant.[25] The degree of output co-movements with the

---

[23]Although the comparison of EMU countries is made vis-à-vis Germany (because Germany was considered the anchor country of European Monetary Union), it bears underscoring that the European Monetary Union ended up being a more symmetric monetary arrangement than initially envisaged. This would not be the case for Central America if it decided to dollarize.

[24]The measure used is the standard deviation of the difference in the logarithm of the real output of country i relative to the real output of country j calculated over different periods for the various pairs of Central American countries and the United States and for various pairs of European countries.

[25]This measure is used in Bayoumi and Eichengreen (1997). Alesina, Barro, and Tenreyro (2002) use a similar measure, but they first estimate a second-order autoregression for the logarithm of relative outputs and then calculate the mean square error using the residuals. The idea is that only the unpredictable part of the shocks is considered. However, if a country has a fixed exchange rate regime, it will not be able to use the exchange rate as an adjustment tool, even when the shocks are predictable.

United States increased in the past decade (1994–2003) compared with the previous one (1984–93) for all the Central American countries except Honduras. On average, co-movement in output increased within the region as well over the same period. The degree of output co-movement of the Central American countries among themselves is on average less pronounced than co-movement between individual Central American countries and the United States.

A comparison between Europe 10 and 20 years before EMU and Central America reveals a similar degree of output co-movement. In fact, the average of all output co-movement measures among the 12 European countries that formed EMU was 0.028 and 0.022 in the decades ending in 1979 and 1989, respectively, compared with 0.025 in Central America in the decade ending in 2003.

The co-movement of output of the Central American countries, as measured by pair-wise correlation, is strongest with the United States, suggesting the importance of the common link with the United States. The average correlation of the Central American countries' output growth with the United States was 0.44 in the decade ending in 2003, while the average pair-wise correlation between Central American countries was only 0.22.[26] Furthermore, the pair-wise correlations in output growth between the Central American countries, after removing the influence of the United States, revealed a significantly lower degree of co-movement, with the average correlation falling to 0.16 (Table 5.A2).[27]

Terms-of-Trade Shocks

The smaller the size of terms-of-trade shocks and the higher the co-movements in the terms of trade, the greater the benefits of a currency union. The correlation of terms-of-trade shocks depends in part on the product composition of trade.

Terms-of-trade shocks are sizable in Central America and much more important than they were for Europe before EMU (Table 5.A3). In fact, at 9.9 percent, the average absolute annual change in the Central American countries' terms of trade over the past decade was more than double that for Europe in the decade ending in 1989 (3.9 percent). The United

States has much smaller terms-of-trade shocks, with an average annual change of 1.5 percent over the past decade. The importance of terms-of-trade shocks for Central America results in part from the fact that these countries still rely heavily on traditional exports, with food being the main export for most of them, followed by manufactured goods.[28] Indeed, over the past decade, the importance of terms-of-trade shocks declined more for those countries that diversified their export base the most: Costa Rica, the Dominican Republic, and El Salvador.[29] On the other hand, the variability of the terms of trade of Guatemala, Honduras, and Nicaragua increased over the same period.

The co-movements in the terms of trade of the Central American countries fell in the past decade, are stronger with the United States than within the region, and are much weaker than in Europe (Tables 5.A4 and 5.A5 in the Appendix).[30] The average correlation among the terms of trade of all Central American countries and the United States fell from 0.2 in 1984–93 to 0.02 in 1994–2003. Furthermore, though the average correlation of the terms of trade of the Central American countries with the United States was 0.12 in the last decade, the average correlation of the terms of trade within the region became very small and negative (–0.01). Nicaragua has all negative correlations; Costa Rica has all negative correlations with Central America, but a very small positive correlation with the United States; Honduras also has several negative correlations. Finally, the correlation in the terms of trade of European countries was significantly stronger than among the Central American countries and the United States.

Currency Substitution in the Economy

The higher the degree of currency substitution of the economy, the smaller the costs of moving to a currency union. This relationship exists because the higher the degree of currency substitution is, the more limited are the effects of nominal exchange rate changes on the real exchange rate. This will happen

---

[26]The exception is Honduras, for which the correlation with the United States was negative in the last decade. Excluding Honduras, the average correlation with the United States is 0.55.

[27]The influence of the United States' business cycle is removed by first regressing the individual countries' output growth on the United States' output growth, and then calculating pair-wise correlations between the residuals of these regressions. Correlation is examined instead of the standard deviation of the country differences in output growth, as was done above, because the latter is by construction always smaller for residuals than the original differences in output growth.

[28]Within the food category, coffee, bananas, and fish/shellfish are the main exports, whereas the countries that have diversified their export base export larger shares of various manufactured goods.

[29]The variability of terms-of-trade shocks also diminished for Panama, even though Panama's exports consist mainly of food.

[30]Although this result may appear at odds with the earlier finding of increased synchronization in business cycles with the United States, it might be because the main transmission channels for the increased synchronization in business cycles do not involve terms-of-trade movements. Possible candidates are financial flows, as well as other current flows such as remittances, which for some Central American countries are as large as exports. Furthermore, increasing trade with the United States can be consistent with both higher synchronization in business cycles and decreasing correlation in the terms of trade if trade is largely at the interindustry level.

not only because the exchange rate will not affect the domestic price of goods whose prices are set in dollars, but also because, in economies with high currency substitution, the pass-through of exchange rate changes to domestically set prices is typically high.

As detailed in Section VI, the degree of currency substitution of the Central American economies is high (although it varies considerably across countries). Excluding the countries that have fully dollarized, financial dollarization amounts to almost 40 percent of total banking system assets, much greater than in Europe in 1979 and 1989.

Inflation Rates and Co-Movements of Prices

The higher and more variable the inflation rate and the higher the degree of co-movements in prices, the greater the benefits of a currency union. That is because the higher the inflation, the greater the benefits of "buying monetary credibility." Also, the larger the co-movements in prices, the smaller the chances of misalignments in competitiveness when the exchange rate is fixed.

Inflation rates and inflation variability have fallen in recent years (Table 5.A6). Inflation rates have declined for all the Central American countries, and for some, rates have converged close to advanced country levels. At the same time, the variability of inflation in individual countries, as well as the cross-country dispersion across Central America, has diminished. Co-movements in prices have increased in Central America in the past decade: they are, however, somewhat less strong than in Europe, as measured both with the anchor country and among all pairs of countries excluding the anchor country (Table 5.A7).

The average inflation rate in Central America in the past decade was 9.5 percent, somewhat higher than the 7.8 percent in Europe in the decade ending in 1989. Similarly, the difference between the average excluding the anchor country (that is, the United States for Central America and Germany for Europe) was greater in the case of Central America.

Factor Mobility

The greater factor mobility, the lower the costs of forgoing exchange rate flexibility. This is because greater factor mobility can lead to resource reallocation that can bring about the necessary adjustment, even in the absence of exchange rate flexibility.

Quantitative information on factor mobility is scarce. An analysis of labor market flexibility is beyond the scope of this section; therefore, only some very crude indicators of labor market flexibility are considered here. The average unemployment rate for the Central American countries was about 8 percent

in the five years up to 2002, somewhat lower than that of European countries in the five years up to 1989 (9.6 percent).[31] Also, according to another measure based on the variability of employment shares in the main sectors of the economy, the Central American countries appear to have greater variability of sectoral employment, perhaps suggesting greater labor market flexibility.[32] Furthermore, emigration from the Central American countries also functions as a shock absorber to a larger extent than in Europe.

Regarding capital mobility, the IMF's *Annual Report on Exchange Arrangements and Exchange Restrictions* suggests that the Central American countries have fairly liberal regimes compared with other emerging markets. Although the same classification is not available for the European countries in 1979 and 1989,[33] it is likely that the Central American countries now have on average a more liberal regime than the European countries had in 1979, but less liberal than the European countries in 1990, the year in which all capital account restrictions among the prospective EMU participants were removed.

Fiscal Flexibility

The greater the fiscal flexibility, the lower the costs of forgoing exchange rate flexibility. Fiscal flexibility is also difficult to measure. International fiscal transfers are very rare; hence, what is more relevant is the extent to which fiscal policy in individual countries can respond flexibly to shocks. Though an in-depth analysis of fiscal flexibility is beyond the scope of this section, a rough measure is the debt-to-GDP ratio, because the higher the debt level is, the less room there is for maneuvering using fiscal policy countercyclically. Nevertheless, comparisons with the European countries based on the debt-to-GDP ratio are not appropriate, as the ability to absorb the debt is much more limited in Central America because of their less advanced domestic financial markets and their intermittent access to international capital markets. The level of debt of most Central American countries suggests little scope for using fiscal policy countercyclically. Even countries whose debt is not high could be constrained by the availability of financing (see Section IV).

---

[31]A higher unemployment rate is considered an indication of a less flexible labor market. Because of data availability problems, these data are only indicative.

[32]Higher variability in the shares of sectoral employment in total employment might indicate greater flexibility of the labor market. For the European countries, the comparison excludes Portugal, as it has a very extreme value, indicating very high variability in sectoral employment.

[33]The Central American countries currently have more restrictive regimes than do the European countries.

Figure 5.1. Nominal Exchange Rate Variability, 1984–2003¹

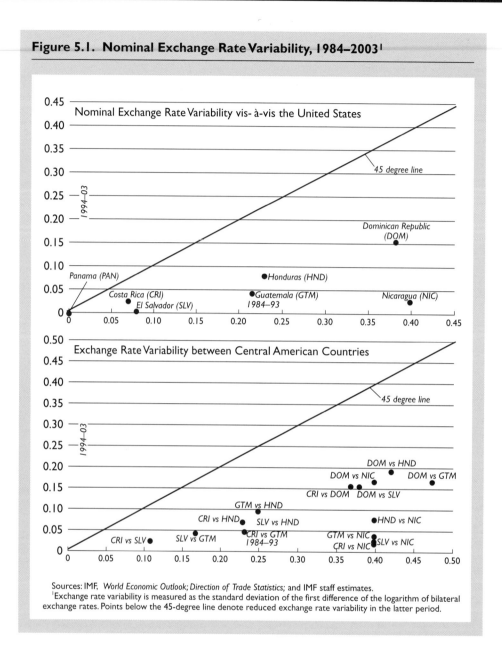

Sources: IMF, *World Economic Outlook; Direction of Trade Statistics;* and IMF staff estimates.
¹Exchange rate variability is measured as the standard deviation of the first difference of the logarithm of bilateral exchange rates. Points below the 45-degree line denote reduced exchange rate variability in the latter period.

Seigniorage

The lower the seigniorage, the smaller the cost of giving up the national currency. Simple calculations indicate that seigniorage in Central American countries is in the range of 1 to 2 percent of GDP on average.[34] Seigniorage has been falling over the years

with inflation and is likely to fall further as inflation is reduced.[35] Hence, this measure of seigniorage is likely to overestimate the costs of dollarization. Furthermore, in comparing a Central American currency union whose currency is pegged to the dollar, the forgone seigniorage is likely to be less, because with

---

[34]This figure represents the average annual increase in base money as a percentage of GDP in 2001–02. The reason for not using a more recent year was that the Dominican Republic had a large increase in seigniorage in 2003, at the same time as inflation spiked as a consequence of the currency and banking crisis. Costa

Rica, the Dominican Republic, Guatemala, Honduras, and Nicaragua are used in the calculations, as El Salvador and Panama are already dollarized.

[35]Estimates of seigniorage losses due to dollarization would decrease further if reserve requirements included in base money were remunerated.

a peg to the dollar, Central America's inflation is likely to be even lower than it would be with a freely floating Central American currency.

Finally, the bilateral exchange rates of the Central American countries reveal reduced variability, which can be interpreted as a summary indicator of the degree of integration. As Figure 5.1 shows, bilateral exchange rate variability of the Central American countries vis-à-vis the United States declined without exception between the periods 1984–93 and 1994–2003.[36] The same is true for all of the possible pairs of Central American countries. This could be interpreted as prima facie evidence of increased synchronization of these economies.

The analysis of this subsection suggests that if the region were to consider a common currency area, it would be more sensible to peg it against the U.S. dollar (or dollarize) rather than float it against the dollar. This is suggested because the Central American countries trade more and are more synchronized with the United States than among themselves. Importantly, CAFTA-DR is expected to boost integration with the United States more than within the region. However, the analysis of the individual factors in this section does not allow conclusions to be reached on Central America's suitability for pegging their exchange rate versus the U.S. dollar or dollarizing. This task is tackled in the next subsection.

Choosing Among the Long-Run Options: An Index Approach

This subsection uses an index approach to formally analyze the suitability of the Central American countries for different exchange rate regimes. The index will provide a summary measure of relative suitability, taking into account most of the factors highlighted above. As underscored in the analysis of the previous subsection, because the Central American countries currently trade more and are more synchronized with the United States than regionally, and because of the potential benefits of anchoring to the United States, this subsection focuses on assessing the relative suitability for dollarization[37] rather than for a Central American currency area with a freely floating currency versus the dollar. In addition, for each Central American country the index will provide information on the choice between dollarization (or a peg to the U.S. dollar) versus a freely floating domestic currency

vis-à-vis the dollar. A low value of the index would denote high suitability for dollarization, while a high value of the index would denote low suitability for dollarization and hence high suitability for a freely floating currency versus the dollar.

An index is constructed to aggregate all the factors relevant to evaluating the long-run suitability for different types of exchange rate regimes. Although the analysis above has analyzed specific factors relevant to the exchange rate regime choice, an index has the advantage of summarizing all the information once the relative weight of the individual factors is estimated from a large cross-section of country data. The index used here adopts an optimum currency area approach and provides a way of formalizing the relative suitability of Central American countries for different exchange rate regimes.[38] Initially, a comparison will be made between these countries' suitability in 1993 and 2003. Projections will then be formulated to evaluate how the Central American countries' suitability might evolve in the future once the macroeconomic effects of CAFTA-DR have fully occurred. Finally, a comparison with EMU member countries before the monetary union will provide a benchmark against which to compare the absolute suitability of Central America for dollarization.

The approach follows Bayoumi and Eichengreen (1997). As detailed in the Appendix, the first step is to estimate an equation that can explain the variability in bilateral exchange rates using variables that are deemed to determine the suitability for an optimum currency area, such as the synchronization of business cycles, the amount of trade, the similarity in the composition of trade, and the size of the countries. The specification of the equations is modified to better fit emerging markets and developing countries (Box 5.2). The regressions use a sample of 53 countries, including the G-7, all Latin American countries, all the European countries that are members of EMU, Australia, and New Zealand. The equations use two different specifications: one with nominal exchange rate variability as the dependent variable and one with the variability of an indicator of exchange market pressure. The latter is defined as an average of the variability of changes in bilateral nominal exchange rates and official reserves. The rationale for this is that some of the countries in the sample maintained a fixed exchange rate regime over the sample period, and hence an indicator of pressure in the foreign exchange market appears more appropriate as a dependent variable.

---

[36]Panama has a variability of zero in both periods because it was dollarized over the entire period.

[37]In the remainder of this subsection, we refer to "dollarization" as the regime choice for anchoring to the United States (which also includes a dollar-peg/currency).

---

[38]Although the index is an optimum currency area index, this should not be construed as an argument in favor of dollarization; rather, it is a common tool to assess relative suitability of exchange rate regimes.

Box 5.2. Regression Results

The estimated equation is specified as follows:

$$y = \beta_0 + \beta_1 SD(Y) + \beta_2 SD(P) + \beta_3 SD(TOT) + \beta_4 TRADE + \beta_5 SIZE, \qquad (1)$$

where y is either the exchange market pressure (*EMP*) indicator—defined as the average of the variability in bilateral exchange rates and official international reserves—or the variability of bilateral exchange rates, denoted by *SD(EXR)*. *SD(Y)* captures the variability in relative output changes, *SD(P)* the variability in relative inflation differentials, *SD(TOT)* the variability in relative changes in the terms of trade, *TRADE* the extent of bilateral trade, and *SIZE* country size measured by the arithmetic average of the log of real GDP in U.S. dollars of the two countries. All variability variables are measured by standard deviations of the underlying variables as described in the Appendix. *TRADE* and *SIZE* represent period averages.

The standard deviations and the means are calculated for a panel of 53 countries over three different sample periods: 1970–2003, 1980–2003, and 1990–2003. With 53 countries, there are 1,378 pairs of countries and hence potentially 1,378 observations in the regressions. In practice, the regressions include 1,308 observations as a result of missing values in the data.

The fact that many countries included in the sample—particularly Central and South American countries—experienced economic turbulence during the sample period suggests that both dependent and independent variables of the regression may be dominated by several outliers. To reduce the influence of outliers, the underlying variables of volatility measures were transformed before calculating their standard deviations.[1]

Table 5.A8 in the Appendix reports the results of regressions estimated for *EMP* and *SD(EXR)* over three different sample periods.

Most of the estimated coefficients have the expected sign and are highly significant. The few coefficients with the wrong sign are generally statistically insignificant. The results also indicate that the goodness of fit of the regressions is highly satisfactory, accounting for 70 to 90 percent of variation in *EMP* and *SD(EXR)*, respectively, when the full sample (1970–2003) was used. Furthermore, the estimated coefficients are relatively stable across different sample periods, supporting their use for forecasting purposes.

---

[1]A monotonic transformation given by $z = x / (1 + x)$ for $x > 0$ and $z = x / (1 - x)$ for $x < 0$ was carried out. This transformation maps the underlying variable x into an interval $(-1, 1)$.

A monetary variable, the variability of inflation differentials, is added to the explanatory variables. This is because the variability of bilateral exchange rates of developing countries (and relative reserve movements) is determined to a large extent by monetary phenomena. Alesina, Barro, and Tenreyro (2002) also stress the importance of co-movements in prices as well as output in determining the suitability of a country for an optimum currency area. Instead of the dissimilarity variable used by Bayoumi and Eichengreen, a variable that captured the variability in the terms of trade was used. Finally, other variables that are discussed in the previous sections, such as indicators of labor market mobility and fiscal flexibility, either did not turn out to be statistically significant (for example, unemployment) or could not be included because of data availability constraints.

As shown in the estimated indices, the Central American countries became more suitable for dollarization between 1993 and 2003. In fact, the indices for all countries became smaller in 1994–2003 than in 1984–93, indicating lower exchange rate variability versus the U.S. dollar and hence greater suitability for dollarization (Figure 5.2 and Table 5.A8 in the Appendix). The index for 1984–93 (1994–2003) was calculated with the values of the explanatory variables over that decade. The greater suitability in

2003 compared with 1993 is explained by the clear increase in the synchronization of business cycles and inflation differentials in the past decade. This result holds when using any of the regressions presented in Table 5.A9 in the Appendix, as well as for all pairs of Central American countries, suggesting also increased suitability for a currency area within the region.[39]

Although all Central American countries became more suitable for dollarization, the degree of change in the index varied among the countries. Nicaragua had by far the largest increase in relative suitability because of its macroeconomic stabilization, followed by Guatemala and the Dominican Republic, and the remaining Central American countries had more modest changes in the indices.

The range of suitability for dollarization does not always reflect the existing exchange rate regimes of the Central American countries. Panama is the country most suited for dollarization, and Guatemala follows (Figure 5.3). Costa Rica and El Salvador are next. The Dominican Republic, Honduras, and Nicaragua are the least suited for dollar-

---

[39]Nevertheless, it is not possible to ascertain whether the greater integration within the region is due to the common greater integration with the United States.

Figure 5.2. Optimum Currency Area Indices, 1984–2003[1]

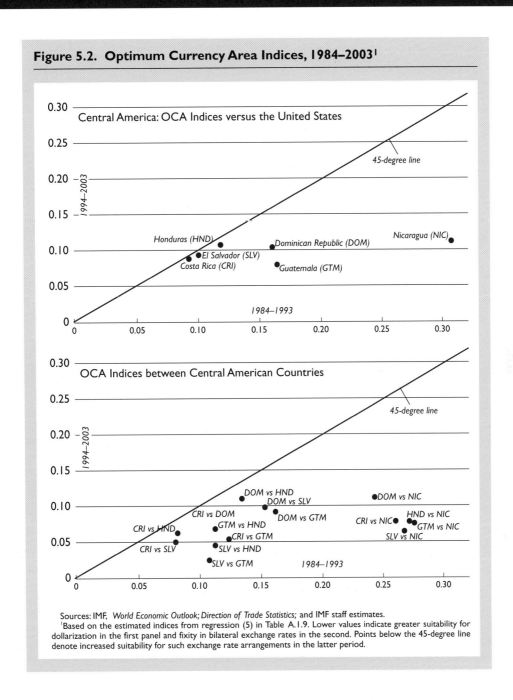

Sources: IMF, *World Economic Outlook; Direction of Trade Statistics;* and IMF staff estimates.
[1]Based on the estimated indices from regression (5) in Table A.1.9. Lower values indicate greater suitability for dollarization in the first panel and fixity in bilateral exchange rates in the second. Points below the 45-degree line denote increased suitability for such exchange rate arrangements in the latter period.

ization and hence the most suited to maintain a flexible exchange rate versus the U.S. dollar).

A comparison of Central America with European countries before EMU reveals that Central America is less suited for dollarization than was Europe for a currency area pegged to the Deutsche mark. To assess the absolute suitability of the Central American countries for dollarization, the indices for Central America vis-à-vis the United States calculated over the period 1994–2003 were compared with the indices for members of EMU vis-à-vis Germany in the 1970s, 1980s,

and 1990s.[40] On average, the estimated indices for Central America in 1994–2003 are higher than those estimated for European countries in all three decades, indicating that the European countries were more suitable for a currency area with Germany than the Central American countries were for dollarization in 2003 (see Figure 5.4 and Table 5.A9 in the Appendix).

[40]The indices for Europe did not show a monotonic convergence over the three periods considered.

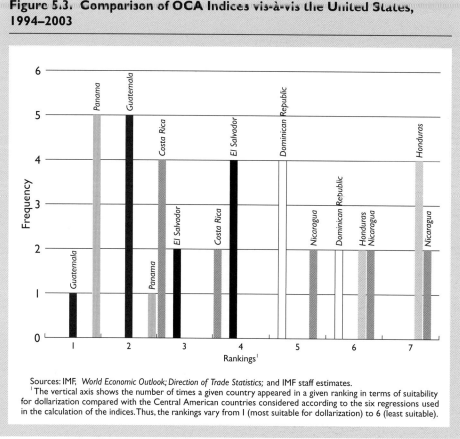

Figure 5.3. Comparison of OCA Indices vis-à-vis the United States, 1994–2003

Sources: IMF, *World Economic Outlook; Direction of Trade Statistics;* and IMF staff estimates.
¹ The vertical axis shows the number of times a given country appeared in a given ranking in terms of suitability for dollarization compared with the Central American countries considered according to the six regressions used in the calculation of the indices. Thus, the rankings vary from 1 (most suitable for dollarization) to 6 (least suitable).

None of the Central American countries has indices comparable to the European countries most suited for a currency union with Germany, such as the Netherlands, Austria, and France. However, some Central American countries have levels of the indices that are comparable to those of the European countries that appeared less suited for EMU, such as Greece, Ireland, Portugal, and Spain, in the 1980s and the 1990s. Considering the average of the indices among Central American countries and comparing them with the average of the indices among Western European countries, excluding Germany, the analysis shows that Central America is less suited to forming a currency union than Europe was in the 1990s. However, depending on the regression used to calculate the indices, the comparison with Europe in the 1980s provides mixed results.

CAFTA-DR and other regional initiatives are likely to make Central America relatively better suited for dollarization. The macroeconomic impact of CAFTA-DR was analyzed in Section II. The results presented in that section projected that trade and synchronicity in business cycles with the United States would increase significantly, thus potentially making the re-

gion more suitable for dollarization.[41] On the basis of Section II's analysis and other assumptions (described in Box 5.3), the indices of the Central American countries are projected to decline, thus making these countries more suitable for dollarization (Table 5.A10). Nevertheless, on average, Central America would still remain less suitable for dollarization than the European countries were for a currency union with Germany in the 1970s, 1980s, and 1990s.[42]

The results presented here should be interpreted with caution. The approach used can provide insights from a long-term perspective but might have some limitations in its application to developing countries. This exercise assumes that the determinants of exchange market pressure and exchange rate variability are the economic variables that have been considered

[41]Also, the variability of output in Central America is projected to decline, increasing the degree of co-movement with the United States. Dynamic effects of currency unions could also be considered, but given the uncertainty in the applicability of the empirical studies conducted so far for advanced economies to developing countries, this is not done here.

[42]The averages presented in Table 5.A10 exclude Panama, as this country does not participate in CAFTA-DR.

Box 5.3. Projections for Indices of Central American Countries

An exercise was conducted to project the indices of the Central American countries for the period 2004–13, taking into account the possible impact of CAFTA-DR. This box describes how the projections for the independent variables were carried out.

As noted by Bayoumi and Eichengreen (1997), projecting optimum currency area indices from the estimated equations is difficult, given that the explanatory variables are standard deviations or averages taken over a decade. In fact, there are at most three nonoverlapping observations for each explanatory variable that can be obtained from the full sample used in this study. As a result of such data limitations and because of the structural breaks observed in many countries in the sample, a simple extrapolation using a deterministic time trend could be misleading in many cases. An exception is the *SIZE* variable, which has exhibited a relatively stable trend over the sample period, and hence was extrapolated using a linear time trend in the projections.

Given these limitations, a less ambitious approach was taken in this study with regard to the projections of the indices for Central America vis-à-vis the United States.

- First, for those explanatory variables for which little empirical or theoretical guidance is available for projections, their actual values over the period of 1994–2003 (the final 10-year period in the sample) were used as projected values. The variability of inflation and the terms of trade fall in this category.

- Second, the variability of relative output was projected by assuming the inception of CAFTA-DR in 2005 and using information taken from Mexico's post-NAFTA experience (see Section II). The standard deviation of each country's real GDP growth was scaled down by the same proportion as the percentage reduction in Mexico's output variability following the inception of NAFTA. Regarding co-

movements in output vis-à-vis the United States, two alternatives were considered for comparison by assuming either no change in output correlation after the inception of CAFTA-DR or an increase to a level comparable to that of post-NAFTA Mexico.[1]

- Finally, the average trade ratio was projected using information taken from Hilaire and Yang (2003), whose simulation results indicate that trade volumes between CAFTA-DR countries and the United States could more than triple after the inception of CAFTA-DR. It is assumed that the trade-promoting impact of CAFTA-DR will occur at an equal and constant rate across all Central American countries, reaching its full effect in five years' time, and each country's GDP is assumed to grow at the same rate as its 10-year historical average. For comparison, an alternative was also considered under which the trade effect of CAFTA-DR progresses more slowly to reach its full effect after only 10 years.

Four sets of projections were carried out and for each of these all six regressions were used; the results are reported in Table 5.A10. The first set of projections assumes that the full effect on trade takes 10 years to materialize and assumes only a reduction in output volatility, with no increase in output correlations. The second set has the same assumptions as the first, but also assumes that output correlations with the United States become the same as Mexico's after NAFTA. The third and fourth sets are the same as the first and the second, respectively, but with the assumption that the full trade effect of CAFTA-DR materializes after five years.

---

[1]The method used for the output variability of individual countries could not be applied to the correlation with the United States because of the initial correlation, which in some cases was negative, as well as the constraint of keeping the correlation in the interval [−1, 1].

---

here as explanatory factors, that is, long-term structural factors. Although in the long run this is a sensible assumption, in the sample period under consideration several other factors (for example political developments and various obstacles to capital flows) could have contributed to exchange rate and exchange market pressure developments and might have persisted long enough to affect the results.

Conclusions

This section analyzed the relative suitability of the Central American countries for various types of exchange rate regimes by adopting a uniform methodology and a regional perspective. It does not recommend or endorse any change of regime; the goal is to

provide analytical background to countries' long-term considerations of their exchange rate regimes as they continue to integrate as a region and globally. Central America has made substantial strides in improving macroeconomic stability and economic integration over the past decade. CAFTA-DR and other regional initiatives are expected to further integration with the United States, and also within the region. These developments need to be taken into account in assessing the long-run exchange rate regime options available to the Central American countries.

The analysis suggests that if Central America were to choose to form a currency area, it would appear more desirable to peg the currency to the U.S. dollar or dollarize rather than adopt a common Central American currency that floats versus the U.S. dollar. This is because the economic links and

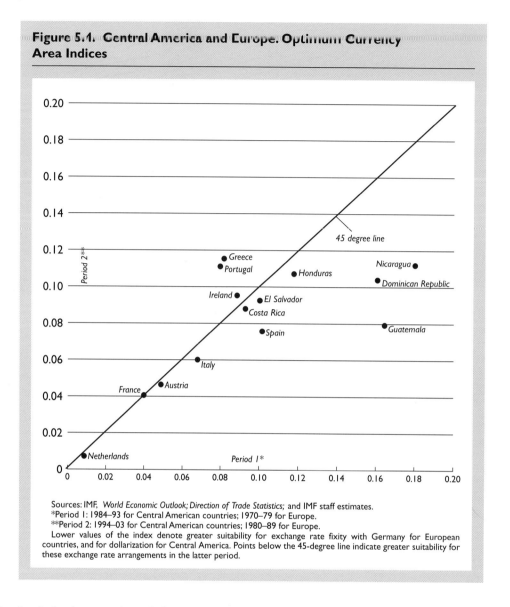

Figure 5.1. Central America and Europe: Optimum Currency Area Indices

Sources: IMF, *World Economic Outlook; Direction of Trade Statistics;* and IMF staff estimates.
*Period 1: 1984–93 for Central American countries; 1970–79 for Europe.
**Period 2: 1994–03 for Central American countries; 1980–89 for Europe.
Lower values of the index denote greater suitability for exchange rate fixity with Germany for European countries, and for dollarization for Central America. Points below the 45-degree line indicate greater suitability for these exchange rate arrangements in the latter period.

synchronization in business cycles existing at present and expected to result from CAFTA-DR are greater with the United States than within the region.

The suitability of Central America for dollarization has increased in the past decade but still falls short of that of European countries for a currency area with Germany. Given the increased synchronization in economic cycles, reduced inflation differentials, and rising trade flows, the Central American countries have become more suitable for dollar peg or dollarization between 1993 and 2003.[43] Despite these develop-

---

[43]The relative suitability for dollarization of different countries does not always reflect these countries' present exchange rate regimes. For example, Guatemala, which has one of the most flexible regimes, appears to be one of the candidates most suited for dollarization. The countries that are relatively less suited for a currency area are Honduras and Nicaragua.

ments, the region still appears less suitable for a currency union than member countries of EMU were in the 1970s, 1980s, and 1990s, even taking into account the predicted effects of CAFTA-DR.

The relative suitability of the Central American countries for dollarization does not always reflect existing exchange rate arrangements. Panama is the most suited country for dollarization, and Guatemala follows. Costa Rica and El Salvador are next. The Dominican Republic, Honduras, and Nicaragua are the least suited for dollarization and hence the most suited for a flexible exchange rate versus the U.S. dollar.

If the Central American countries were to choose dollarization as their long-term objective, the prerequisites and convergence criteria should be considered carefully. This is particularly important in light of the fact that fiscal discipline is key when adopting an inflexible exchange rate regime. Indeed, the Maastricht fiscal convergence criteria have been important milestones for EMU. In addition to fiscal discipline, several other structural and institutional reforms are also prerequisites for dollarization, in particular, reforms that increase the flexibility of factor markets and strengthen the financial sector. For economies already dollarized, the focus should be on policies that ensure adequate competitiveness and the sustainability of regimes, including through appropriate wage policies.

Shorter-term considerations regarding the choice of exchange rate regimes and country-specific circumstances may lead to conclusions that differ from those suggested in this section. Existing constraints may limit the choices of exchange rate regimes in the short run or simply make a different choice more desirable. Whatever the exchange rate regime chosen in the short run, consolidating prudent economic management, introducing the necessary structural reforms, and building institutions would ensure that policymakers have, in the longer run, the option to choose among the full range of possible exchange rate regimes.

Appendix. Technical Appendix

The Bayoumi and Eichengreen Optimum Currency Area Index

Bayoumi and Eichengreen developed a procedure to operationalize the optimum currency area theory. They have applied this approach to several parts of the world, but the paper taken as a specific reference in this section is the one that applies it to Western Europe (Bayoumi and Eichengreen, 1997).

Bayoumi and Eichengreen first estimated an equation that relates exchange rate variability to variables that are deemed to determine a country's suitability for participating in a currency area. They focused on the variability of nominal bilateral exchange rates, because a currency union would be equivalent to fixing the nominal exchange rates. The explanatory variables are a proxy for the synchronization of output movements, the extent of bilateral trade, the dissimilarity in the commodity composition of exports, and the size of the economies. Other variables that the optimum currency area literature has identified, such as factor mobility and automatic stabilizers, have not played an important role across national borders, and hence were not included in this specification.

The exact definitions of the variables employed by Bayoumi and Eichengreen are as follows. The dependent variable, $SD(E)$, is the standard deviation of the difference in the logs of the bilateral exchange rates over a given sample period. Hence, the higher this variable, the higher the exchange rate variability

between the currencies of the two countries and the less suitable they are for a currency union. The independent variables are the following:

$SD(Y)$, the standard deviation of the differences of the relative output of the two countries over a given sample period—the higher this variable, the less synchronized business cycles are.

$TRADE$, the mean of the bilateral exports to GDP over the given sample period—the higher this variable, the larger the extent of bilateral trade.

DIS, the sum of the absolute differences between the shares of five categories of export commodities in total exports in the two countries over a given sample period—the higher this variable, the larger the dissimilarity in the export composition.

$SIZE$, the mean of the logs of the GDP of the two countries in dollars, reflecting the countries' size.

This is a cross-section equation with as many observations as there are pairs of countries. The sample period determines over which time horizon the standard deviations and means are calculated.

The expected signs are all positive, except for that on bilateral trade. The higher the standard deviation of relative output movements, the greater the dissimilarity in the composition of trade; and the larger the size of the countries, the greater the expected exchange rate variability, and hence the less suited these countries are to forming a currency union. On the other hand, the trade variable is expected to have a negative sign, as the more countries trade with each other, the smaller the expected exchange rate variability.

The equation estimated by Bayoumi and Eichengreen is

$$SD(E_{ij}) = -0.09 + 1.46 \, SD(Y_{ij}) + 0.022 \, DIS_{ij}$$
$$\quad (0.02) \ (0.21) \qquad (0.006)$$

$$\quad - 0.054 \, TRADE_{ij} + 0.012 \, SIZE_{ij},$$
$$\quad (0.006) \qquad (0.001)$$

$R^2 = 0.51$, number of observations = 210

where the subscripts $_{ij}$ denote the pair formed of countries i and j. Standard errors are reported in brackets.

Bayoumi and Eichengreen then used the estimated equation to predict the optimum currency area indices. The latter are the predicted value of the dependent variable (the standard deviation of the difference in the logs of the bilateral exchange rates) obtained by using a projected value of the explanatory variables, which are projected by extrapolating the trend. They calculated optimum currency area indices for 1987, 1991, and 1995, and reported those against Germany for 15 western European countries. Smaller values for this index denote greater suitability for a currency area.

Table 5.A1. Co-Movements in Output[1]

Central America and the United States[2]

	United States	Costa Rica	Dominican Republic	El Salvador	Guatemala	Honduras	Nicaragua	Panama
United States		0.026	0.045	0.021	0.031	0.023	0.049	0.077
Costa Rica	**0.021**		0.032	0.024	0.023	0.024	0.039	0.070
Dominican Republic	**0.022**	0.035		0.050	0.040	0.035	0.056	0.089
El Salvador	**0.017**	0.024	**0.028**		0.025	0.027	0.045	0.071
Guatemala	**0.010**	**0.022**	**0.022**	**0.010**		0.027	0.045	0.073
Honduras	0.029	0.043	0.035	0.032	0.027		0.047	0.076
Nicaragua	**0.015**	**0.029**	**0.023**	**0.018**	**0.015**	**0.035**		0.037
Panama	**0.017**	**0.027**	**0.026**	**0.029**	**0.022**	**0.031**	**0.025**	

Europe[3]

	Germany	France	Italy	Spain	Portugal	Belgium	Luxembourg	Ireland	Netherlands	Austria	Finland	Greece	Denmark	Sweden	United Kingdom
Germany		0.011	0.020	0.029	0.025	0.018	0.017	0.031	0.015	0.019	0.027	0.030	0.012	0.029	0.016
France	0.035		0.020	0.021	0.028	0.013	0.016	0.029	0.007	0.016	0.025	0.034	0.019	0.025	0.019
Italy	0.042	**0.014**		0.033	0.030	0.020	0.019	0.033	0.020	0.025	0.033	0.049	0.027	0.032	0.027
Spain	0.031	**0.013**	**0.017**		0.037	0.022	0.030	0.035	0.022	0.026	0.031	0.041	0.030	0.033	0.028
Portugal	0.052	**0.023**	**0.024**	**0.023**		0.028	0.030	0.032	0.032	0.028	0.036	0.043	0.031	0.045	0.028
Belgium	0.042	**0.011**	**0.007**	**0.016**	**0.021**		0.011	0.035	0.011	0.021	0.027	0.039	0.022	0.027	0.025
Luxembourg	0.037	0.024	0.026	**0.022**	0.033	0.024			0.016	0.025	0.025	0.040	0.024	0.025	0.026
Ireland	0.038	**0.015**	**0.017**	**0.019**	**0.025**	**0.016**	**0.027**		0.034	0.036	0.042	0.050	0.038	0.048	0.031
Netherlands	0.030	0.007	**0.015**	**0.015**	**0.031**	0.011	0.016	**0.018**		0.018	0.028	0.037	0.021	0.024	0.023
Austria	0.039	**0.011**	**0.016**	**0.017**	**0.025**	**0.015**	0.025	**0.020**	**0.016**		0.026	0.041	0.023	0.030	0.029
Finland	0.042	**0.009**	**0.010**	**0.016**	**0.021**	**0.008**	0.029	**0.015**	**0.018**	**0.012**		0.039	0.032	0.018	0.029
Greece	0.040	**0.019**	**0.017**	**0.025**	0.044	**0.015**	**0.022**	**0.021**	**0.018**	**0.022**	**0.019**		0.029	0.040	0.028
Denmark	0.035	0.025	0.025	0.028	**0.029**	0.028	0.038	0.032	0.024	0.023	0.026	**0.028**		0.034	0.019
Sweden	0.038	**0.014**	**0.010**	**0.016**	0.037	**0.013**	0.029	**0.019**	**0.014**	**0.015**	**0.012**	**0.021**	**0.019**		0.032
United Kingdom	0.025	0.022	0.025	0.016		0.027	0.030	0.031	0.020	0.024	0.026	0.031	0.021	**0.022**	

Sources: IMF, *World Economic Outlook*; and IMF staff estimates.

[1] The co-movements in output are measured as the standard deviation of the difference in the logarithm of the real output of two countries. Lower values indicate greater co-movement.

[2] In the upper part of the matrix the period is 1984–93; in the lower part 1994–2003. Bold indicates that output co-movements increased in later period.

[3] In the upper part of the matrix the period is 1970–79; in the lower part 1980–89. Bold indicates that output co-movements increased in later period.

Table 5.A2. Source of Output Co-Movements

	Correlations of Output Growth							
	United States	Costa Rica	Dominican Republic	El Salvador	Guatemala	Honduras	Nicaragua	Panama
United States		0.230	0.125	0.327	−0.463	0.246	−0.284	−0.387
Costa Rica	0.599		0.699	0.363	0.425	0.405	0.380	0.069
Dominican Republic	0.533	0.114		−0.147	0.399	0.641	0.120	−0.224
El Salvador	0.311	0.409	0.154		0.104	0.048	0.015	−0.040
Guatemala	0.592	0.524	0.550	0.809		0.383	0.022	−0.106
Honduras	−0.184	−0.436	0.058	−0.226	−0.012		−0.103	−0.249
Nicaragua	0.523	0.153	0.522	0.429	0.547	−0.324		0.881
Panama	0.719	0.388	0.428	−0.067	0.327	0.132	0.244	

	Correlations of Output Growth After Eliminating the United States' Influence[1]						
	Costa Rica	Dominican Republic	El Salvador	Guatemala	Honduras	Nicaragua	Panama
Costa Rica		0.694	0.307	0.645	0.311	0.498	0.225
Dominican Republic	−0.149		−0.198	0.522	0.606	0.177	−0.162
El Salvador	0.292	0.003		0.294	−0.037	0.119	0.099
Guatemala	0.433	0.456	0.616		0.490	−0.067	−0.248
Honduras	−0.458	0.102	−0.188	−0.075		−0.064	−0.205
Nicaragua	0.066	0.449	0.289	0.637	−0.348		0.876
Panama	0.266	0.305	−0.200	0.517	0.023	0.431	

Sources: IMF, World Economic Outlook; and IMF staff estimates.
Note: The upper part of each matrix reports correlations over the period 1984–93, while the lower part refers to the period 1994–2003.
[1]To eliminate the United States' influence, the output growth series were first regressed over U.S. growth and the correlations taken on the residuals.

Table 5.A3. Terms of Trade[1]

	1984–93	1994–2003		1970–79	1980–89
Central America	8.18	9.94	Europe	4.43	3.95
Costa Rica	7.37	0.32	Austria	1.67	2.35
Dominican Republic	14.29	2.72	Belgium	1.92	1.82
El Salvador	14.03	12.46	Finland	...	...
Guatemala	6.57	7.71	France	3.53	3.20
Honduras	4.86	8.25	Germany	3.11	4.13
Nicaragua	5.35	35.21	Greece	13.37	7.24
Panama	4.77	2.93	Ireland	6.14	2.41
			Italy	3.82	3.97
United States	1.83	1.48	Luxembourg	...	...
			Netherlands	1.53	1.66
			Portugal	4.14	7.72
			Spain	5.07	5.03

Sources: IMF, World Economic Outlook; and IMF staff estimates.
[1]Averages of absolute annual percentage changes in the terms of trade.

Table 5.A4. Co-Movements in the Terms of Trade[1]

Central America and the United States[2]

	United States	Costa Rica	Dominican Republic	El Salvador	Guatemala	Honduras	Nicaragua	Panama
United States		0.026	0.045	0.021	0.031	0.023	0.049	0.077
Costa Rica	**0.019**	0.090	0.179	0.172	0.074	0.096	0.067	0.058
Dominican Republic	0.028	**0.037**	0.199	0.128	0.053	0.130	0.125	0.084
El Salvador	0.176	0.182	**0.168**	0.190	0.189	0.255	0.213	0.193
Guatemala	0.087	0.091	**0.077**	0.183	0.117	0.219	0.204	0.151
Honduras	**0.091**	**0.096**	**0.086**	**0.197**	**0.031**	0.128	0.114	0.057
Nicaragua	0.413	0.402	0.421	0.492	0.435	**0.440**	0.088	0.111
Panama	**0.039**	**0.036**	**0.046**	0.191	0.086	**0.085**	0.406	0.085

Europe[3]

	Germany	France	Italy	Spain	Portugal	Belgium	Luxembourg	Ireland	Netherlands	Austria	Finland	Greece
Germany		0.033	0.032	0.062	0.072	0.048	...	0.078	0.036	0.035	...	0.188
France	**0.030**		0.047	0.055	0.069	0.050	...	0.070	0.046	0.047	...	0.196
Italy	**0.031**	**0.031**		0.053	0.081	0.056	...	0.080	0.045	0.053	...	0.186
Spain	**0.038**	**0.040**	**0.036**		0.083	0.070	...	0.071	0.064	0.075	...	0.182
Portugal	0.107	0.125	0.126	0.117		0.101	...	0.119	0.122	0.126	...	0.211
Belgium	0.049	0.047	0.052	**0.065**	0.041		...	0.089	0.022	0.024	...	0.195
Luxembourg	...	...	...	...	...	...		...	...	...	...	...
Ireland	**0.044**	**0.034**	**0.051**	**0.056**	0.119	**0.039**	...		0.081	0.088	...	0.178
Netherlands	0.058	0.044	0.058	0.072	0.122	0.028	...	**0.035**		0.024	...	0.185
Austria	0.057	0.046	0.053	**0.064**	0.126	0.038	...	**0.035**	0.031		...	0.187
Finland	0.152	0.135	0.147	0.163	0.220	0.140	...	0.135	0.117	0.128		...
Greece	**0.091**	**0.100**	**0.095**	**0.109**	**0.100**	**0.076**	...	**0.107**	**0.097**	**0.108**	0.185	

Sources: IMF, World Economic Outlook; and IMF staff estimates.

[1]The co-movements in terms of trade are measured as the standard deviation of the difference in the logarithm of the terms of trade of two countries. A lower number indicates greater co-movement. Bold indicates that terms of trade co-movements increased in later period.

[2]In the lower part of the matrix the period is 1984–93; in the upper part of the matrix the period 1994–2003.

Table 5.A5. Correlations of Terms of Trade

Central America and the United States[1]

	United States	Costa Rica	Dominican Republic	El Salvador	Guatemala	Honduras	Nicaragua	Panama
United States		0.532	0.411	0.635	0.602	-0.464	-0.089	0.307
Costa Rica	0.033		0.144	0.760	0.848	0.003	-0.157	0.549
Dominican Republic	**0.615**	-0.265		0.481	0.210	-0.750	-0.287	0.059
El Salvador	0.238	-0.570	0.406		0.887	-0.209	-0.143	0.692
Guatemala	0.253	-0.314	**0.536**	0.207		-0.154	-0.176	0.753
Honduras	**0.312**	-0.305	**0.416**	**0.075**	**0.947**		0.285	-0.174
Nicaragua	-0.590	**-0.092**	-0.512	-0.337	-0.278	-0.309		0.012
Panama	-0.014	-0.375	**0.115**	-0.269	0.287	**0.450**	-0.091	

Europe[2]

	Germany	France	Italy	Spain	Portugal	Belgium	Luxembourg	Ireland	Netherlands	Austria	Finland	Greece
Germany		0.816	0.820	0.669	-0.078	0.097	...	0.617	0.506	0.576	...	0.205
France	**0.871**		0.650	0.744	0.224	0.458	...	0.706	0.658	0.587	...	0.074
Italy	**0.872**	**0.860**		0.766	-0.053	0.248	...	0.562	0.651	0.327	...	0.254
Spain	**0.873**	**0.882**	**0.890**		0.308	0.572	...	0.693	0.881	0.419	...	0.331
Portugal	**0.486**	0.163	**0.194**	**0.388**		0.704	...	0.052	0.047	0.267	...	-0.225
Belgium	**0.645**	0.422	**0.544**	**0.602**	**0.867**		...	0.423	0.562	0.525	...	-0.059
Luxembourg	...	...	...	...	...	...	...	...	...	...	...	...
Ireland	**0.706**	**0.760**	0.537	**0.753**	**0.235**	0.220	...		**0.815**	**0.507**	...	**0.388**
Netherlands	0.296	0.561	0.313	0.398	**0.115**	0.271	...	0.341		0.342	...	0.395
Austria	0.376	0.480	0.476	**0.603**	0.006	0.070	...	0.442	0.255		...	0.282
Finland	-0.258	-0.076	-0.157	-0.413	-0.522	-0.493	...	-0.348	0.482	-0.028		...
Greece	**0.378**	**0.155**	**0.304**	0.197	**0.602**	**0.770**	...	-0.214	-0.050	-0.356	-0.554	

Sources: IMF, *World Economic Outlook*; and IMF staff estimates.

[1] In the upper part of the matrix the period is 1984–93; in the lower part, 1994–2003. Bold indicates that terms of trade correlation increased in later period.

[2] In the upper part of the matrix the period is 1970–79; in the lower part, 1980–89. Bold indicates that terms of trade correlation increased in later period.

Table 5.A6. Inflation Performance

	Average[1]		Coefficient of Variation	
	1984–93	1994–2003	1984–93	1994–2003
Central America	467.90	9.46		
Costa Rica	17.23	12.99	0.33	0.33
Dominican Republic	27.83	9.50	0.69	0.70
El Salvador	19.67	4.75	0.33	0.85
Guatemala	17.22	7.88	0.94	0.32
Honduras	10.79	15.66	0.94	0.48
Nicaragua	3,181.73	14.37	1.47	0.69
Panama	0.84	1.09	0.74	1.09
United States	3.80	2.45	0.32	0.27

	Average[1]		Coefficient of Variation	
	1970–79	1980–89	1970–79	1980–89
Europe	8.76	7.78	...	...
Austria	6.10	3.80	0.34	0.54
Belgium	7.13	4.90	0.47	0.59
Finland	10.41	7.28	0.26	0.45
France	8.92	7.34	0.55	0.41
Germany	4.88	2.75	0.56	1.59
Greece	7.13	12.30	0.21	0.17
Ireland	12.75	9.26	0.26	0.63
Italy	12.46	11.38	0.37	0.61
Luxembourg	7.00	4.72	0.80	1.32
Netherlands	7.07	2.84	0.50	1.21
Portugal	7.13	16.56	0.33	0.17
Spain	14.12	10.25	0.24	0.76

Sources: IMF, *World Economic Outlook*; and IMF staff estimates.
[1]In percent, period average.

Table 5.A7. Co-Movements in Prices[1]

Central America and the United States[2]

	United States	Costa Rica	Dominican Republic	El Salvador	Guatemala	Honduras	Nicaragua	Panama
United States		0.045	0.146	0.058	0.139	0.082	1.787	0.011
Costa Rica	**0.036**		0.136	0.083	0.137	0.065	1.763	0.046
Dominican Republic	**0.057**	**0.071**		0.163	0.164	0.135	1.685	0.154
El Salvador	**0.036**	**0.025**	**0.071**		0.135	0.113	1.782	0.058
Guatemala	**0.023**	**0.032**	**0.066**	**0.026**		0.109	1.756	0.141
Honduras	**0.063**	**0.033**	**0.094**	**0.039**	**0.052**		1.754	0.085
Nicaragua	**0.079**	**0.078**	**0.103**	**0.064**	**0.069**	**0.076**		1.794
Panama	0.013	0.044	**0.060**	**0.039**	**0.023**	**0.068**	**0.076**	

Europe[3]

	Germany	France	Italy	Spain	Portugal	Belgium	Luxembourg	Ireland	Netherlands	Austria	Finland	Greece
Germany		0.026	0.051	0.055	0.025	0.025	0.026	0.038	0.014	0.011	0.039	0.025
France	**0.024**		0.030	0.038	0.020	0.020	0.022	0.027	0.027	0.022	0.029	0.020
Italy	**0.039**	**0.017**		0.027	0.036	0.036	0.037	0.030	0.047	0.045	0.027	0.036
Spain	**0.023**	**0.013**	**0.023**		0.048	0.048	0.050	0.048	0.053	0.052	0.042	0.048
Portugal	0.062	0.065	0.075	0.063		0.000	0.004	0.019	0.018	0.016	0.018	0.000
Belgium	**0.015**	0.018	0.033	**0.016**	0.053		0.004	0.020	0.018	0.015	0.018	0.000
Luxembourg	**0.017**	0.019	0.032	**0.019**	0.078	0.008		0.018	0.018	0.017	0.019	0.004
Ireland	0.045	0.024	0.015	0.032	0.063	0.041	0.039		0.030	0.045	0.020	0.019
Netherlands	**0.012**	0.016	0.030	0.014	0.061	0.013	0.016	0.037		**0.009**	0.030	0.018
Austria	0.011	0.024	0.038	0.020	0.066	0.015	0.021	0.045	0.030		0.031	0.018
Finland	**0.012**	0.017	0.030	0.019		0.016	0.017	0.037	**0.010**	**0.014**		0.018
Greece	0.068	0.087	0.100	0.080	0.099	0.075	0.080	0.107	0.074	0.068	0.076	

Sources: IMF, World Economic Outlook; and IMF staff estimates.

[1] The co-movements in prices are measured as the standard deviation of the difference in the logarithm of the price levels of two countries. A lower number indicates greater co-movement.

[2] In the upper part of the matrix the period is 1984–93; in the lower part, 1994–2003. Bold indicates that price co-movements increased in later period.

[3] In the upper part of the matrix the period is 1970–79; in the lower part, 1980–89. Bold indicates that price co-movements increased in later period.

Table 5.A8. Optimum Currency Area Index: Regression Results

Dependent Variable	Regressor[1]						Sample[2]	R^2	NOBS[3]
	Constant	SD(Y)	SD(P)	SD(TOT)	TRADE	SIZE			
1. Exchange Market Pressure[4] (EMP)									
Regression (1)	0.106***	1.072***	0.558***	0.028	−1.699***	0.005***	1970–2003	0.703	1,308
Regression (2)	0.137***	0.635***	0.609***	−0.008	−1.988***	0.001	1980–2003	0.663	1,308
Regression (3)	0.125***	0.825***	0.552***	−0.020	−1.483***	0.000	1990–2003	0.536	1,308
2. SD(EXR)[5]									
Regression (4)	−0.003	0.493***	0.920***	0.081***	−1.355***	0.007***	1970–2003	0.871	1,308
Regression (5)	0.020***	0.372***	0.914***	0.014	−1.824***	0.006***	1980–2003	0.811	1,308
Regression (6)	0.024***	0.377***	0.894***	−0.029*	−1.586***	0.005***	1990–2003	0.808	1,308

Sources: IMF, *World Economic Outlook, Direction of Trade Statistics*; and IMF staff estimates.

Note: One, two, and three asterisks indicate significance at 10, 5, and 1 percent, respectively.

[1] For the definitions of regressors, see Box 5.1.

[2] All variables included in the regressions are calculated over the specified sample period.

[3] With 53 countries covered by the sample, there are 1,378 observations in total, out of which 1,308 observations are used in estimation after excluding missing values.

[4] EMP is defined as the average of standard deviations of percentage changes in bilateral exchange rate and foreign reserves.

[5] SD(EXR) refers to the standard deviation of percentage changes in bilateral exchange rate.

Table 5.A9. Optimum Currency Area Indices for Central America and Europe vis-à-vis Anchor Country

1. Central America[1]

	Regression (1)		Regression (2)		Regression (3)		Regression (4)		Regression (5)		Regression (6)	
	1984–93	1994–2003	1984–93	1994–2003	1984–93	1994–2003	1984–93	1994–2003	1984–93	1994–2003	1984–93	1994–2003
Costa Rica	0.176	0.169	0.174	0.169	0.162	0.157	0.083	0.075	0.092	0.088	0.088	0.086
Dominican Republic	0.235	0.180	0.225	0.179	0.212	0.167	0.158	0.092	0.160	0.104	0.152	0.101
El Salvador	0.179	0.171	0.177	0.169	0.163	0.155	0.094	0.086	0.100	0.093	0.093	0.086
Guatemala	0.226	0.157	0.224	0.158	0.209	0.144	0.155	0.069	0.164	0.079	0.159	0.075
Honduras	0.191	0.189	0.191	0.185	0.177	0.173	0.109	0.099	0.118	0.107	0.113	0.102
Nicaragua	0.324	0.184	0.328	0.181	0.306	0.163	0.300	0.114	0.307	0.112	0.299	0.099
Panama	0.213	0.157	0.190	0.158	0.188	0.145	0.084	0.060	0.089	0.073	0.087	0.071
Average	**0.221**	**0.173**	**0.216**	**0.171**	**0.203**	**0.158**	**0.140**	**0.085**	**0.147**	**0.094**	**0.142**	**0.089**
Average of own indices[2]	0.229	0.162	0.236	0.168	0.224	0.159	0.161	0.070	0.167	0.074	0.162	0.070

2. EMU Countries[1,3]

	Regression (1)			Regression (2)			Regression (3)			Regression (4)			Regression (5)			Regression (6)		
	1970–79	1980–89	1990–98	1970–79	1980–89	1990–98	1970–79	1980–89	1990–98	1970–79	1980–89	1990–98	1970–79	1980–89	1990–98	1970–79	1980–89	1990–98
France	0.119	0.136	0.147	0.110	0.116	0.122	0.109	0.121	0.127	0.039	0.045	0.051	0.040	0.041	0.045	0.043	0.045	0.048
Italy	0.145	0.156	0.154	0.136	0.135	0.130	0.134	0.139	0.133	0.066	0.062	0.058	0.068	0.060	0.054	0.070	0.063	0.055
Spain	0.183	0.167	0.171	0.176	0.157	0.152	0.166	0.150	0.149	0.094	0.068	0.068	0.102	0.076	0.070	0.098	0.074	0.069
Portugal	0.166	0.208	0.186	0.164	0.194	0.174	0.153	0.187	0.167	0.069	0.107	0.086	0.079	0.111	0.093	0.076	0.107	0.090
Ireland	0.177	0.186	0.199	0.174	0.180	0.180	0.164	0.171	0.177	0.079	0.086	0.081	0.088	0.095	0.087	0.085	0.093	0.085
Netherlands	0.096	0.105	0.138	0.085	0.085	0.114	0.091	0.096	0.122	0.013	0.016	0.040	0.009	0.007	0.034	0.015	0.013	0.038
Austria	0.138	0.148	0.147	0.133	0.132	0.130	0.128	0.134	0.131	0.042	0.046	0.047	0.049	0.046	0.047	0.050	0.048	0.049
Greece	0.173	0.201	0.191	0.165	0.191	0.179	0.155	0.182	0.171	0.078	0.110	0.091	0.081	0.115	0.098	0.076	0.111	0.095
Average	**0.150**	**0.163**	**0.167**	**0.143**	**0.149**	**0.148**	**0.138**	**0.147**	**0.147**	**0.060**	**0.068**	**0.065**	**0.064**	**0.069**	**0.066**	**0.064**	**0.069**	**0.066**
Average of own indices[2]	0.170	0.167	0.150	0.166	0.167	0.150	0.157	0.156	0.140	0.070	0.079	0.057	0.078	0.088	0.068	0.075	0.085	0.067

Sources: IMF, *World Economic Outlook; Direction of Trade Statistics;* and IMF staff estimates.

[1]The United States is considered the anchor country for Central America, and Germany for Europe.

[2]Average of optimum currency area indices constructed for pairs of countries, excluding United States for Central America and Germany for EMU countries.

[3]Belgium, Finland, and Luxembourg are excluded because of missing values in trade related data.

Table 5.A10. Central America: Projections for the Optimum Currency Area Indices vis-à-vis the United States

	OCA Index						Difference Between Projected Index and Index in 1994–2003[1]					
	1	2	3	4	5	6	1	2	3	4	5	6
Simulation 1												
Costa Rica	0.164	0.164	0.152	0.074	0.087	0.085	−0.005	−0.005	−0.005	−0.001	−0.001	−0.001
Dominican Republic	0.172	0.171	0.159	0.087	0.098	0.096	−0.009	−0.008	−0.007	−0.005	−0.005	−0.005
El Salvador	0.167	0.165	0.151	0.084	0.090	0.084	−0.004	−0.004	−0.004	−0.002	−0.002	−0.002
Guatemala	0.155	0.154	0.141	0.067	0.077	0.073	−0.003	−0.003	−0.004	−0.002	−0.002	−0.002
Honduras	0.180	0.177	0.166	0.093	0.101	0.097	−0.009	−0.008	−0.008	−0.005	−0.006	−0.006
Nicaragua	0.183	0.180	0.163	0.114	0.111	0.098	−0.001	−0.001	−0.001	0.000	−0.001	−0.001
Average	**0.170**	**0.169**	**0.155**	**0.087**	**0.094**	**0.089**	**−0.005**	**−0.005**	**−0.005**	**−0.002**	**−0.003**	**−0.003**
Simulation 2												
Costa Rica	0.161	0.162	0.149	0.072	0.085	0.083	−0.009	−0.007	−0.008	−0.003	−0.003	−0.003
Dominican Republic	0.167	0.168	0.155	0.085	0.097	0.095	−0.014	−0.011	−0.011	−0.007	−0.007	−0.007
El Salvador	0.160	0.161	0.146	0.081	0.088	0.081	−0.011	−0.008	−0.009	−0.005	−0.005	−0.005
Guatemala	0.152	0.153	0.139	0.066	0.076	0.072	−0.005	−0.005	−0.005	−0.003	−0.003	−0.003
Honduras	0.167	0.169	0.155	0.087	0.096	0.092	−0.022	−0.016	−0.018	−0.011	−0.011	−0.010
Nicaragua	0.179	0.177	0.159	0.111	0.109	0.096	−0.006	−0.004	−0.005	−0.003	−0.002	−0.002
Average	**0.164**	**0.165**	**0.151**	**0.084**	**0.092**	**0.087**	**−0.011**	**−0.008**	**−0.009**	**−0.005**	**−0.005**	**−0.005**
Simulation 3												
Costa Rica	0.163	0.163	0.151	0.072	0.085	0.083	−0.007	−0.006	−0.006	−0.003	−0.003	−0.003
Dominican Republic	0.169	0.169	0.157	0.085	0.096	0.094	−0.011	−0.010	−0.009	−0.007	−0.008	−0.007
El Salvador	0.166	0.164	0.150	0.082	0.088	0.082	−0.005	−0.005	−0.005	−0.003	−0.004	−0.004
Guatemala	0.153	0.153	0.140	0.066	0.075	0.071	−0.004	−0.005	−0.004	−0.003	−0.004	−0.004
Honduras	0.178	0.175	0.164	0.091	0.098	0.095	−0.011	−0.011	−0.010	−0.007	−0.009	−0.008
Nicaragua	0.183	0.180	0.163	0.113	0.110	0.098	−0.001	−0.001	−0.001	−0.001	−0.001	−0.001
Average	**0.168**	**0.167**	**0.154**	**0.085**	**0.092**	**0.087**	**−0.007**	**−0.006**	**−0.006**	**−0.004**	**−0.005**	**−0.004**
Simulation 4												
Costa Rica	0.159	0.161	0.148	0.070	0.083	0.082	−0.011	−0.008	−0.009	−0.005	−0.005	−0.004
Dominican Republic	0.164	0.166	0.153	0.082	0.094	0.092	−0.016	−0.013	−0.013	−0.009	−0.010	−0.009
El Salvador	0.159	0.160	0.145	0.079	0.086	0.080	−0.012	−0.010	−0.010	−0.007	−0.007	−0.006
Guatemala	0.150	0.151	0.138	0.065	0.074	0.070	−0.007	−0.007	−0.006	−0.004	−0.005	−0.005
Honduras	0.164	0.167	0.154	0.085	0.094	0.090	−0.025	−0.019	−0.020	−0.013	−0.013	−0.012
Nicaragua	0.178	0.177	0.159	0.111	0.109	0.096	−0.006	−0.004	−0.005	−0.003	−0.003	−0.003
Average	**0.162**	**0.164**	**0.149**	**0.082**	**0.090**	**0.085**	**−0.013**	**−0.010**	**−0.010**	**−0.007**	**−0.007**	**−0.007**

Sources: IMF, *World Economic Outlook; Direction of Trade Statistics;* and IMF staff estimates.

Note: See Box 5.3 for a description of how the projections are calculated. 1–5 indicate regression numbers.

[1]Negative values denote greater suitability for dollarization in projections than in indices for 1994–2003.

References

Alesina, Alberto, and Robert Barro, 2002, "Currency Unions," *Quarterly Journal of Economics* (May), pp. 409–36.

———, and Silvana Tenreyro, 2002, "Optimal Currency Areas," NBER Working Paper No. 9072 (Cambridge, Massachusetts: National Bureau of Economic Research).

Bayoumi, Tamim, and Barry Eichengreen, 1997, "Ever Closer to Heaven? An Optimum-Currency-Area Index for European Countries," *European Economic Review*, Vol. 41 (April), pp. 761–70.

Broda, Christian, 2001, "Coping with Terms of Trade Shocks: Pegs Versus Floats," *American Economic Review, Papers and Proceedings*, Vol. 91 (May), pp. 376–80.

Bubula, Andrea, and Inci Ötker-Robe, 2002, "The Evolution of Exchange Rate Regimes Since 1990: Evidence from De Facto Policies," IMF Working Paper 02/155 (Washington: International Monetary Fund).

Calvo, Guillermo, and Frederic Mishkin, 2003, "The Mirage of Exchange Rate Regimes for Emerging Market Countries," *Journal of Economic Perspectives,* Vol. 17 (November), pp. 99–118.

Calvo, Guillermo, and Carmen Reinhart, 2002, "Fear of Floating," *Quarterly Journal of Economics*, Vol. 117 (May), pp. 379–408.

Collins, Susan, 1996, "On Becoming More Flexible: Exchange Rate Regimes in Latin America and the Caribbean," *Journal of Development Economics*, Vol. 51 (October), pp. 117–38.

Corbo, Vittorio, 2002, "Exchange Rate Regimes in the Americas: Is Dollarization the Solution?" *Monetary and Economic Studies*, Vol. 20 (December), pp. 91–111.

Dornbusch, Rudi, 2001, "Fewer Monies, Better Monies," *American Economic Review, Papers and Proceedings*, Vol. 91 (May), pp. 238–42.

Fischer, Stanley, 2001, "Exchange Rate Regimes: Is the Bipolar View Correct?" *Journal of Economic Perspectives*, Vol. 15 (Spring), pp. 3–24.

Frankel, Jeffrey, 1999, "No Single Exchange Rate Regime Is Right For All Countries or At All Times," Essays in International Finance No. 215 (Princeton, New Jersey: International Finance Section, Department of Economics, Princeton University).

———, 2004, "A Currency Union for East Asia," in *Monetary and Financial Integration in East Asia: The Way Ahead*, Vol. 2, ed. by Asian Development Bank (New York: Palgrave Macmillan).

———, and Andrew Rose, 2002, "An Estimate of the Effect of Common Currencies on Trade and Income," *Quarterly Journal of Economics*, Vol. 117 (May), pp. 437–66.

Garcia-Lopez, Cristina, Felipe Larrain, and José Tavares, 2001, "Exchange Rate Regimes: Assessing Central America's Options," in *Economic Development in Central America*, Vol. 1, ed. by Francisco Larrain (Cambridge, Massachusetts: Harvard University Press).

Ghosh, Atish Rex, Anne-Marie Gulde, and Holger Wolf, 2003, *Exchange Rate Regimes: Choices and Consequences* (Cambridge, Massachusetts: MIT Press).

Goldberg, Linda, 2002, "Comment" to "Exchange Rate Regimes in the Americas: Is Dollarization the Solution?" *Monetary and Economic Studies*, Vol. 20 (December), pp. 112–17.

Hilaire, Alvin, and Yongzheng Yang, 2003, "The United States and the New Regionalism/Bilateralism," IMF Working Paper 03/206 (Washington: International Monetary Fund).

IMF, *Annual Report on Exchange Arrangements and Exchange Restrictions* (Washington: various issues).

———, 2003, *Exchange Arrangements and Foreign Exchange Markets—Developments and Issues*, World Economic and Financial Surveys Series (Washington).

———, 2004, "From Fixed to Float—Operational Aspects of Moving Toward Exchange Rate Flexibility" (Washington, November 19). Available via the Internet: http://www.imf.org/external/NP/mfd/2004/eng/111904.htm.

Kose, Ayhan, Alessandro Rebucci, and Alfred Schipke, 2004, "Macroeconomic Implications of CAFTA-DR: Trade, Growth, and Business Cycles," Section II in *Central America: Global Integration and Regional Cooperation*, ed. by Markus Rodlauer and Alfred Schipke (Washington: International Monetary Fund).

Levy-Yeyati, Eduardo, and Federico Sturzenegger, 2001, "Exchange Rate Regimes and Economic Performance," *IMF Staff Papers*, Vol. 47 (Special Issue), pp. 62–98.

———, 2005, "Classifying Exchange Rate Regimes: Deeds vs. Words," *European Economic Review,* Vol. 49 (August), pp. 1603–35.

Mundell, Robert, 1961, "A Theory of Optimum Currency Areas," *American Economic Review*, Vol. 51 (September), pp. 657–65.

Obstfeld, Maurice, and Kenneth Rogoff, 1995, "The Mirage of Fixed Exchange Rates," *Journal of Economic Perspectives*, Vol. 9 (Fall), pp. 73–96.

Palerm, Angel, 2002, "Comment" to "Exchange Rate Regimes in the Americas: Is Dollarization the Solution?" *Monetary and Economic Studies*, Vol. 20 (December), pp. 117–20.

Papaioannou, Michael, 2002, "Exchange Rate Regimes: The Experience of Six Central American Countries" (unpublished; Washington: International Monetary Fund).

———, 2003, "Determinants of the Choice of Exchange Rate Regimes in Six Central American Countries: An Empirical Analysis," IMF Working Paper 03/59 (Washington: International Monetary Fund).

Reinhart, Carmen, and Vincent Reinhart, 2003 "Twin Fallacies about Exchange Rate Policy in Emerging Markets," NBER Working Paper No. 9670 (Cambridge, Massachusetts: National Bureau of Economic Research).

Reinhart, Carmen, and Kenneth Rogoff, 2004, "The Modern History of Exchange Rate Arrangements: A Reinterpretation," *Quarterly Journal of Economics*, Vol. 119 (February), pp. 1–48.

Rennhack, Robert, Erik Offerdal, and Valerie Mercer-Blackman, 2004, "Choice of Exchange Rate Regimes," in *The Macroeconomy of Central America*, ed. by Robert Rennhack and Erik Offerdal (New York: Palgrave Macmillan).

Ricci, Luca, 1997, "A Model of an Optimum Currency Area," IMF Working Paper 97/76 (Washington: International Monetary Fund).

Rodlauer, Markus, 2004, "Perspectives for Economic Integration in Central America," Remarks made at the 40th Anniversary of the Central American Monetary Council, Tegucigalpa, Honduras, February 27. Available via the Internet: www.imf.org/external/np/speeches/2004/022704a.htm.

Rogoff, Kenneth, Aasim Husain, Ashoka Mody, Ray Brooks, and Nienke Oomes, 2004, *Evolution and Performance of Exchange Rate Regimes*, IMF Occasional Paper No. 229 (Washington: International Monetary Fund).

Rose, Andrew, 2000, "One Money, One Market: The Effect of Common Currencies on Trade," *Economic Policy*, Vol. 15 (April), pp. 9–45.

Schaechter, Andrea, Mark Stone, and Mark Zelmer, 2000, "Adopting Inflation Targeting: Practical Issues for Emerging Market Countries," IMF Occasional Paper No. 202 (Washington: International Monetary Fund).

Tenreyro, Silvana, and Robert Barro, 2003, "Economic Effects of Currency Unions," NBER Working Paper No. 9435 (Cambridge, Massachusetts: National Bureau of Economic Research).

Truman, Edwin, 2003, *Inflation Targeting in the World Economy* (Washington: Institute for International Economics).

VI Regional Integration and Financial System Issues

R. Armando Morales and Alfred Schipke

Central America has made good progress over the past decade in stabilizing the macroeconomic environment and establishing a sound and efficient financial system. Macroeconomic stability and measures to address financial sector weaknesses have contributed to increased intermediation and improvements in key financial sector indicators.

At the same time, credit to the private sector from locally licensed banks remains relatively low and the ability of banks to withstand shocks would benefit from improved financial sector risk management.[1] Dollarized balance sheets and lending to a largely unhedged private sector make some systems vulnerable, particularly to adverse exchange rate movements, underscoring the need for further crisis-proofing. This is particularly important in countries with high debt levels and in a region that is susceptible to shocks such as commodity price movements and natural disasters.

Financial sector integration brings important benefits, but it also poses new risks and challenges. Ongoing financial sector integration and consolidation will help the region take advantage of economies of scale and promote competition and efficiency. At the same time, however, financial sector integration without appropriate regulations and supervision could undermine adequate prudential monitoring of bank activities and allow undue risk-taking. Harmonizing prudential norms and financial supervision between countries and strengthening the capacity to conduct consolidated supervision to keep pace with the growth of cross-border banking activities will help the region capitalize on the opportunities that integration offers.[2]

Financial Sector Development and Structure

Macroeconomic Policies and Resilience to Shocks

Financial stability in Central America has benefited from the stabilization gains achieved in the region. During the 1990s, the region experienced a recovery in growth, lower inflation rates, and improved external positions arising from higher exports and remittances. These developments were accompanied by efforts to reduce fiscal deficits and the debt burden.

Lower spreads on sovereign debt in recent years have reduced financing costs for countries that have access to international capital markets but they have also caused renewed borrowing. In the face of weakening growth from the late 1990s (except in Costa Rica), underlying weaknesses in the public finances reemerged in some countries, also reflecting contingent liabilities arising from costly pension systems and problem banks. This led to a renewed increase in public debt, in particular foreign debt, in recent years (Figure 6.1).

Given these vulnerabilities, the capacity of the Central American economies to absorb shocks is still limited, which in turn affects the financial system. This is of particular importance since the region has historically been subject to large exogenous shocks related to price fluctuations in primary product markets (such as coffee) and natural disasters such as hurricanes and earthquakes.

Structure of the Financial Systems

Increasing confidence in the financial system has spurred financial intermediation. Credit to the private sector has been rising from an average of about 14 percent of GDP in 1996 to about 38 percent of GDP in 2003, similar to levels in countries that joined the European Union in 2004 (Figure 6.2). Central America's banking systems are almost exclusively privately owned (except in Costa Rica).

---

[1]In some countries, banking crises have occurred (Dominican Republic and Nicaragua); in others, the banking system has experienced episodes of stress (Costa Rica, Guatemala, and Honduras).

[2]This section is largely based on the results of (bilateral) Financial Sector Assessment Programs (FSAPs) carried out by the IMF and the World Bank for all Central American countries in recent years.

Figure 6.1. Central America: Public Debt, 1990–2003
(In percent of GDP)

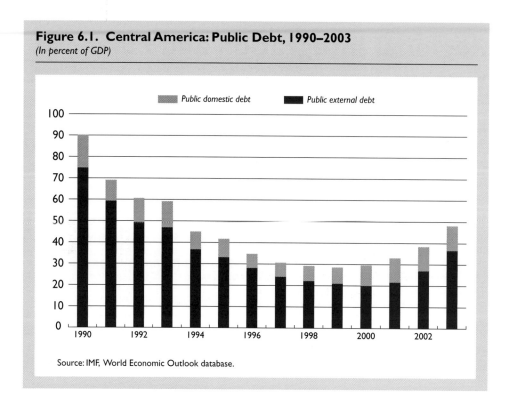

Source: IMF, World Economic Outlook database.

Figure 6.2. Central America: Financial Sector Development

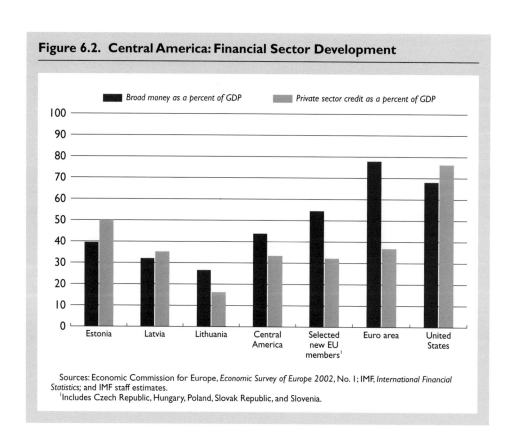

Sources: Economic Commission for Europe, *Economic Survey of Europe 2002*, No. 1; IMF, *International Financial Statistics*; and IMF staff estimates.
[1] Includes Czech Republic, Hungary, Poland, Slovak Republic, and Slovenia.

Figure 6.3. Banking Sector Dollarization, 2003
(Percent of total assets/deposits)

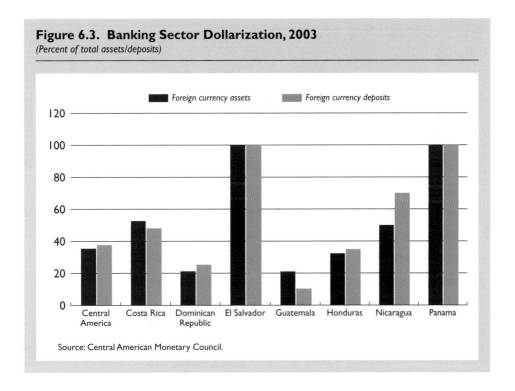

Source: Central American Monetary Council.

The share of assets managed by public banks has decreased on average from about 8 percent of GDP in 1996 to less than 3 percent in 2003.

However, access to credit remains limited and financial systems in Central America continue to be largely bank based. Also, given the relatively large number of banks compared with the small size of the countries concerned (Table 6.1), the region is likely to be faced with consolidation pressures.

Despite the stabilization gains and reforms, a history of inflation and exchange controls, regulatory burdens, and lingering uncertainty about the future direction of policies have spurred informal dollarization and offshore or parallel financing transactions.[3] These factors induced a strong preference of depositors for keeping assets in foreign currency, while some borrowers and bankers sought to avoid taxation and strengthened prudential regulations by moving activities to foreign jurisdictions (Figure 6.3).

Financial dollarization

Financial dollarization in Central America has increased significantly in recent years. As of 2003,

40 percent of total assets (in countries not officially dollarized) were in dollars, and almost 55 percent when Panama and El Salvador are included.[4] The high degree of dollarization reflects a history of high inflation (Costa Rica) or even hyperinflation (Nicaragua), regulatory biases against domestic currency intermediation, and lingering uncertainty about the future direction of economic policy.

Other factors have also contributed, especially on the lending side. Financial sector integration and cross-border lending, including through banks conducting cross-border operations, increased competition in dollar intermediation, which in turn spurred dollarization. As locally licensed banks have been trying to compete with external intermediaries by reducing their net interest margin on dollar-denominated loans, U.S. dollar loans have become more attractive.

The choice of a particular exchange rate system to anchor expectations appears to have contributed to some degree to the dollarization of loans. Countries in Central America show a wide variety of exchange rate arrangements, ranging from official dollarization (El Salvador and Panama), to prean-

---

[3]Spontaneous dollarization (or partial dollarization) is an endogenous process that differs from the use of the U.S. dollar as legal tender in Panama and El Salvador. In the rest of this section, the term dollarization is used to describe spontaneous dollarization.

[4]Dollarization for transaction purposes is somewhat less pronounced, but in some countries certain contracts (such as mortgages, rents, and suppliers' contracts) are predominantly in U.S. dollars.

Table 6.1. Central America: Structure and Performance of the Financial Sector, 1996–2003[1]

	1996	1997	1998	1999	2000	2001	2002	2003
Number of banks	26	25	25	24	23	21	19	20
Total assets								
Private banks	20	19	21	20	18	16	16	16
Total assets of private banks (percentage of GDP)	33.8	36.0	49.5	45.7	47.4	49.9	52.2	43.4
Public banks	3	2	2	2	2	2	1	2
Total assets of public banks (percentage of GDP)	5.5	5.2	1.7	1.5	1.4	1.2	1.1	2.0
Foreign banks	2	2	2	2	2	2	2	2
Total assets of foreign banks (percentage of GDP)	0.7	0.7	1.0	1.2	1.4	1.7	1.6	1.8
Bank concentration								
Number of banks accounting for at least:								
25 percent of total assets	2	2	2	2	2	1	2	2
75 percent of total assets	7	7	9	8	8	8	7	7
Dollarization and maturity structure								
Banking system assets as percentage of GDP	41.9	45.4	56.9	54.9	55.4	57.9	57.5	65.5
Assets in foreign currency as percentage of banking system assets	37.8	38.8	38.2	35.9	35.0	37.1	37.7	35.4
Foreign currency deposits as percentage of banking system deposits	20.2	19.1	22.5	23.2	23.5	27.9	32.3	31.1
Deposits with less than 30 days maturity as percentage of total deposits	51.3	43.1	48.8	46.7	49.1	50.1	51.7	51.4
Contingent and off–balance sheet accounts								
as percentage of total assets	5.5	4.2	5.8	6.9	6.5	6.9	7.6	11.3
Contingent and off–balance sheet accounts in foreign currency as percentage of total assets	3.3	2.4	6.2	7.5	7.4	7.0	8.4	8.4
Capital								
Ratio of capital to risk-weighted assets	13.8	11.7	10.6	14.0	15.1	14.7	16.3	15.5
Asset quality								
Credit to the private sector as percentage of GDP	13.9	27.9	35.8	38.6	39.9	37.7	32.9	37.6
Ratio of nonperforming loans to total loans	4.0	3.9	4.4	7.3	5.5	4.9	4.1	3.1
Provision coverage								
Ratio of provisions to total loans	4.9	3.7	3.3	3.5	3.7	3.5	3.9	3.5
Ratio of provisions to nonperforming loans	12.8	92.0	59.2	56.4	61.6	72.9	70.9	119.5
Ratio of foreign currency credit to total private credit	15.7	15.7	16.8	15.7	19.1	22.8	26.1	28.0
Ratio of real estate loans to total loans	12.5	19.8	26.0	22.1	22.2	23.4	25.2	24.5
Management								
Ratio of administrative expenses to total assets	4.8	4.5	5.6	5.6	5.1	5.0	4.8	3.2
Profits per employee (in thousands of U.S. dollars)	3.5	10.4	14.9	12.1	15.3	13.5	11.7	5.0
Profitability								
Pre-tax return to average equity	25.8	15.2	12.4	14.2	12.3	13.5	12.6	11.2
Pre-tax return to average total assets	1.8	1.3	1.2	1.5	1.2	1.0	1.1	1.1
Liquidity								
Ratio of loans to deposits	72.2	77.0	84.0	83.9	75.6	75.8	74.5	77.0
Ratio of liquid assets to deposits	46.6	37.7	43.7	40.7	42.5	39.5	41.4	43.8
Central bank credit to banks as percentage of banking assets	0.1	0.4	0.6	0.5	0.3	0.3	0.0	0.0
Interest margin								
Annual average financial spread (percentage)	6.9	7.1	9.1	9.2	8.9	8.7	7.3	5.7

Sources: Central banks; country authorities; and IMF staff estimates.
[1]Average (median) excluding the Dominican Republic and Panama.

Box 6.1. Institutions Conducting Cross-Border Financial Transactions in Central America

Several types of financial institutions operate regionally throughout Central America, with varying implications for how strictly regional financial groups are supervised.

- Branches of foreign banks have an identifiable head office located abroad. Some foreign banks operate regionally from branches located in one particular Central American country (Panama and Honduras). These banks are normally first-rate institutions (for example, Citibank, HSBC, and Primer Banco del Istmo).

- Bank subsidiaries are incorporated under the law of the host country. Operations are consolidated in the corresponding parent company's host country. Salvadoran banks and one Nicaraguan bank operate through subsidiaries or affiliates (local banks in which they have purchased a majority share). In recent years, regional financial groups have chosen to locate in Panama, to take advantage of that country's status as a well-supervised international financial center.

- Parallel banks are banks licensed in different jurisdictions that have the same beneficial owners and consequently often share common managed and interlinked business, although they are not part of the same financial group for regulatory consolidation purposes.[1] For example, many Nicaraguan financial groups include a parallel bank that conducts local Nicaraguan activities, but they are not subject to consolidated supervision.

- Offshore banks, for the purposes of this section, are those banks licensed in offshore financial centers that are allowed to conduct business only with clients that are not residents of the licensing jurisdiction. Offshore financial centers are improving supervisory standards, making dubious operations less likely.

- Shell banks are banks that have no physical presence in the country where they are incorporated and licensed, and are not affiliated with any financial services group that is subject to effective consolidated supervision. Management is located in another jurisdiction, often in the offices of an associated entity or sometimes in a private residence.[2]

[1]Basel Committee on Banking Supervision, 2003, *Shell Banks and Booking Offices*, Basel Committee Publications No. 94 (Basel, January).
[2]Basel Committee on Banking Supervision, 2003, *Parallel Owned Bank Structures,* Basel Committee Publications No. 95 (Basel, January).

nounced crawling pegs (Costa Rica and Nicaragua), a de facto crawling peg (Honduras), and a float (Dominican Republic and Guatemala). However, among countries that are not formally dollarized, those with an announced crawling peg show the highest degree of dollarization of loans and other financial assets.[5]

Financial sector dollarization is associated with substantial risks in those countries that have not officially adopted the U.S. dollar. Although banks are broadly hedged—foreign currency assets are broadly matched by foreign currency liabilities—lending to unhedged private sector entities leaves the banks exposed to credit risk, and borrowers are exposed to exchange rate risk. Large devaluations could therefore adversely affect banks' capital positions.[6]

---
[5]This phenomenon can be explained partly by the fact that preannounced crawling pegs have been associated with a reduction in exchange rate volatility while the volatility of domestic interest rates remains high.
[6]The high degree of dollarization, in turn, has reduced the authorities' freedom to move toward greater exchange flexibility.

Regional financial sector integration and cross-border lending

Financial sector integration gained momentum over the past few years. Some financial institutions that originally focused on the home market have expanded throughout the region by establishing offices, branches, or subsidiaries or by using other arrangements (Box 6.1). The percentage of assets held by regionally operating banks is particularly high in El Salvador, Nicaragua, and Panama. The most important groups are the Cuscatlán Group (El Salvador), Primer Banco del Istmo (Panama), and the Banco de América Central (Nicaragua) (Table 6.2).

Consolidation of regional financial operations is only partial. Only one Nicaraguan financial group is formally consolidated in Panama, and Salvadoran and Panamanian banks operate through subsidiaries (see, for example, the structure of Cuscatlán, in Figure 6.4). The rest of cross-border financial intermediation takes place on an unconsolidated basis.

The establishment of subsidiaries and branches of financial institutions foreign to the region is still limited. Citibank and Scotiabank are the only institutions with capital from outside the region, and only

Table 6.2. Regional Banks, 2003
(In millions of U.S. dollars)

Regional Banks	Costa Rica	El Salvador	Guatemala	Honduras	Nicaragua	Central America Total
Banks with regional capital	1,287	6,084	603	1,112	1,603	10,689
Grupo Pacific-Banco Uno	39	188	143	137	200	707
Banco de América Central	488	371	122	216	337	1,534
Banpro	124	115	...	85	559	883
Banco Cuscatlán	174	2,418	153	...	...	2,745
Lloyds Bank	...	...	185	68	...	253
Banco Agrícola	...	2,992	...	...	84	3,076
Banco del Itsmo	462	...	...	606	...	1,068
Bancentro	...	...	...	...	424	424
Banks with capital outside the region	281	582	118	69	0	1,051
Citibank	75	182	118	69	...	445
Scotiabank	206	400	...	...	...	606
Total assets of regional banks	1,568	6,666	722	1,181	1,603	11,740
Memorandum item:						
Total assets of banking system	21,779	18,728	9,483	19,248	2,123	71,361

Sources: Bankscope, EDSS, and FitchSearch.

Scotiabank operates at the retail level. However, given the experiences of other regions, including the European Union, implementation of CAFTA-DR will likely lead to increased presence of foreign financial institutions.

The formation of regional conglomerates and cross-border lending allows financial institutions to take advantage of economies of scale and provide services to customers across countries. However, it also represents to some extent regulatory arbitrage, since prudential requirements are different across Central America.[7] Capital requirements are highest in El Salvador and lowest in Panama (Table 6.3). Substantial differences also exist with respect to reserve requirements, which are only 10 percent in Costa Rica but are 20 percent in the Dominican Republic, amounting to an additional implicit tax.[8] Moreover, the regionalization of financial services can lead to gaps in monitoring that can create new vulnerabilities, warranting increased cooperation among regulators and supervisors.

Increased regionalization of banking services could limit the capacity of country authorities to reg-ulate their respective financial systems effectively. For example, a tightening of capital requirements in one country could encourage financial institutions to establish a holding company in another country with lower capital requirements, and then operate through branches or subsidiaries. Differences in prudential requirements can also encourage "adverse selection," as strong banks might opt to establish holding companies in countries that have a reputation of strong regulation and supervision. By doing so, these institutions signal that they are financially sound. This rationale might explain, for example, why an increasing number of Central American banks have opted to incorporate in Panama (Box 6.2). On the other hand, weaker institutions might have an incentive to move their headquarters to the countries with less demanding financial sector regulations and supervision requirements.

Challenges for Financial Regulation and Monitoring

IMF Financial Sector Assessment Programs (FSAPs) in Central American countries took place during periods marked by varying degrees of stress in the respective systems (Table 6.4). In Costa Rica and El Salvador, tensions were building at the time

---

[7]Avoidance of prudential supervision and cross-border activities also pose the risk that it might be associated with money laundering and the financing of terrorism.

[8]Substantial differences also exist in the area of deposit insurance.

Figure 6.4. Organizational Structure of Cuscatlán

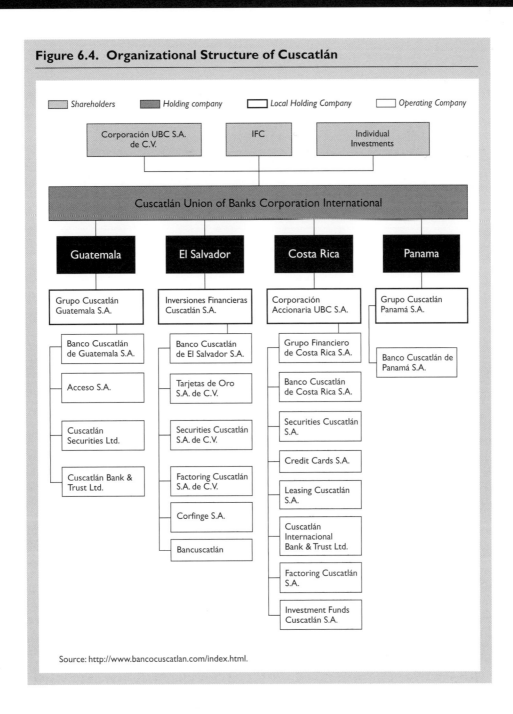

Source: http://www.bancocuscatlan.com/index.html.

of the FSAP, as economic growth was slowing down, and as the external current account and fiscal deficits were rising, all of which raised the banking system's vulnerability to risks. In Guatemala and Honduras, the FSAP took place in a period when prudential indicators were weakening as a result of increasing nonperforming loans, insufficient provisioning, and deteriorating capital adequacy and profitability. In Nicaragua, the FSAP was conducted during a process of consolidation following the 2000–01

banking crisis. In the Dominican Republic, the 2001 FSAP found moderate stress and inadequate information, which obscured elements that underlay the banking crisis that erupted two years later (Box 6.3).

Efforts to upgrade banking supervision and regulation have been made in response to increasing stress. In some cases, new regulations were prepared with the support of other multilateral organizations, chiefly the Inter-American Development Bank (IDB). In several countries, noticeable progress has

Table 6.3. Prudential Requirements

	Capital Requirements	Reserve Requirements		Liquid Asset Requirements	
		Domestic currency	Foreign currency	Domestic currency	Foreign currency
Costa Rica	10 percent	10 percent	10 percent	...	...
Dominican Republic	10 percent	20 percent[1]	20 percent	8 percent[2]	none
El Salvador[3,4]	12 percent	20–25 percent	not applicable	3 percent[5]	not applicable
Guatemala	10 percent	14.6 percent	14.6 percent	none	none
Honduras	10 percent	12 percent	12 percent	none	38 percent
Nicaragua	10 percent	16.25 percent	16.25 percent	...	...
Panama[3]	8 percent	none	not applicable	35 percent	not applicable

Source: Country authorities.

[1]Includes cash in vault (up to a maximum of 5 percent of liabilities subject to reserve requirements).

[2]Compulsory investment requirement equivalent to 8 percent of bank's deposits. To be held at the central bank yielding 15 percent.

[3]El Salvador and Panama are fully dollarized economies.

[4]Upon dollarization, reserve requirements were substituted by remunerated liquidity requirements.

[5]Since January 1, 2005, banks were required to hold an additional 3 percent of the daily average of deposits of the previous month in foreign securities.

taken place in on-site and off-site supervision, including the initiation of steps toward a risk-based supervision framework (Costa Rica and Nicaragua). In El Salvador, a new banking law allows for implementation of consolidated supervision, and in Guatemala, offshore banks have been brought into the regulated system and a new bank resolution framework has been put in place. Many countries (El Salvador, Guatemala, Panama, and Nicaragua) concluded agreements with supervisory authorities in countries where banks owned by residents were incorporated. In a few countries, market risk became a factor for the determination of capital requirements in recent years (Dominican Republic and Nicaragua). Moreover, all countries embarked on efforts to comply with anti–money laundering standards.

The main problems facing the financial sector are associated with credit risk, which often is not reflected in the level of nonperforming loans until it comes to the fore after a downturn in economic activity and/or external shocks. High credit risk is generally found to be related to sector concentration and related lending, and it is often compounded by the small scale of intermediation, as high transaction costs are reflected in wide interest rate spreads. In the presence of an economic slowdown or a sizable external shock (for example, the decline in coffee prices in recent years), the corresponding deterioration of the loan portfolio could be rapid. Moreover, unhedged foreign currency lending is a common practice, other than in the two countries that formally adopted the dollar (El Salvador and Panama). Regulatory action in these areas has been delayed

partly because of a lack of specific guidelines under the Basel framework.

Other problems affecting financial institutions in Central America included significant exposure to government bonds, especially in countries with high public debt. The risks associated with holding government securities are in turn compounded by liabilities of the government emerging from pension system reforms, and in some cases from bank restructuring.

An important deficiency in the regulatory framework is the limited supervisory coverage of cross-border financial operations. The highest risk is in cases in which unsupervised entities could be used as vehicles for dumping impaired assets or generating fictitious capital for supervised institutions. However, financial problems may arise even if all financial institutions belonging to a group are supervised, but on a nonconsolidated basis. When the soundness of financial groups is difficult to ascertain, regulators do not know the extent to which domestic activities are financed through triangular operations or what the potential spillover effects of difficulties in a different location might be. In 2001, other countries had begun producing general information with a view to facilitating the integration of related institutions under the umbrella of their national supervisory authorities (Costa Rica and Guatemala).[9] Other groups, such as some Nicaraguan and Salvadoran financial groups, have consolidated in Panama, presumably to take

---

[9]Guatemala has since brought its offshore banks into the regulatory framework as part of licensed and supervised financial conglomerates.

Box 6.2. Panama's Financial System and Regional Offshore Center

Panama's financial system is the most developed and sound in Central America. Total bank assets amount to 250 percent of GDP, of which more than 50 percent are managed by foreign institutions. Banks are liquid, show low nonperforming loans, and are capitalized well above Basel standards. An important regional offshore center has developed, with 32 internationally licensed banks (six banks are headquartered in Panama) out of a total of 73 banks.[1] An IMF assessment of Panama's offshore financial sector in 2001 found a high level of compliance with the Basel Core Principles. Since then the authorities have introduced measures to address a few remaining weaknesses.

The 1998 banking law provides an adequate framework for banking supervision. The superintendency has the power to supervise conglomerates, including nonbank affiliates, on a consolidated basis. Offices of foreign banks are subject to consolidated supervision by their home country supervisors. Given that a number of Panamanian banks have subsidiaries and affiliates in

other Central American countries, and that Central American banks are establishing their legal domicile in Panama for supervisory purposes, the Superintendency of Banks has signed memoranda of understanding (MOU) with other superintendencies in the region. These MOUs provide the legal foundation to ensure the sharing of information among supervisors across countries and to allow on-site inspections. The superintendency also allows foreign supervisors from jurisdictions without MOUs to conduct on-site inspections in Panama upon request and on a case-by-case basis.

Panama's financial system has been resilient to shocks (including from the financial crisis in Argentina), despite the lack of a lender-of-last-resort facility and the absence of a deposit insurance scheme. The authorities rely on market forces for financial sector workouts, and the government has refrained from bailing out failing institutions. Main prudential concerns relate to the vulnerability to corporate failures due to high loan concentration, a heavy reliance on interest income as opposed to income from fees or commissions, and overbanking. A challenge in the coming years will be the capacity to absorb increasing bank consolidation resulting from increased financial sector integration and cross-border financial intermediation in Central America.

---

[1] Panama's offshore legislation requires that internationally licensed banks establish a physical presence in Panama and maintain an office with local staff. Internationally licensed banks cannot lend to or take deposits from residents.

Panama: Financial Sector Indicators[1]
(In millions of U.S. dollars unless otherwise indicated)

	1996	2000	2003
Structure			
Number of banks	90	75	73
Of which: foreign banks	66	52	54
Total bank assets (in percent of GDP)	411.5	387.0	250.0
Of which: foreign banks	291.8	231.0	132.1
Private banks	365.6	345.0	216.1
Public banks	46.0	42.0	33.9
Credit to the private sector as percentage of GDP	79.4	98.6	74.6
Bank concentration			
Number of banks accounting for at least			
25 percent of total assets	2	2	3
75 percent of total assets	24	23	20
Capital			
Ratio of capital to risk-weighted assets	...	16.0	18.5
Asset quality			
Ratio of nonperforming loans to total loans	1.1	1.6	2.7
Provision coverage			
Ratio of provisions to total loans	1.4	2.0	3.5
Ratio of provisions to nonperforming loans	134.9	124.1	127.7
Management			
Ratio of administrative expenses to total assets	0.6	0.8	1.0
Profits per employee (in thousands of U.S. dollars)	51.0	38.0	55.8
Profitability			
Pre-tax return to average equity	22.2	14.0	21.3
Pre-tax return to average total assets	1.5	1.3	2.4
Liquidity			
Ratio of loans to deposits	82.0	80.0	77.0
Ratio of liquid assets to deposits	3.5	38.1	30.5
Interest margin			
Annual average financial spread (percentage)	1.8	1.6	2.9

Sources: Superintendency of Banks; and Central America Monetary Council.
[1] Includes general license banks and international license banks.

Table 6.4. Financial Sector Assessment Programs

	Original	Update	Offshore
Costa Rica	8/1/2002		
Dominican Republic	11/1/2001		
El Salvador	12/1/2000	3/9/2004	
Guatemala	7/1/2001		
Honduras[1]	4/28/2003		
Nicaragua[2]	2/2/2004		
Panama			8/31/2001

[1]The Financial System Stability Assessment (FSSA) was issued on April 28, 2003. The FSAP report is ongoing.
[2]The date is for the second FSAP mission. All the reports are ongoing.

advantage of its position as an international financial center.

Financial Soundness

Stress in the financial system has not always been reflected in bank statements. This was to a large extent a result of reporting deficiencies, such as the high percentage of loans reclassified during inspections, which reflect inadequate risk management practices by banks. Financial stress has generally been reflected in the financial statements only when a crisis was imminent. Intervention of banks experiencing financial difficulties did not occur until several years after the first signs of stress started to show. Also, particular shocks and pressures from interest groups led to special treatment of specific segments of the loan portfolio.

Capital positions and profitability are often reported to be comfortable, but these measures were often inflated, primarily because of underprovisioning. Moreover, because financial statements of many financial groups are not consolidated, it has not yet been possible to assess the effective solvency of such groups. Other specific weaknesses in individual countries include exemptions to provisioning rules, exclusion of provisions from total expenditure in the banks' income statements, and lax definitions of nonperforming loans.

Spontaneous dollarization entails higher liquidity and credit risk. Direct access to foreign currency deposit holdings fosters an eventual deposit drain in the face of financial uncertainties. However, it may not be a decisive factor. In Nicaragua, deposits stayed within the system following the 2000–01 banking crisis (with "flight-to-quality" shifts within the domestic banking system), possibly supported by a blanket

Box 6.3. Dominican Republic: Banking Crisis and Financial Reform

The Dominican banking system came under severe stress in 2003 following financial scandals, which involved unreported liabilities in a separate set of accounts, at one large and two medium-sized banks. All three banks (including Baninter) have been resolved without imposing losses on depositors, which has helped contain deposit outflows and avoided a systemic crisis, albeit at a high cost. Behind the banking crisis were weaknesses in transparency, accounting procedures, and fiscal control.

Currently, banking reforms are taking place in the following five broad areas: (1) institutional arrangements (including the creation of an asset recovery unit at the central bank); (2) legal and regulatory changes (new law on bank resolution under systemic risk and update of prudential norms in line with international best practices); (3) actions for the resolution of weak banks; (4) rules for the provision of emergency liquidity; and (5) restructuring of public banks to ensure equal treatment with respect to private institutions.

Additional reform priorities include (1) bank recapitalization; (2) establishment of an independent asset management unit; (3) strengthening of the superintendency of banks; (4) development of a plan for savings and loans, development banks, and public banks; and (5) regulatory changes to bring the prudential framework in line with international best practices.

government guarantee on deposits. Unhedged foreign currency lending had increased more markedly in countries with a pre-announced crawling peg (Costa Rica and Nicaragua), possibly reflecting moral hazard behavior in the face of an exchange rate guarantee. In Honduras, where dollarization is moderate relative to other Central American countries, the authorities adopted specific prudential measures against dollarization risks, including higher liquidity requirements on foreign currency deposits, and restrictions on lending in foreign currency to unhedged borrowers. However, attempts to prevent dollarization by legal means could be damaging; in Costa Rica and Guatemala, a legal prohibition on conducting financial transactions in foreign currency induced the emergence of unsupervised offshore banking.[10]

Legal and Regulatory Framework

Deficiencies in legal and institutional arrangements undermine the autonomy of supervisory au-

---

[10]Offshore operations continued once foreign currency deposits were allowed.

thorities. Supervisory authorities are often institutionally weak against the courts. Supervisory authorities in some cases cannot close a bank, suspend its operations, or revoke its license without a court ruling; in other cases, critical judicial determinations rule on how the superintendency should proceed. Moreover, some interinstitutional arrangements discourage effective banking supervision. This problem is compounded by the absence of legal protection for bank supervisors.

Consolidated supervision constitutes a major challenge. In jurisdictions where consolidated supervision has been pursued, the legal structure of companies has sometimes complicated this effort. Also, a careful assessment is needed of the definition of financial groups, and accounting criteria for consolidating financial statements need to be clear. However, in most jurisdictions consolidation was still partial. In one case, companies were required only to consolidate their reporting for entities in which they had a majority interest. In most countries, not all nonbank financial institutions were included in legal provisions for consolidated supervision. To mitigate the risks associated with the slow progress toward effective consolidated supervision, second-best ring-fence measures have been implemented.[11] However, these measures are still imperfect substitutes for regional consolidated supervision.

Prudential supervision and enforcement remain in need of further improvement in the following areas:

- effective prevention of excessive related lending;

- adequate rules for valuation of loans and the norms of provisioning in most countries;

- narrowly focused on-site inspection and off-site analysis (not yet fully integrated into a risk-based approach);

- oversight of sales or transfers of significant shares of a bank's capital;

- harmonization of accounting standards with a view to bringing them in line with international standards;

- greater reliance on external auditors, with appropriate accountability provisions;

- a centralized credit information system;

- a system of prompt corrective action with appropriate sanctions and remedial measures; and

- fit and proper criteria.

Crisis management frameworks suffer from several deficiencies. Systemic liquidity has often been made

unduly available for institutions with solvency problems, to support failed banks for extensive periods and in relatively large amounts. Appropriate triggers for prompt correction have generally been absent; as a result, intervention in banks generally serves only as a first step toward their liquidation. Existing legislation has not allowed the supervisory authority to impose a graduated regime of prompt correction.

Corporate reorganization and liquidation proceedings are hindered by a slow judicial process, disincentives for creditor participation, and the lack of effective out-of-court solutions. Execution of both unsecured and secured claims is often cumbersome and requires the use of inefficient judicial enforcement proceedings. The legal framework for insolvency neither facilitates the reorganization of viable enterprises nor allows the efficient liquidation of nonviable ones. Some countries show positive features: in El Salvador, the real estate registration system is well advanced, and Nicaragua possesses an expedient process to execute collateral when the creditor is a bank.

Supervision of public banks is generally weaker than that applied to private institutions. In some cases, public banks and their affiliates did not report consolidated accounts, reported nonperforming loans showed data inconsistencies, and the provisions coverage of bad loans was low. This has led to quasi-fiscal exposures arising from public banks.

Some basic legislation has recently been modified. Central bank, banking, and bank supervision laws were updated in the Dominican Republic and Guatemala following the FSAP. The purpose was to eliminate inconsistencies in prevailing practices in financial markets and to strengthen the autonomy of the central bank and supervisory bodies in monitoring and regulating the financial system. At the time of the FSAP update in El Salvador, the authorities had made some progress in establishing troubled bank resolution procedures, although those procedures have not yet been tested. In Nicaragua, the legal framework is being overhauled, to bring it in line with most standards and best practices.

Key Policy Recommendations

The legal framework for financial intermediation should be improved. This would entail strengthening the functions and structure of the supervisory authority, removing bank secrecy in lending operations, and introducing legal protection of supervisors. In several countries the national authorities have secured approval of new legislation or have prepared draft legislation for consideration by legislatures.

Consolidated supervision requires action and coordination at the regional level, with strict enforce-

---

[11]Ring fences are temporary, stricter-than-normal prudential measures aimed at preventing noncompliance with other norms that are more difficult to enforce.

ment at the domestic level. This is a key element for compliance with the Basel Core Principles for Effective Supervision. Country authorities are well aware of the advantages of consolidated supervision, although they still lack the capacity to implement it individually. Effective regional coordination toward consolidated supervision would be a significant step forward in the prudential monitoring capacity of supervisors in the region.

Bank supervision should move to a risk-based approach as soon as possible. In this process, the following steps need to be taken: improve loan classification and provisioning rules, enhance interaction between supervisors and external auditors, strengthen oversight of "fit-and-proper" attributes, implement international accounting standards, and enhance supervision for anti–money laundering and combating of terrorism financing. Country authorities have already taken some steps in this direction.

Crisis management frameworks need significant improvement in most countries in the region. Some reforms were introduced in countries more recently affected by a banking crisis. However, implementation of these reforms is still pending in most cases, as is the integration of emergency liquidity facilities and supervisory action.

Insolvency and creditor rights also require significant improvement. To the extent that the rights of creditors are not fully enforced, there will be limitations to further progress in financial development.

Recent Progress and Looking Forward

Important steps have been taken in recent years toward improving the framework for financial activities in Central American countries. In addition to advances in legislation, countries are making efforts to improve rules for the valuation of loans and provisioning, to integrate on-site inspection and off-site analysis, and to fully adopt fit-and-proper criteria. Country authorities are also actively restructuring their bank resolution frameworks. Some other specific measures aimed at improving the framework for financial activities are as follows.

- In Costa Rica, information requirements have been upgraded to put more emphasis on consolidated reports. Also, international accounting standards are being introduced, and the supervisory framework is moving toward a risk-based approach. Moreover, draft regulations on external audit and corporate governance have been prepared.

- In El Salvador, the definition of "financial conglomerate" was revised, and new supervisory

guidelines were issued to make consolidated supervision more effective. Improvements were made in on-site and off-site bank examinations, and anti–money laundering procedures were introduced. Emphasis has been placed on developing a friendly environment for microfinancing operations.

- In Guatemala, the authorities have undertaken a comprehensive financial sector-restructuring program, including a modernization of the legal framework with new central bank, banking, monetary, and financial supervision laws. Also, unregulated (offshore) financial intermediaries are being brought into the regulated system. On-site examinations have become more focused and a CAMEL-type methodology is helping improve the effectiveness of off-site surveillance. Starting May 2004, a central database of debtors is accessible to banks.

- In Honduras, new banking legislation was introduced at the end of 2004. The authorities are working to strengthen the rules of loan classification and provisioning, with a view to aligning them with international standards. The authorities are also considering introducing stricter standards for provisioning foreclosed assets and the restructured agricultural portfolio.

- In Nicaragua, the superintendency is taking steps toward a risk-based approach for banking supervision. Regulations introduced include a norm on liquidity management based on maturity mismatches, and capital requirements for an open foreign currency position (to be phased in over two years).

Regional efforts are necessary to consolidate progress at the country level, especially on consolidated supervision. The Inter-American Development Bank is supporting coordination among Central American countries to harmonize regulations that would help put in place a common framework for supervising financial groups. Effective cooperation among Central American countries in this area would help eliminate incentives for regulatory and tax arbitrage.

The development of a regional market for government securities would facilitate better liquidity management by financial institutions. This is especially important for Central America, where domestic debt is increasing as a result of pension reforms, a shift away from external debt, and in some cases the need to finance bank restructuring. Some steps have been taken to strengthen the primary market, including standardizing securities and developing a basic public debt management strategy. Further steps are necessary to develop interbank markets, secondary markets, and the infrastructure for security settlements, and to regulate collective investment.

Central American countries have an opportunity to integrate workers' remittance flows into the financial sector. It is estimated that only about one-tenth of remittances are intermediated by the banking system. A common effort in improving the infrastructure to provide better remittance-related services would help reduce transaction costs and facilitate financial deepening.

Significant economies of scale could be achieved by adopting common standards for countries' payment systems. Regulations to process checks and securities, common standards for book entry systems, and the development of a common framework for electronic payments and settlements would contribute to the development of the regional financial system and would help to better integrate cross-border financial transactions.

Central American countries need to develop the insurance sector, since their economies are subject to large shocks, such as natural disasters and crop diseases. Lack of insurance against major disasters is one factor limiting credit flows to small firms, particularly in rural areas. There may be an advantage in regionally based insurance that would help pooling risks over a larger and more diverse area. There may be a similar unmet demand for hedging of commodity price movements that could best be met by a regional initiative, and for securitized mortgages.

Conclusions

Central America has made good progress in establishing sound financial systems, which in turn has contributed to increased financial intermediation and improvements in key financial sector indicators. Credit to the private sector has been rising, from an average of 14 percent of GDP in 1996 to almost 40 percent of GDP in 2003. However, for certain sectors, access to credit remains limited, and the financial systems continue to be largely bank based. Bank resolution frameworks have been strengthened in a number of countries, but the actual implementation continues to lag behind. Thus, financial systems still face significant vulnerabilities associated with a high degree of dollarization, balance sheet mismatches, nonperforming loans, unregulated offshore activities, related lending, and supervisory weaknesses and forbearance.

Over the past few years, regional financial sector integration has been accelerating and cross-border activities have increased. Some financial institutions that initially focused on the home market have expanded throughout the region. Assets of these regionally operating banks amounted to more than 15 percent of GDP in 2003. Financial sector integration and consolidation will help the region to take advantage of economies of scale and promote competition and efficiency. At the same time, financial sector integration increases the risk of spillovers leading to contagion in the case of a banking crisis, and the regionalization of financial services reflects, in part, regulatory arbitrage. Increased policy attention to the regional aspects of financial sector activities is therefore a priority. Since consolidation of regional financial operations is only partial, and most cross-border financial intermediation takes place on an unconsolidated basis, it is essential that the region move forward with consolidated supervision at both the domestic and regional levels.

VII   Regional Issues in Macroeconomic Statistics

Lorraine Ocampos

Central America has made significant efforts in recent years to improve data quality and provision, with a view to ensuring sound economic policymaking and to fostering investors' confidence (see Box 7.1).[1] The countries that are already issuers of sovereign bonds in international capital markets are well aware of the need to provide timely and adequate statistical information to market participants (see Table 7.A1).[2] Thus, Panama and Costa Rica, followed by El Salvador, are at the forefront of data compilation and use of cutting-edge methodologies.

El Salvador subscribed to the Special Data Dissemination Standard (SDDS)[3] in 1998 and Costa Rica subscribed in 2001; Panama began participating in the General Data Dissemination System (GDDS) in 2000,[4] and Guatemala began in 2004. Honduras and Nicaragua are adapting their statistical frameworks to international standards, including by preparing to participate in the GDDS and regional initiatives to facilitate cross-country comparisons and data exchange. Nicaragua and Honduras have also made some progress in improving the quality of statistics, especially with respect to the national accounts and the monetary statistics. The drive for more harmonized statistics is motivated in particular by the trend toward increased economic integration and policy coordination in the region.

Despite the progress so far, statistical deficiencies remain, with uneven data quality across sectors and countries. Outdated methodologies, poor source data, and inconsistency across sectors affect countries to different degrees, hampering policy formulation and monitoring. A key advantage throughout the region is that the fiscal statistics generally cover the entire nonfinancial public sector, although precise identification of the overall balance by level of government is problematic in some countries.

The quality of legal frameworks for compiling and disseminating statistics varies. In Honduras, a new law that came into effect in 2000 contains comprehensive provisions that strongly support the compilation of statistics, whereas in El Salvador the national statistical law is outdated and suffers from significant gaps. The legal framework in Costa Rica does not grant compilers legal power to collect data from the nonfinancial private sector and to impose sanctions for noncompliance. Such limits hamper, for example, the collection and analysis of balance of payments data, especially on capital flows. Penalties for noncompliance are adequate in only a few countries, such as Honduras, where the real value of penalties is protected by indexation to the minimum wage. However, compilers seldom invoke laws and resort to penalties when requesting data, preferring to rely on persuasion, with different degrees of success. Therefore, an improvement in macroeconomic statistics requires both a more rigorous application of existing laws and—in most countries—changes in legal frameworks.

In most countries in the region there is scope to improve coordination among statistical agencies and for a targeted increase in resources to improve statistical output. In particular, greater coordination among the central bank, the finance ministry, and the national statistical agency would help governments better assign responsibilities for data sets, strengthen the collection of basic data, and improve the timeliness of certain data, including on the general government. There are significant disparities in resources available to support statistical production: central banks are generally better endowed than national statistical agencies and finance ministries.

---

[1] Although geographically the Dominican Republic is not part of Central America, it has joined a number of regional initiatives, including the Central American Free Trade Agreement (CAFTA-DR). Statistical issues for the Dominican Republic are summarized in Box 7.2 and noted as memorandum items in tables.

[2] Costa Rica, the Dominican Republic, El Salvador, Guatemala, and Panama have issued sovereign bonds in international capital markets. Although Honduras and Nicaragua have not issued sovereign bonds, a number of private residents of these countries have issued securities internationally.

[3] The SDDS was established in 1996 to guide countries that have, or that might seek, access to international capital markets in the dissemination of data to the public. Subscribers must fully meet the requirements of the SDDS at the time of subscription.

[4] The GDDS was established in 1997 to guide countries in providing the public with comprehensive, timely, accessible, and reliable data. The GDDS, which provides recommendations on good practices in compilation and dissemination, is less demanding than the SDDS because it requires progress in statistical improvement over the medium term.

Box 7.1. Main Data Issues in Central America

National Accounts

Outdated methodologies and an obsolete base year affect the quality of the national accounts in El Salvador, Guatemala, and Honduras. Concepts and definitions in El Salvador follow the 1968 System of National Accounts (SNA) with 1990 as base year. In Honduras compilation is conducted under the 1953 SNA with 1978 as the base year. Guatemala is currently implementing the 1993 SNA and is changing the base year of the national accounts to 2001. All countries still face problems with limited source data, although efforts are under way to broaden coverage. For instance, Panama is completing a revision of its national accounts, adopting the 1993 SNA and changing the base year from 1982 to 1996. Coverage has been extended to activities that did not exist in 1982, and the accounts now include resident banks and enterprises operating in the Colón Free Zone (ZLC). In the same vein, Nicaragua recently conducted a census of enterprises in urban areas plus surveys of small enterprises and the informal sector, in the context of the implementation of the 1993 SNA (see Table 7.A1).

Prices

In general, the consumer price index (CPI) is based on internationally accepted practices and standards. Moreover, most countries have updated weights according to recent household expenditure surveys. In addition, Costa Rica, El Salvador, Honduras, and Panama publish a producer price index (PPI), and also publish related date (except for Honduras). However, coverage of the PPI is limited in most cases to the manufacturing sector and excludes key sectors such as maquila, mining, and electricity.

Government Finance Statistics (GFS)

To facilitate financial programming, countries compile fiscal data on a cash basis following the *Manual on Government Finance Statistics 1986 (GFSM 1986)*. Some countries in the region report GFS (on a cash basis) in the format of the *Government Finance Statistics Manual 2001 (GFSM 2001)* for publication in the *Government Finance Statistics Yearbook (GFSY)*. Costa Rica, El Salvador and Panama are planning to review their accounting systems to incorporate the analytical framework of the *GFSM 2001*, which includes recording transactions on an accrual basis. Main shortcomings in most countries relate to coverage (exclusion of certain extrabudgetary operations and social security funds), classification, basis of recording (a mixed basis of cash and accrual), and discrepancies between the overall balance and financing data.

Monetary Statistics

Monetary statistics are reliable, but uneven coverage is an issue. Costa Rica, El Salvador, and Panama follow, to a large extent, the *Monetary and Financial Statistics Manual (MFSM)*, though its adoption lags behind in Guatemala, Honduras, and Nicaragua. However, the latter countries are working with the IMF to improve their databases. In general, the main shortcomings are lack of information on offshore operations of bank conglomerates and investment funds (particularly important in Costa Rica), and difficulties in obtaining detailed sectorized deposit and credit data from banks. The latter hampers the reliability of the estimates of the public sector financing by levels of government. Costa Rica publishes a monetary survey comprising the monetary authorities and other depository corporations, as well as data on other financial corporations (such as cooperative development bank and mortgage banks). Monetary statistics in El Salvador also include data on nonmonetary financial corporations, whereas an expansion of coverage is needed in Panama to ensure inclusion of data on other nonbank institutions such as cooperatives.

Balance of Payments

Lack of sufficient source data hinders the reliability of the balance of payments in some countries. Costa Rica, El Salvador, and Panama compile the balance of payments in conformity with the methodology recommended in the fifth edition of the *Balance of Payments Manual (BPM5)*, which is more demanding regarding the need for reliable source data. In contrast, compilation in Honduras and Guatemala is still based on the *BPM4*, although a move toward adoption of *BPM5* is under way. Guatemala is in the transition between *BPM4* and *BPM5*, and has adopted significant *BPM5* recommendations, in particular for the current account. Costa Rica and Panama compile and disseminate quarterly balance of payments and annual International Investment Position (IIP) statistics, whereas El Salvador disseminates annual and quarterly balance of payments and IIP data. In spite of substantial progress in coverage and timeliness of balance of payments data by these countries, certain deficiencies remain as a result of the lack of reliable source data on services and financial account transactions. Sizable data revisions may suggest that there is room for improvement in quality control, even though this may also reflect improvements in coverage such as in Panama.

Data Suitability for Analytical Purposes

Despite these shortcomings, the quality of statistical data is broadly adequate for analytical purposes,

particularly in the case of Panama and Costa Rica. Data are somewhat less suitable in Guatemala and Honduras, while they have improved considerably in Nicaragua. Until recently, El Salvador enjoyed a reputation for having a good statistical system in relation

---

Box 7.2. Dominican Republic: Data Issues

Main Data Issues and Their Suitability for Analytical Purposes

The Dominican Republic has made some progress in improving the quality of its macroeconomic statistical framework and, along with Honduras and Nicaragua, is in the process of participating in the GDDS initiative. Nonetheless, several shortcomings remain that hamper the use of the GDDS for analytical purposes.

A revision of the *national accounts* is being undertaken in line with *1993 SNA* and an updated base year (1991). The quarterly series have, however, outdated conceptual and methodological frameworks that make them unreliable for analysis. *Price statistics* have new consumer price indices based on updated and more accurate consumption baskets, with weights based on the 1997–98 national household survey.

Government finance statistics are collected from various institutions but the lack of interinstitutional coordination creates serious problems for matching above-the-line data on expenditures and revenues to below-the-line financing from foreign and domestic sources. This gap is represented in some years as about 5 percent of GDP. Moreover, data on the operations of public enterprises are often partial and available with excessive delays.

Along with price statistics, the *monetary statistics* data set is one of the most reliable. It broadly follows the *MFSM*, although deficiencies in the data collection system, being addressed through the setup of a new

database with automated data processing, will not be solved until the end of 2004.

Balance of payments statistics, despite being compiled in conformity with methodological standards of *BPM5*, have serious data sources constraints related mainly to coverage of imports, capital transfers, and income and financial accounts that generate large errors and omissions.

The debt data set has coverage and classification problems that have led to sizable underestimations of stocks (see Tables 7.A1 and 7.A2).

Statistics Technical Assistance

Since the inception of the data initiatives (1996), the Dominican Republic has received 16 STA technical assistance missions, which, compared with the Central American countries, place it as one (along with Costa Rica) of the major beneficiaries of STA technical assistance missions (vis-à-vis an average of 10 missions per Central American country during the same period). The bulk of the missions were on balance of payments and national accounts statistics. As a result, the compilation of balance of payments follows *BPM5* and national account statistics have been revised. No mission has been fielded so far for government finance statistics. One multisector mission took place in 2002, and a data ROSC mission was requested by the authorities after a recent monetary and financial statistics mission, which also included a follow-up in other statistical areas (see Table 7.A3).

---

to regional practices. However, since dollarization in 2001, the ensuing streamlining of the functions of the central bank—the main provider of economic statistics—and an erosion of financial and human resources deployed to statistics have had some adverse effects, including the discontinuation of several key surveys. This has affected, in particular, the national accounts and the balance of payments (see Table 7.A2).

Monetary statistics are the most reliable and suitable for analysis and financial programming, although coverage and sectorization gaps continue to be a matter of concern. Closing these gaps would require substantial effort, as covering offshore operations and the needed modifications to the chart of accounts for financial institutions in some countries would entail resource costs and require further technical assistance (see also Section VI, on offshore financial transactions).

Shortcomings in the national accounts (the SNA) and the balance of payments complicate the analysis of sources of economic growth, national savings, output gap, and external sustainability. The national accounts are considered more reliable in Panama and Costa Rica. In Nicaragua, recent implementa-

tion of the *1993 SNA* has updated the base year and introduced numerous surveys to broaden coverage, thus increasing data reliability. Although the balance of payments is considered more reliable than the national accounts, large and volatile errors and omissions introduce uncertainty to estimates and projections, particularly in Guatemala and Nicaragua.

Fiscal statistics are considered acceptable for analysis in most countries. However, the coverage of public enterprises is incomplete, and data are untimely in some countries, particularly in Nicaragua. Discrepancies between the overall balance and financing data, particularly in El Salvador and Nicaragua, have resulted at times in a gap of about 2 percent of GDP.

Cross-sectoral consistency is a major issue in the region. This affects especially the national accounts, balance of payments, and government finance statistics. For example, in Costa Rica, data on the operations of large nonfinancial enterprises have been affected by unreliable estimates of changes in inventories and imports. In Guatemala, operations of the *maquila* enterprises are included in the balance of payments, although reflected on a net basis, but excluded from the national accounts. In Nicaragua, the new series of national accounts include better estimates of capital and current expenditures than in the government finance statistics, for which overestimation of capital expenditures is a concern. Good progress to improve intersectoral consistency is being made in Panama, where reconciliation of data on capital flows between banking sector and balance of payments statistics is being conducted following a compilation method introduced by the Superintendency of Banks in 2002.

Analysts strongly support the implementation of up-to-date methodologies, but are concerned about possible breaks in the series. They consider that the implementation of more advanced methodologies improves data classification and sectorization, thereby facilitating the use of data for analytical purposes. They caution, however, that breaks in the series could complicate intertemporal analysis.

Moving Toward a Harmonized Statistical Framework

Deepening economic integration of the region should be supported by compilation of consolidated macroeconomic statistics for the region. Coordination of macroeconomic policies would, at the outset, require the exchange of statistical information among members so as to compare data sources and methodologies for classification and sectorization. Given the lack of an integrated statistical database for the Central American countries, there is a need to develop a coordinated, consolidated, and harmonized statistical system.

Some efforts in this direction have been undertaken by the Central American Monetary Council (CAMC), which has created working groups to deal with statistical issues. These groups are preparing working papers on estimating the co-circulation of domestic and foreign currency and analyzing operations of offshore banks. A working group on the national accounts is tasked with researching the determinants of economic growth in the region, and another group is working on a common definition of money in Central America.[5] Also, the CAMC is working on a project to disseminate debt data of the central governments and central banks.

Some progress in harmonizing monetary statistics has been fostered by the policy needs of regional central banks. Monetary and financial policy issues common to the countries in the region are being discussed in the context of the CACM, with a focus on

avoiding unexpected capital movements across the region. Accordingly, data sources, level of coverage, and data classification and sectorization have been assessed across countries to determine the degree of comparability. This project has been implemented with support from the IMF's Statistics Department (STA) in the framework of the GDDS initiative.

The Partnership in Statistics for Development in the 21st Century (Paris 21) has also been promoting regional integration of Central American statistics.[6] Workshops to strengthen the statistical capacity of Central American countries, organized by the Secretariat of Paris 21, took place in El Salvador (May 2003) and Panama (April 2004). The principal recommendations arising from these meetings include creation of a regional authority for statistical coordination and standardization of regional definitions and methodologies.

Methodological convergence is needed for a consolidated and a harmonized statistical system across the region. Regionwide implementation of the *1993 SNA* would help in the preparation of consolidated accounts for Central America. This and further improvements to the national accounts would require better source data through a strengthening of the statistical institutions, the establishment and maintenance of statistical registers, and the regular conduct of economic surveys and censuses. Similarly, in the area of fiscal statistics, countries would be well advised to update the *Government Finance Statistics Manual*, budget, and accounting systems based on the *GFSM 2001*. Some countries should also improve fiscal data coverage, in particular by including extrabudgetary units, social security funds, and local governments. Guatemala, Honduras, and Nicaragua need to make further progress in the adoption of the *MFSM* and in compiling the balance of payments in conformity with the methodology recommended in *BPM5*.

Technical Assistance to the Region

Since the inception of the data standards initiatives (SDDS, GDDS, and data ROSCs), the IMF has fielded 88 missions to Central America and the Dominican Republic to assist in the improvement of the

---

[5]For information on research papers and working groups, see www.secmca.org/documentos.asp?mnu=11.

[6]Paris 21 was launched at a meeting of statisticians and policymakers, which was held in Paris in November 1999. The meeting was an initiative of the United Nations, the Organization for Economic Coordination and Development (OECD), the IMF, the World Bank, and the European Commission in response to a UN Economic and Social Council resolution. This global consortium aims to help promote a culture of evidence-based policymaking and monitoring, especially in poor countries. The initial focus is on helping countries to prepare national Poverty Reduction Strategy Papers (PRSPs).

macroeconomic statistics. Costa Rica and the Dominican Republic received the most (15 missions each), followed Guatemala and Honduras (12 each), Panama (11), El Salvador (10), and Nicaragua (9) (Table 7.A3). Most missions were related to monetary statistics, followed by balance of payments and national accounts.

Data ROSC missions have visited Costa Rica, El Salvador, Honduras, Guatemala, and Nicaragua and have prepared detailed assessments of statistical practices based on international standards.[7] In addition, several missions and seminars are taking place in 2004 to assist the Dominican Republic, Guatemala, Honduras, and Nicaragua in preparing to participate in the GDDS. These missions and seminars explain the modalities and benefits of using the GDDS as a framework to improve their national statistical systems and have assisted in (1) documenting compilation methods and sources (metadata), (2) identifying deficiencies in the compilation and dissemination process, (3) documenting the plans for improvement over the short and medium term, and (4) identifying technical assistance needs in the short and medium term. Metadata for the external and monetary sectors have already been finalized, whereas those for the real and fiscal sectors are being drafted.

Technical assistance has helped strengthen statistical systems in the region. A good example is Nicaragua, which has made considerable progress in updating the statistical methodologies. Nicaragua has significantly improved its monetary statistics (in particular central bank aggregates), publishes national accounts data that are compatible with the *1993 SNA,* and presents fiscal data to the IMF in the format of the *GFSM 2001.*

Technical assistance could play a role in the support of regional integration. To this end, technical assistance will need to attach priority to strengthening methodological convergence and to making statistics comparable across countries. The IMF could provide technical assistance to regional institutions for creating coordinated and harmonized statistical systems. Given the high level of trade integration in the region, future technical assistances should also focus on harmonizing balance of payment statistics.

Conclusions

Deepening economic integration and increased macroeconomic policy coordination should be mirrored in a strengthening and methodological convergence of statistical systems in Central America. In the medium term, this could be supplemented through the development of an integrated statistical database for the region. Convergence of statistics should take place at the most advanced level, guided by those countries that already have access to international capital markets and that subscribe to the SDDS.

Overall, Central America has a good record of providing data to the IMF and has made progress in improving statistical frameworks. Among the Central American countries, Costa Rica and Panama are at the forefront of data compilation and use of cutting-edge methodologies. Costa Rica and El Salvador subscribe to the SDDS, whereas Panama and Guatemala subscribe to the GDDS. The other countries are preparing to participate in the GDDS. Statistical deficiencies remain, however, with uneven data quality across sectors and countries, including the use of outdated methodologies.

Appendix. Statistical Issues, Suitability of Data for Analytical Purposes, and Technical Assistance Missions

The following tables provide detailed information on statistical issues for each country.

---

[7]Starting in 2001, the data module of Reports on the Observance of Standards and Codes (data ROSCs) includes an assessment of data quality based on the IMF's Data Quality Assessment Framework (DQAF).

Table 7.A1. Statistical Issues

	SDDS/GDDS	National Accounts	Price Index	Government Finance Statistics	Monetary Statistics	Balance of Payments
Costa Rica	Subscribed to SDDS in November 2001	New series of accounts compiled in accordance with *1993 SNA* with 1991 as base year. Weaknesses remain in the source data (informal sector not explicitly estimated; input-output ratios from 1991 used for estimating 80 percent of value added; limitations in coverage and quality of data for compiling the expenditure approach of GDP), which affects the quarterly estimates.	Overall structure of consumer price index (CPI) based on internationally accepted practices and standards. Product classification according to household consumption expenditure classification of *1968 SNA*. Producer price index (PPI) coverage limited to manufacturing sector output for the domestic market (excludes businesses operating under special customs regimes—*maquila*).	Methodology for compiling GFS for policy analysis follows the guidelines of the *GFSM 1986*. A committee in the Ministry of Finance (MoF) has been created to prepare a migration plan and implement the *GFSM 2001* guidelines. The MoF reported cash data in *GFSM 2001* format for publication in the *GFSY*. The MoF does not consolidate data for the central government. Local government and university financing data are not included. Problems in reconciling above-the-line with below-the-line (financing flows) figures. Financing and debt classifications not fully in line with *GFSM 1986*. Breakdown of financing is not disseminated regularly.	Analytical framework broadly follows the *MFSM*, after several TA improvements made to the classification, coverage, and timeliness of money and banking statistics, in particular of the central bank. Enhanced monetary data for publication in *IFS* include balance sheets of cooperatives, savings and loans institutions, and private financing corporations. Main shortcomings: sectorized source data from other depository corporations need significant improvements, and offshore operations of resident banks need coverage.	Compiled in conformity with methodology recommended in *Balance of Payments Manual* (*BPM5*). Substantial progress in the application of appropriate methodologies in the compilation of balance of payment (BOP) statistics, including the preparation of quarterly BOP and annual International Investment Position (IIP) data. Shortcomings: (1) incomplete coverage of long-term liabilities of private banks and equity holdings abroad; (2) limited coverage of services, especially in the quarterly series; and (3) statistical techniques needed to eliminate effects of valuation changes for banking flows.
Dominican Republic	In the process of participating in GDDS	A revision is being undertaken in line with *1993 SNA* and an updated base year (1991).	New indices for consumer prices based on updated and more accurate consumption baskets, and weights based on the 1997–98 national survey on household income and expenditure. There are no available series for producer prices, industrial production, or wages (except minimum wages).	Fiscal data are collected from various institutions, but with limited coordination and consistency in classification. Information on public enterprises is often incomplete and available only with long delays. Data are collected on a cash basis. Data on fiscal revenues and expenditures lack consistency with data on financing, resulting in statistical discrepancies. The implementation of the Integrated System of Financial Management project is expected to improve both coverage and classification of the public accounts and introduce the accrual concept.	Analytical framework reflects concepts and definitions that broadly follow the *MFSM*. Coverage includes banking institutions as well as other depository institutions. A new database, to be operational by the end of 2004, will substantially improve timeliness and the methodological soundness of monetary statistics. A major shortcoming is the lack of data on offshore banks and financial cooperatives.	Compiled in conformity with methodological standards of *BPM5*. IIP statistics should become available in 2005. Main shortcomings: problems in coverage remain in imports, capital transfers, income, and the financial account, giving rise to large errors and omissions.

Table 7.A1 *(continued)*

	SDDS/GDDS	National Accounts	Price Index	Government Finance Statistics	Monetary Statistics	Balance of Payments
El Salvador	Subscribed to SDDS in June 1998	Concepts and definitions follow the *1968 SNA* with 1990 as base year. The authorities intend to migrate to *1993 SNA*. Source data are scarce. Last agricultural census conducted in 1971 and annual economic surveys interrupted in 1999. Coverage curtailed significantly when compilation of institutional sector accounts partially suspended in 1995.	Monthly price data for CPI and industrial price index (IPRI) are adequate and collected in a timely and efficient manner. CPI with sound methodological basis and coverage representing 85 percent of urban population. CPI weight based on the 1990/91 NHIE survey. PPI weight based on the 1993 economic census, which also included goods produced under special customs regimes (*maquila*) (13 percent of manufacturing sector). However, this production is not covered by the PPI or by goods produced for export.	Concepts and definitions based on *GFSM 1986* for internal use and for reporting to Western Hemisphere Department (WHD) in the IMF. Accounting system under review for incorporating *GFSM 2001* analytical framework. All units of the nonfinancial public sector are covered, except some decentralized institutions such as the Salvadoran Institute of Municipal Development. Mutual funds are wrongly included. Classification in accordance with the recommendations of the *GFSM 1986* with some exceptions, such as inconsistent treatment of inflows from privatization and recording of guaranteed debt in the consolidated central government. The MoF reported GFS cash and accrual data in *GFSM 2001* format for publication in the *GFSY*.	Analytical framework reflects concepts and definitions that broadly follow the *MFSM*. Good periodicity and quality of data, though several financial institutions do not distinguish transactions by residents and nonresidents. Main shortcomings: depository corporations' survey does not include credit and savings cooperatives; loans and other accounts are not fully sectorized; offshore operations of resident banks are not covered; and estimates of money need to be improved by incorporating a measure of dollars circulating in the economy.	Compiled in conformity with methodological standards of *BPM5*. Annual and quarterly dissemination, including the IIP. Data sources broadly sufficient to compile major items of BOP. Significant improvements in coverage and timeliness of BOP data in recent years. Significant progress in compiling trade and insurance data and data on services, workers' remittances, foreign direct investment, private external debt, and goods for processing, as well as data for IIP statistics. Interest, dividends, and external debt transactions are still recorded on a cash basis.
Guatemala	Participating in the GDDS since December 2004	Compilation based on *1953 SNA* with 1958 as base year. Coverage is limited, especially for services. 1958 input-output ratios used for estimating more than 80 percent of value added. Central bank in the process of implementing the *1993 SNA* with a recent base year.	New CPI since Feb. 2001 based on weights from a household expenditure survey of 1998/99. No compilation of PPI.	Methodology follows the guidelines of the *GFSM 1986*. No migration plan for moving to *GFSM 2001*. Problems in reconciling the government public sector balance (above-the-line) with that from financing flows (below-the-line). Little progress in improving statistics of the social security fund and public corporations. Overall nonfinancial public sector data not compiled on a regular basis. The MoF reported GFS cash data in *GFSM 2001* format for publication in the *GFSY*.	Significant shortcomings in the implementation of the *MFSM*. Main shortcomings: coverage excludes deposit and credit cooperatives; depository corporations still unable to provide fully sectorized data; off-shore operations of resident banks not covered. Steps toward developing an integrated database have been re-initiated in the context of the GDDS.	Classification and presentation according to *BPM4*. Some progress has been made in the transition to the methodology of *BPM5*. Main source of data—for compiling services, transfers, and private capital transactions (despite major deficiencies of this data source)—is International Transactions Reporting System (ITRS) reported by banks. Guatemala does not compile IIP statistics. A recent TA mission recommended overall to improve the quality of ITRS and to implement enterprise surveys.

Honduras	In the process of participating in GDDS	Compilation based on 1953 SNA with 1978 as base year. Central Bank of Honduras implementing a four-year program for adopting 1993 SNA and changing the base year to 2000. Lack of coverage and deficient quality of data sources (informal sector not explicitly estimated; the reliance on input-output ratios from 1978 in some industries is excessive; deficient statistical techniques for compiling the expenditure approach of GDP).	CPI compiled following internationally accepted concepts, practices, and standards. New indices published since April 2000 with revised basket and updated weights in basis of a household income and expenditure survey conducted on 1998/99. CPI covers eight principal cities, and its basket includes 282 goods and services. Although unpublished, the PPI broadly follows international guidelines with respect to concepts and definitions. Coverage, however, limited to the manufacturing sector, excluding key sectors such as maquila, mining, and electricity.	GFS classification not completely in line with the GFSM 1986 recommendations. No migration plan for moving to GFSM 2001. Discrepancies between central bank and MoF data. Statistical discrepancy between above-the-line and financing estimates of the fiscal deficit. Integrated system of finance administration in process. This integrated system does not have a payroll module. There is no common sectorization of GFS within the MoF. Contrary to recommendations in the GFS manuals, statistics on the consolidated central and general government are not prepared. Only central administration data are disseminated, which exclude operations of social security funds and some extrabudgetary units.	MFSM not fully adopted. Intention is to revise compilation methodology and procedures in line with MFSM. Monetary survey consolidates balance sheet of the central bank, commercial bank, development banks, saving and loan institutions, and finance companies but does not include credit cooperatives. Main shortcomings: lack of coverage of deposit and credit cooperatives and offshore operations of residents; lack of fully sectorized balance sheet for depository corporations.	Compiled in broad conformity with BPM4. In transition to BPM5. Principal shortcomings: several deviations from the classification recommended by BPM5, such as (1) the treatment of goods for processing, (2) lack of breakdown of transportation service, and (3) transfers not disaggregated into current and capital transfers. There is a need for improvement of statistical techniques for estimating workers' remittances, profits of maquila firms, freight and insurance on goods imports, and undercoverage of goods. Improvements in BOP surveys are also required.
Nicaragua	In the process of participating in GDDS	New national accounts series for 1994–2000 compatible with 1993 SNA was adopted in March 2003 with 1994 as base year. New figures entail an expansion of data sources and broader coverage of industries and the informal sector. Supply and use tables are also provided.	CPI, with new weights referencing 1999 since 2001, covers Managua and eight other cities. The current IPRI is a good proxy of the PPI, although it only covers agriculture, fishing, and manufacturing sectors.	Methodology follows the guidelines of the GFSM 1986. The MoF reported GFS cash data in GFSM 2001 format for publication in the GFSY. Some shortcomings: discrepancies between deficit/surplus balances and financing items (from domestic and external sources) and misclassification of current and capital expenditure. Institutional coverage is incomplete, owing to the exclusion of some extrabudgetary funds. Coverage of the consolidated central and general governments is incomplete because it does not include decentralized and autonomous entities, as well as para-statal enterprises.	Significant improvements in timeliness of analytical accounts for the central bank. Main shortcomings: difficulties in properly sectorizing the public sector accounts of the deposit money banks (in central government, nonfinancial public enterprises, and local governments); lack of coverage of credit and saving cooperatives and offshore operations of resident banks.	In transition between BPM4 and BPM5. Significant BPM5 recommendations, in particular for the current account, have been implemented. Data are reported to the Statistics IMF's Department for publication in the Balance of Payments Statistics Yearbook, following the standard BPM5 format. No compilation of IIP. Coverage somewhat incomplete. Financial account incomplete especially owing to insufficient enterprise surveys. In current account, details for some services and income items not available. Data of central government debt are good. Improvement needed for external debt of public enterprises, banks, and private sector.

Table 7.A1 (concluded)

	SDDS/GDDS	National Accounts	Price Index	Government Finance Statistics	Monetary Statistics	Balance of Payments
Panama	Participating in GDDS since December 2000. Metadata posted on the DSBB.	National accounts published according to *1968 SNA* with 1982 as base year. Authorities completing a revision of national accounts with a change in the base year from 1982 to 1996, based on the *1993 SNA*. The project entails an update on the measurement of certain activities and the implementation of a new sectoral classification system. Coverage extended to activities that did not exist in 1982, such as resident banks and enterprises operating in the Colón Free Zone (ZLC) by strictly applying the residency criterion of the BOP and the national accounts.	Weights underlying the CPI were derived from a household budget survey conducted in 1983/84. Authorities plan to introduce a new CPI in the first half of 2004 based on weights of the 1997/98 household survey. Consumer price data are available through October 2003.	Methodology used for compiling GFS by the MoF and the General Comptroller Office (GCO) follows the guidelines of the *GFSM 1986*. Plans are under way to implement the *GFSM 2001* guidelines. The integrated financial administration system (SIAFPA) coverage of the central government accounts was completed in 2003. Work is under way to incorporate decentralized agencies such as the Social Security Agency in the SIAFPA. Data on nonfinancial public sector are compiled on a cash basis by the MoF and on a mix of cash and accrual bases by the GCO. In 2003, after the handover of the Panama Canal, the authorities decided to include its operational balance in the nonfinancial public sector statistics. There is a need to broaden SIAFPA's scope of coverage; to address the issue of unrecorded expenditures, some of them likely due to accumulation of arrears; and to improve the quality of the data sources and economic and functional classifications.	Analytical framework broadly follows the *MFSM*. In the past two years, a joint effort of the banking system and the superintendency of banks improved the timeliness of monetary statistics production and minimized errors through better information technology. A wider coverage of financial soundness indicators improved the transparency of the banking system statistics. Main shortcomings: lack of consistent data prepared on the financial position of the National Mortgage Bank and of the Agricultural Development Bank.	Compiled in conformity with methodology recommended in *BPM5*. Substantial progress in the application of appropriate methodologies in the compilation of BOP statistics, including improved compilation procedures and systems, reduced lags in data collection, reconciliation of external debt statistics discrepancies with multilateral lenders, and systematized procedures for quality control. IIP data for 1995–2003 have been compiled. Despite substantial progress, a main shortcoming is the sizable revision of data, particularly of merchandise imports and foreign direct investment. Revisions may reflect improvements in coverage, but they also suggest that there is room for improvement in quality control procedures.

Key: BOP = Balance of payments; CPI = Consumer price index; GDDS = General Data Dissemination System; GFSM = *Manual on Government Finance Statistics*; GFSY = *Government Finance Statistics Yearbook*;
IFS = *International Financial Statistics*; IIP = International Investment Position; IPRI = Industrial price index; MoF = Ministry of Finance; PPI = Producer price index; SDDS = Special Data Dissemination System;
SNA = *System of National Accounts*; TA = technical assistance; CAMC = Central American Monetary Council; * = forthcoming missions.

Table 7.A2. Suitability of Data for Analytical Purposes

Countries	General Comments	National Accounts	Government Finance	Monetary Statistics	Balance of Payments and External Debt
Costa Rica	Statistics overall of good quality and publicly available in a timely fashion, though sometimes some adjustments are needed for WHD purposes. Economic statistics are mostly produced by Central Bank. Consistency of time series over time is considered more important than the adoption of cutting edge methodologies. New manuals should include an executive summary of most important recommendations and changes that should be implemented with urgency to increase quality and transparency.	In general, good quality with satisfactory coverage by means of periodic surveys. Nonetheless, some shortcomings remain, such as constant and sizable revisions throughout the year and consistency with fiscal and BOP data (though reconciled in final version). Main issue is the treatment of the operations of INTEL, particularly adequate registration of change in inventories and imports that affects the real sector as well as the BOP statistics.	Information of central government is pretty reliable. No big problems in reconciling above-the-line with below-the-line (financing flows). Differences are minor and identifiable. Main shortcoming is the lack of complete and timely data of state-owned enterprises.	Quality is good and reliable except for the lack of consistent information on offshore operations (very important for Costa Rica). Data of offshore operations are deficient, owing to variability of coverage and timeliness.	The quality of BOP is quite good but has similar problems to real sector statistics. A need exists to strengthen efforts for adequately registering INTEL operations. Other shortcomings: insufficient coverage of net private capital flows, mainly portfolio investments, which are underestimated. Public debt database is good for availability of consolidated external and domestic debt. Nonetheless, a breakdown by holder (resident and nonresident) is needed. Lack of information on private sector debt; staff should therefore develop own database.
El Salvador	In general, the statistical system is well rated. Since dollarization in 2001, though, insufficient human resources at the Central Reserve Bank (CRB) have led to discontinuance of several surveys. This affects the quality of statistics, mainly national accounts and balance of payments. Use of manual is specifically relevant in the case of monetary statistics; improves transparency.	National accounts statistics follow out-of-date standards. Time series at current prices are disseminated in dollars; however, series at constant 1990 prices are published in colones dollars. The basket of goods to measure poverty is no longer representative.	Large statistical discrepancies between above-the-line and financing estimates of the fiscal deficit (in 2003, approximately 2 percentage points of GDP).	Detailed accounts of the CRB are not publishec; only available upon request Lack of information on offshore banking operations.	No major comments.
Guatemala	In general, the quality of statistics has serious deficiencies. In particular, real sector statistics are not reliable, since the base year is obsolete. Rather than use cutting-edge methodologies, the problems of coverage should be prioritized.	The use of an obsolete manual (SNA 1953) and an out-of-date base year (1958) make national accounts highly unreliable. Estimates of GDP growth have constant and large changes until publication of the final version, which may imply acute quality constraints. Data on trade exclude maquila sector, which reduces coverage of national accounts.	Data generally of good quality, but only cover the budgetary central government.	In general, good. An important unresolved issue is the treatment of offshore banking operations, which are not consolidated with on-shore operations.	Main shortcomings: large unexplained amounts of private capital flows.

Table 7.A2 (concluded)

Countries	General Comments	National Accounts	Government Finance	Monetary Statistics	Balance of Payments and External Debt
Honduras	Quality of statistics with serious deficiencies. Major problems observed in real sector and government finance statistics. Serious cross-sectoral consistency difficult analysis and generally must be fixed during WHD missions.	Despite efforts to change the base year, the use of an out-of-date base year (1978) is considered a major hurdle to use national account for analytical purposes. This is reflected in constant and considerable revisions (e.g., in some years up to 1 percentage point of GDP)	Serious problems of accountability and institutional coordination. Efforts have been made to overcome these shortcomings. With the expansion of the integrated financial administration system, coverage and reliability of the central government have improved substantially. Still serious difficulties in obtaining good quality and timely data from public enterprises and municipalities, which are reflected in large and unexplained above-the-line discrepancies and financing estimates.	By far the most reliable data set. Presentation is user-friendly. Major problem: revisions that go back one year have changed levels of aggregates. Commercial banks do not have the recommended sectorized balance sheet and only differentiate between central administration and rest of the public sector. This makes it difficult to carry out consistency analyses.	Efforts to improve periodicity have been made, though quarterly data still not available. Major problems with workers' remittances that given its weight generates large variability of the current account (up to 1 percentage point of GDP). Large and constant revisions (that may take up to two years) make BOP statistics unsuitable for analytical purposes.
Nicaragua	Considerable improvement in national accounts statistics, as well as monetary and banking statistics. The fiscal sector is the area with more shortcomings, followed by balance of payments. Statistical presentations are not always very useful for analytical purposes. Efforts that are under way in the monetary division of STA are reducing the gap between statistical and analytical purposes. Need for technical assistance in integrated databases.	Considerable improvements in national accounts with the implementation of SNA 1993 with new base year, expanded coverage, and input-output tables. Better estimation of capital and current expenditures than government finance statistics. Need to finish quarterly presentation.	Large statistical discrepancies between above-the-line and below-the-line flows. Poor breakdown. Institutional coverage is incomplete: only a few nonfinancial public corporations (2 out of more than 30) included, and only 1 municipality (Managua, representing 30 percent of the country) included. Budget not on accrual basis. Overestimation of capital expenditures. Bad and insufficient information on domestic public debt.		Areas with main shortcomings: imports over-estimated, perhaps owing to nonregistered transshipments (reexports); migrants' transfers underestimated, owing to insufficient source data; FDI only of large enterprises. As a result, considerable errors and omissions. Very good external debt data. Lack of external and domestic consolidated public debt.

Panama	In general, statistics are adequate for analysis. The Panamanian statistical system is highly rated among Central American countries. There is a calendar of revisions, but significant publication delays persist. Follow-up of STA TA is important for continuity of improvements.	Considerable improvement with the implementation of *SNA 1993* with 1996 as base year. In general, national accounts are reliable. Main shortcomings are the lack of statistics from the demand side and constant and considerable revisions (in some years representing about 2 percentage points of GDP).	Although considered generally good for analytical purposes, many problems in data sources and classifications still persist.	They are considered of good quality and suitable for analysis. A shortcoming, though minor, is the lack of information on other non-bank institutions, such as cooperatives.	BOP statistics have improved considerably, though significant revisions may represent a constraint for analysis.
Memorandum item: Dominican Republic	In general, the quality of statistics for analytical purposes has serious deficiencies. Serious problems with cross sectoral consistency. Public external debt flows differ between fiscal and balance of payments. Public investment figures differ between the real and the fiscal sector. Exports and imports are inconsistent between the real and the BOP sector.	It is expected that the revision process under way will improve the quality of national accounts. A major constraint is the quarterly series, which are considered unreliable owing to measurement deficiencies.	Serious deficiencies hamper analysis. Large discrepancies between above and below-the-line (in 2003 represented about 5 percentage points of GDP). Significant problems of coverage and consistency owed mainly to institutional hurdles. The budget office works relatively well but it does not receive information of the entire public sector. Particularly, capital expenditures are decentralized and they are not included in the budget.	Follows the *MFSM*. Thanks to STA TA considerable progress have been done in monetary sectorization, but follow-up is necessary. Reporting problems to follow the program exist owing mainly to lack of full computerized reporting systems.	Despite the use of *BPM 5* considerable shortcomings persist that hampers the analysis. Problems are mainly related with the tourism sector and debt registration. As a result errors and omissions are considerably high (2004 QI: approximately US$500 million). Serious problems with the debt data base.

Table 7.A3. Statistics Technical Assistance Missions, 1995–end-January 2005[1]

	Costa Rica	Dominican Republic	El Salvador	Guatemala	Honduras	Nicaragua	Panama	CAMC Members	Total
SDDS	1999, 2001		1998						3
GDDS		2004		2004	2004	2004	1999	2004	6
National accounts	1999, 2004	Jan. 2002, Oct. 2002, Jan. 2004, Apr. 2004	2004	1997, 1998 1999, 2000	1999, 2005	2000, 2001	1997, 2001		17
Price statistics				2000					1
Government finance statistics	1999, 2004	2005*			2004		2004, 2005		5 + 1*
Money and banking statistics	Apr. 1998, Dec. 1998, 2001, 2003	1997, 2003, 2004	2001	1998, 2001, 2004	1998, 2000, 2001, 2004	1997, 1999, 2001, 2003		1998, 2001	21
Balance of payments	1999, 2000, 2005	Jan. 1996, Jun. 1996, 1998, 2002, 2003, 2004	1998, 1999	2004	1995, 2004	1998	1996, Jun. 1997, Oct. 1997, 1998, 1999, 2002		21
Multisector missions	1996	2002	1998	1997					4
Integrated databases	2002								1
Legal and institutional framework			1999, 2000						2
ROSC missions	2002		2003	2004	2003	2005			5
ROSC—follow-up			2004		2005				2
Total	16	15 + 1*	10	12	12	9	11	3	88

[1]An asterisk represents "forthcoming missions."

VIII The Political Economy of Implementing Pro-Growth and Anti-Poverty Policy Strategies in Central America

Luis Breuer and Arturo Cruz

As described in the previous sections of this paper, Central America has made significant political, economic, and social progress since the start of the 1990s, but considerable challenges remain. Although the region has made important advances with economic reforms, there have also been major setbacks, and policy implementation has been fitful in some countries. Why is it that governments across the region have often found it difficult to implement their policy agendas, focused as they are on the goals of rapid growth, macroeconomic stability, and poverty reduction—goals that appear to be widely supported in the society? This section looks at the complex political, institutional, and social landscape in those countries. It highlights the main obstacles in the political process as governments try to integrate the interests of diverse groups into policies that are more firmly based on a broad national consensus. It also makes some recommendations for the work of the IMF—how it can fulfill its role of supporting institutional strengthening to underpin sound economic policies, and how it can incorporate lessons from the political economy of the region into its program work.

Setting

Viewed against the experience of the 1980s, Central America—which here refers to Costa Rica, El Salvador, Guatemala, Honduras, and Nicaragua—has achieved much during the past decade and a half. During the 1980s, much of the region was caught in protracted civil conflicts or subject to autocratic rule. The conflicts, coupled with frequent economic shocks and often inappropriate economic policies, caused profound economic dislocation and a sharp rise in poverty. After the civil wars ended, during the 1990s democracy took hold throughout the region, and orderly political successions were achieved. At the same time, macroeconomic policies were strengthened and structural reforms gained momen-

tum, leading to a recovery of output, lower inflation, and stronger external positions. Rising nontraditional exports helped diversify the region's economic base.

However, since the end of the 1990s, the recovery has slowed. Adverse shocks (hurricanes, earthquakes, worsening terms of trade, and the global slowdown) compounded domestic problems as some countries found it difficult to sustain the reform effort, fiscal positions deteriorated, and some banking systems came under stress. As a result, growth slowed in much of the region (see Section I).

In 2003–04 growth rebounded, spurred by the global recovery, and most countries launched a new effort at fiscal consolidation and structural reforms. These reforms, if sustained, will provide a good basis for continued growth, supported also by the free trade agreement with the United States (CAFTA-DR). Nevertheless, the region remains vulnerable to shocks and policy reversals, and it faces increased competition in the global market for textiles and clothing since trading quotas were lifted at the beginning of 2005. To remain competitive and prosper as the region further integrates into the global economy, Central America will need to deal with the political fragmentation and vested interests that at times have stood in the way of a domestic consensus on key structural reforms.

Despite a notable improvement during the 1990s, social conditions continue to lag (except in Costa Rica). Poverty has fallen in relative terms (percentage of population) while it has increased in absolute terms (number of poor) (PNUD, 2003), and about half of the region's population continues to live in poverty (Table 8.1). Poverty tends to be concentrated in rural areas where access to basic public services (including health and education) is inadequate in most countries, and is often linked to underemployment or low-wage employment in the informal sector. Poverty and a lack of economic opportunities have fueled emigration, and in some countries worker remittances have be-

Table 8.1. Comparative Social Indicators

	Costa Rica	El Salvador	Guatemala	Honduras	Nicaragua	Average for Latin America and the Caribbean
Rank in UNDP Human Development Index (out of 177 countries)	45	103	121	115	118	79
GDP per capita PPP, U.S. dollars (2002)	8,840	4,890	4,080	2,600	2,470	7,223
People not expected to survive to age 40 (in percent of population) (2000–05)	3.7	9.9	14.1	13.8	10.3	9.7
Life expectancy at birth (years) (2002)	78.0	70.6	65.7	68.8	69.4	70.5
Infant mortality (per 1,000 live births) (2002)	9	33	36	32	32	27
Percent of population without access to safe water (2000)	5	23	8	12	23	14
Per capita health exp. in PPP, U.S. dollars (2001)	562	376	199	153	158	...
Physicians per 100,000 people (1990–2003)	160	126	109	87	62	...
Adult illiteracy (2002)	4.2	20.3	30.1	20	23.3	11.4
Primary school net enrollment (2001/02) (in percent of relevant age of the population)[1]	91	89	85	87	82	94
Secondary school net enrollment (2001/02) (in percent of relevant age of the population)[1]	51	46	28	36	37	61
Share of income or consumption (in percent)[2]						
Poorest 10 percent	1.4	0.9	0.9	0.9	1.2	...
Richest 10 percent	34.8	40.6	48.3	42.2	45	...
Gini index (Human Development Report, 2004)[3]	46.5	53.2	48.3	55.0	55.1	...
Percentage of population below the poverty line[3]	18.5	37.2	56.0	63.9	47.9	44.7

Sources: UNDP, Human Development Report 2001, 2002, 2003, and 2004.

[1]Data of net enrollment ratios are based on the new International Standard Classification of Education, adopted in 1997 (UNESCO, 1997), and may not be strictly comparable with those for earlier years. Data for some countries may refer to national or UNESCO Institute for Statistics estimates. For details, see http://www.uis.unesco.org. Because data are from different sources, comparisons across countries should be made with caution.

[2]Survey based on income.

[3]Data refer to the most recent year available during the period specified. The average is for Central America.

come a major source of foreign exchange. Literacy rates and health indicators have been improving, albeit from low levels. In some countries, urban crime and violence are endemic; although delinquency has been reduced recently in some countries (such as El Salvador and Honduras), it remains a serious concern and is often related to drug trafficking, which has become a significant problem.

With the advent of peace and democracy, social expectations have risen. Urbanization has increased the demand for public services, and increased political openness has allowed for greater dissent, social criticism, and open expression of social demands. The increased availability of information about higher living standards outside the region tends to raise expectations. At the same time, many institutions remain hobbled by political polarization fueled by a simmering distributional conflict that tends to permeate the political discourse. The associated social tensions have tended to stymie the political process and set back efforts to move economic reforms forward and to fulfill the rising expectations.

Governance problems continue to exacerbate the weakness of institutions in much of the region, despite notable progress over the past decade (Table 8.2). Corruption, lack of transparency, and questions about legal protection have tended to undermine the business climate and discourage foreign investment.[1] Cor-

---

[1]In the 2004 corruption perception index, produced by Transparency International (2004) on the basis of surveys, Costa Rica and El Salvador have the lowest perception of corruption among Central American countries (see www.transparency.org).

ruption also tends to affect the poor and disadvantaged disproportionately and frustrate their efforts at economic and social progress. Most countries also face a need to strengthen institutions and build confidence in judicial processes. Court decisions have at times complicated the pursuit of consistent economic policies—for example, by creating an unpredictable tax environment (Guatemala) and by delaying banking reforms. Governments across the region have recognized this challenge and made better governance one element of their economic and social reform strategies.

The unequal distribution of income and power in most of the region constrains social capital and generates pressures for redistribution.[2] Inequality weakens social cohesion, and most countries have yet to build the social cohesion needed to reduce political polarization. Distrust has made consensus more difficult to achieve, especially on policies and reforms that have distributional implications, and there is uncertainty about which groups receive their benefits. Sustained unfulfilled—and at times unrealistic—demands for redistribution strain the political process and undermine the economic policymaking process.

Political Support for Pro-Growth and Anti-Poverty Strategies

Recent research on Central America has highlighted the key elements of a comprehensive policy strategy that would help boost growth and reduce poverty (see Box 8.1).[3] The following are key elements of that strategy:

- Securing macroeconomic stability and reducing economic vulnerabilities. Large macroeconomic imbalances have had adverse effects on growth and poverty reduction in some countries.

- Improving the investment climate. Strengthening the rule of law (including contract enforcement) and the property rights regime and improving governance have been cited as key to achieving this.

- Expanding public investment, including investment in physical and social infrastructure (education and health).

- Improving social programs to expand coverage of educational and health services to the poor.

- Broadening access to credit.

- Using trade integration as an engine of growth and catalyst for institutional reform, in particular the regional integration and implementation of CAFTA-DR.

- Improving emergency preparedness, particularly by adopting measures to mitigate the costs of natural disasters.

There is broad consensus in the region on the strategic economic policy goals—maintaining macroeconomic stability by reducing economic vulnerabilities, boosting growth, and reducing poverty—and on the key elements of the strategy to reach those goals. Recent elections in all countries have echoed these objectives as well as the broad strategy for achieving them.

At the same time, the sociopolitical context in Central America creates challenges for the implementation of sound economic policies. In some countries there is distrust of the integrity of public institutions and politicians. Governments at times have a bias toward policies with short-term impact (consumption over investment) because of short election cycles and rules that do not allow for the possibility of (consecutive in most cases) reelection of presidents. Powerful interest groups put pressure on governments and legislatures, thus constraining policy reforms, while divided or fragmented legislatures hamper efficient policymaking. Adversarial relationships between executive and legislative branches often undermine the kind of constructive dialogue needed to build consensus on key issues, and widespread earmarking of public resources often reflects a relationship that is not only adversarial but also distrustful. Finally, in some countries the judicial branch has tended to rule on matters with serious economic impact (such as court decisions on tax policy in Guatemala or bank resolution in Nicaragua).

Fiscal Policy

Weaknesses in the public finances remain a common source of vulnerability in the region. Despite progress in several countries in reducing fiscal deficits over the past few years, public debt remains high in all countries (except Guatemala), tax systems are narrowly based, and tax compliance is poor. Public expenditures are subject to capture by interest groups, including through widespread earmarking, thereby constraining the availability of resources for growth and anti-poverty programs.

Although significant progress has been made on fiscal policymaking in recent years, much remains to

---

[2]Social capital refers to the institutions, relationships, and norms that shape the quality and quantity of a society's social interactions. According to the World Bank, there is increasing evidence that social cohesion is critical for societies to prosper economically and for development to be sustainable (www.worldbank.org/social-capital).

[3]See for instance Agosin, Machado, and Nazal (2004), Loayza, Fajnzylber, and Calderón (2002), De Ferranti and others (2003), and World Bank (2004).

Table 8.2. Comparative Governance Indicators[1]

	Voice and Accountability	Political Stability	Government Effectiveness	Regulatory Quality	Rule of Law	Control of Corruption
Costa Rica						
2004	84.0	83.0	68.3	71.4	65.7	77.3
2002	84.8	86.5	66.5	72.7	72.2	79.4
1997/98	87.8	81.2	73.5	90.9	71.5	76.6
El Salvador						
2004	53.4	39.8	47.6	68.5	42.5	43.8
2002	51.5	56.8	35.6	56.2	39.7	36.6
1997/98	49.4	48.1	44.5	99.4	29.7	41.6
Guatemala						
2004	36.4	21.8	18.8	48.8	18.8	27.1
2002	35.4	32.4	32.0	52.1	21.6	30.9
1997/98	33.1	22.1	45.8	66.7	10.3	18.8
Honduras						
2004	46.1	26.7	27.9	39.4	33.8	30.0
2002	46.0	38.4	27.3	41.8	23.7	27.3
1997/98	51.2	36.4	36.1	43.6	17.0	11.0
Nicaragua						
2004	48.5	41.7	27.4	46.3	30.4	46.3
2002	52.0	47.6	17.5	39.7	32.0	39.7
1997/98	57.6	37.7	29.7	37.0	25.5	18.2
Average for Central America						
2004	53.7	42.6	38.0	54.9	38.2	44.9
2002	53.9	52.3	35.8	52.5	37.8	42.8
1997/98	55.8	45.1	45.9	67.5	30.8	33.2
Average for Latin America and the Caribbean						
2004	60.5	58.3	55.6	57.6	54.3	57.4
2002	61.2	51.2	53.3	58.4	53.2	54.9
1997/98	59.1	45.0	48.3	66.4	43.9	46.7

Source: Kaufmann, Kraay, and Mastruzzi (2005).
[1]Percentile rank with a higher number denoting better governance.

be done to achieve fiscal sustainability, strengthen the tax effort, and improve the quality of spending. Improvements in revenues depend on addressing tax compliance and strengthening tax administrations, broadening the tax base, reducing tax incentives and widespread exemptions, and, in some cases, on implementing selective increases in tax rates. The quality of spending can be improved by enhancing transparency, reducing earmarking, and better focusing subsidies, while also reforming the civil service, pension systems, and public enterprises. Progress on these issues is being made, including in the following cases:

• El Salvador, Honduras, and Nicaragua have recently implemented tax reforms, and tax initiatives have been under way in Costa Rica and Guatemala for some time.

• Virtually all countries are implementing programs to strengthen public expenditure management. Programs focus on enhancing the information systems and making them more transparent and on modernizing the budget process.

Nonetheless, important challenges remain in strengthening public finances:

• Business groups have resisted higher taxation in many countries, partly because of their distrust of public institutions and the belief that public spending is inefficient and captured by interest groups, and therefore not supportive of growth or social objectives.[4] To address this situation,

---

[4]Some events feed into the belief that the public sector is a poor custodian of the nation's resources. For example, unions representing public sector employees in Honduras (for example, teachers and health workers) have succeeded in raising the government wage bill by about 5 percent of GDP over a recent five-year period, and major corruption scandals have surfaced in several countries in recent years.

Box 8.1. Institutional Aspects of Strategies to Boost Growth and Reduce Poverty

A successful growth and anti-poverty agenda should incorporate the following core elements.

1. Ensuring macroeconomic stability. The following are key reforms:

   • *Promote financial sector stability* by strengthening regulation and supervision of the banking system, and improving bank resolution procedures and the payment system.

   • *Ensure fiscal discipline and sustainability* through fiscal rules, including passing fiscal responsibility laws, eliminating tax incentives and exemptions, reducing earmarking of revenues, strengthening public debt management, integrating budgets with medium-term plans, and improving the quality of the public investment.

   • *Ensure low inflation* by directing central bank activity to control inflation.

   • *Improve the wage-setting mechanisms* by ensuring that wage increases are linked to productivity increases, including by strengthening dialogue.

2. Improving the functioning of markets. The following reforms are needed to enhance productivity:

   • *Streamline the investment approval process*, simplify entry and exit procedures, and reduce the reliance on taxes and other concessions to attract investments.

   • *Establish strong regulatory mechanisms* for utility companies and other monopolies.

   • *Further liberalize trade* to facilitate greater integration with the region and the world.

   • *Further integrate regional financial markets* by harmonizing prudential regulations and coordinating the supervision of cross-border banking.

   • *Improve accounting and business reporting standards* for greater market discipline.

   • Reduce the transaction cost in transferring property, especially collateral.

3. Redefining the role of the public sector. To strengthen fiscal performance, the following key measures should be pursued:

   • *Strengthen the management of public expenditures* by eliminating nonproductive expenditures and shifting resources to investment and anti-poverty programs.

   • *Divest public services* that are unconnected to core functions of the public sector.

   • *Improve accountability and financial management* of public enterprises.

   • Enhance public sector transparency in reporting to the general public.

4. Strengthening disaster mitigation and management. Domestic agencies must strengthen capacity and preparedness. Regional coordination will improve with mechanisms for cooperating and exchanging information, especially during multicountry events that require coordinated responses.

---

governments are devoting greater effort to building domestic consensus for tax reform.[5]

• Interest groups have succeeded in capturing segments of the national budgets (for example, public universities in Honduras and Nicaragua, and teachers in Honduras and Guatemala) through the earmarking of spending that is sometimes provided for in the constitution.

Financial Sector Reforms

After a period of financial stress, the region has made important progress in reforming the financial sector (see Section VI). With the exception of El Sal-

vador, all countries have experienced banking crises (Nicaragua) or episodes of banking stress (Costa Rica, Guatemala, and Honduras) in recent years. This has led to considerable efforts to upgrade prudential norms and improve banking supervision. All countries are moving toward a risk-based supervision framework, and most have concluded agreements to exchange information among supervisory authorities. Legal and bank resolution frameworks for the financial sector are being upgraded throughout the region. Recent moves toward financial integration and competition in the financial sector have heightened the awareness of the need for harmonizing financial norms in the region to prevent regulatory arbitrage and other distortions that affect competitiveness.

Despite the progress achieved, further efforts are needed. Banking systems remain fragile and a source of vulnerability.[6] Addressing this fragility

---

[5]These efforts (for example, in Guatemala, Honduras, and Nicaragua) have linked higher taxes with higher social spending and have been combined with assertive anti-corruption campaigns. Notwithstanding these efforts, tax reforms have so far made only modest progress in some countries (Costa Rica and Guatemala), and in others the reforms have been limited because governments were able to secure congressional support for only limited reforms and had to compromise on their initial objective of significantly expanding the tax base (El Salvador, Honduras, and Nicaragua).

[6]Banking fragility is reflected in highly nonperforming loans, balance sheet mismatches, less well-supervised offshore and parallel banking activities, and limited supervisory capacity.

Box 8.2. Consolidated Supervision of the Financial Sector

Regional financial conglomerates have emerged that successfully compete with international banks (see Section VI). The main factors behind this development include increased regional economic integration, political risk in some countries, economies of scale, and the facilities offered by Panama (particularly international licenses to conduct operations throughout the region).

Although financial integration is a positive development, it gives rise to the need for consolidated supervision and harmonization of norms and regulations to avoid the emergence of regulatory arbitrage and distortions of competitiveness. Financial integration would allow the assessment of the soundness of the whole financial conglomerate as well as the systemic and contagion risks associated with potential insolvency of a group. In the absence of consolidated supervision, intra-group transactions that inflate capital could go undetected for long periods of time.

Introducing effective consolidated supervision will require a concerted regional effort, including estab-

lishing minimum standards, strengthening the exchange of information among supervisors, and harmonizing core prudential regulations (such as on related lending).

However, important challenges remain in introducing consolidated supervision:

- Banks are likely to resist this process because it would reduce their discretion in choosing whether and where to consolidate their operations.

- Bankers are likely to oppose the consolidation in countries that are perceived as higher risk as a result of lingering political polarization (for example, El Salvador and Nicaragua).

- Applying regional limits to related lending would also create tensions, given the size and limited diversification of the region's economy.

- Regulators have tended to be reluctant to share information, in part because of limited legal protection.

---

will require actions on various fronts, including further strengthening of loan classification, prudential standards, bank resolution frameworks, and upgrading of supervisory capabilities, particularly consolidated supervision in both domestic and cross-border operations of related financial firms (Box 8.2). Widespread informal dollarization presents particular challenges that require a comprehensive policy strategy to restore the attractiveness of local-currency assets.[7]

A number of challenges remain to strengthen the financial sector.

- At times, bank stockholders have been reluctant or unable to increase bank capital to levels that allow for appropriate loan classification and provisioning while maintaining statutory capital adequacy ratios. Banks are an influential pressure group, and in some cases they have succeeded in delaying the introduction of more rigorous prudential norms and secured public funding for deposit insurance schemes (for example, Guatemala and Honduras). Granting bank supervisors appropriate legal protection is also an urgent priority.

- Applying limits to related lending creates tensions in many countries. Banks are often owned by a few large business groups that are also the banks' clients (for example, in El Salvador, Guatemala, Honduras, and Nicaragua).

- The presence of state banks (Costa Rica and Guatemala), which in the past have enjoyed special privileges (such as offering dollar deposits or enjoying an implicit full state guarantee of deposits) and may have engaged in political lending, may weaken the authority of supervisory agencies.

Trade Openness

The movement toward regional integration has gained momentum, most recently with the signing of a free trade agreement with the United States (CAFTA-DR) and with the efforts to complete a customs union in the region. Since the 1990s, the Central American Common Market has seen substantive progress with the virtual elimination of all intraregional tariffs, and a common external tariff currently covers 95 percent of all imports, with an average rate of less than 5 percent. These international trade agreements can be an important external anchor and catalyst for institutional change by breaking through domestic impediments to reforms.

The main support for CAFTA-DR comes from the export sectors, whereas opposition is centered on a coalition of political, civil society, and selective business groups. Among other things, CAFTA-DR

---

[7]The response to the challenges posed by informal dollarization includes strengthening macroeconomic policies to boost confidence in the domestic currencies, modifying prudential rules to reflect the risks of dollarization and minimize the risk of currency mismatches; and increasing cushions against possible deposit outflows by raising international reserves and/or arranging for international credit lines.

will make permanent the current trade preferences extended to the region by the United States under the Caribbean Basin Initiative. CAFTA-DR is therefore strongly supported by business groups representing the export processing zones (*maquilas*) and commercial agriculture. Most of the opposition has come from a coalition of groups that are skeptical about forging closer ties with the United States on political grounds, public sector unions, and civil society and interest groups concerned about the conditions negotiated in the agreement and its impact on some sectors, including the traditional agricultural sector. In addition, selected agro-industrial firms (for example, meat, dairy, and poultry industries) have expressed concern about losing their protected positions under CAFTA-DR.

To reduce the opposition to CAFTA-DR and garner support for the agreement, selected groups are being afforded continued protection. Gradual tariff reductions and quotas were used to cushion the impact on sensitive sectors. For example, poultry producers will be protected through tariffs and quotas for a transition period of up to 20 years. Similarly, corn (maize) has been excluded from the agreement with Nicaragua, and in Honduras quotas (beyond which a high tariff applies) have been established.

Generating Consensus on a Long-Term Reform Strategy

A broad national debate is generally needed to forge a consensus on policy strategies. This consensus must be entrenched in a policy framework based on credible and enduring rules. The fairly wide underlying agreement on long-term goals (growth, stability, and poverty reduction) provides a mandate and opportunity for governments to lay down medium-term policy markers and objectives. The consensus needs to be reflected in institutional arrangements and legislation as anchors to policymaking, which could include fiscal pacts, fiscal responsibility laws, and procedural safeguards. To achieve this, policymakers need to better communicate the benefits of the pro-growth and anti-poverty policies, including discussing the short-term costs versus the long-term benefits.

Key institutions that serve the long-term goals need to be strengthened. Countries need to focus on building the kinds of institutions and processes that deliver better policy outcomes and help sustain them over time. The status quo sometimes delivers inferior outcomes as key interest groups make ad hoc policy decisions that focus on short-term goals. For policies to improve, they need to be framed in a wider context and constrained by rules-based and accountable processes and institutions that push for long-term

goals. Though institutional reforms do not always lend themselves to "best practice" formulations because of the diversity of specific country circumstances and conditions, recent research has highlighted the importance of strong institutions for economic growth.[8] In particular, institutional arrangements that are growth enhancing tend to share the following elements.

- *Fiscal policies* supportive of macroeconomic stability and focused on key spending priorities (investment and social programs). Institutions must focus on countering the classic threats to fiscal discipline, including the common-pool and intertemporal problems,[9] which, if left unchecked, could result in weak public sector balance sheets, destabilizing deficits, and unsustainable debt.

- *Monetary policy* and institutions that give priority to achieving and sustaining price stability. These have to overcome potential obstacles such as the lack of central bank independence; fiscal dominance; and pursuit of multiple or even contradictory policy objectives.

- *Financial sector policies* and institutions that contribute to sound and efficient banking systems. These basically have to counter problems of asymmetric information and moral hazard in banking by providing adequate incentives to banking system participants to act as if a government bailout would be an event both very rare and costly for them,

- *Trade policy* and institutions that promote open trade regimes. Trade policy is the classic arena for rent-seeking since protection can bring large benefits to individual firms and industries, while the costs of protection are borne in the form of more widely and thinly spread economic dislocations and inefficient allocation of resources.

There is a need to strengthen the political process and governance. Often, political responsibility is diluted in regimes where the executive and legislative branches are controlled by different groups and do not function in a coordinated or effective way. Current discussions on political change have centered on lengthening electoral cycles (such as by allowing one consecutive reelection of the president), modify-

---

[8]See, for instance, Chapter 2 of Kalter and others (2004) and Chapter 3 of IMF (2003).

[9]Common-pool problems arise when particular groups lobby for public sector actions to their own benefit without internalizing the associated costs (for example, subnational governments with inadequate budget constraints). Intertemporal problems include inadequate incentives to be concerned with future implications of policies, which are often attributed to situations of very frequent political turnover.

ing the financing of elections, strengthening technical capabilities of legislatures and political parties,
and taking other measures to improve cooperation
between branches of government.[10]

External factors can help to promote and anchor
policy reform and possibly contribute to improving
the political process. The requirements of CAFTA-
DR, the World Trade Organization, the IMF and other
international financial institutions, and the donor
community can help catalyze institutional reforms,
lock in best practices, and bring greater transparency
to public policies. The latter might contribute to improving the political process by making the system
more accountable. Effective support of these policy
strategies could perhaps benefit from better focus of
external assistance and associated conditionality on a
few core (institutional) issues in the reform agenda.
Donor financing can help foster reforms, while also
helping to finance social safety nets to cushion any
short-term adverse effects of reforms.

Implications for the IMF

The IMF should remain engaged in Central America through its various operational modalities. The
focus of the IMF's work in the region, and elsewhere,
has increasingly concentrated on crisis prevention and
institutional strengthening to help entrench macroeconomic stability and lay the conditions for economic
growth. The IMF has developed a framework of internationally agreed-upon standards and codes in the
areas of public finance, banking, and statistics that
serve as benchmarks for institution building. Besides
providing bilateral surveillance and program support—such as Poverty Reduction and Growth Facility
(PRGF) arrangements in Honduras and Nicaragua
and two Stand-By Arrangements in Guatemala in the
past few years—the IMF has strengthened the regional dimension of its work in Central America, including by increasing research on key policy issues
for the region, expanding technical assistance, engaging in outreach activities, and organizing regional
conferences and seminars.

The IMF should leverage these efforts to help promote a strong policy agenda, primarily in the following ways:

- Help promote national debate on pro-growth and
anti-poverty agendas. The IMF should encourage the authorities to strengthen their efforts to
explain and build support for appropriate poli-

cies. Open public debate, transparency, and better communication of policy strategies would
help raise public awareness of key policy issues
and the opportunity cost of reforms, thus promoting ownership. Resident representative offices should play a key role in these efforts.

- Intensify outreach with main actors in the political process. The IMF's engagement—focused
and well timed—with congressional leaders,
labor unions, business leaders, civil society
groups, media, donors, and the public at large
can be very helpful to crystallize policy options
and catalyze well-informed policy consensus. In
an effort to strengthen the constituency for reforms, the IMF can do this through outreach
seminars, op-ed articles in newspapers, and bilateral meetings with IMF missions. In this
work, the IMF can bring to the region its experience on best practices in Latin America and
world-wide.

- Support regional integration efforts with technical assistance in the areas of the IMF's expertise:

  - Address relevant macroeconomic issues that
  require a regional approach, such as tax harmonization and coordination, consolidated banking supervision, and cooperation on economic
  statistics.

  - Support the creation and strengthening of regional institutions and collaboration.

  - Step up efforts to help authorities identify
  sources of, and obstacles to, growth (for example, by helping to develop the reforms necessary to harness the potential benefits of
  CAFTA-DR).

- For the IMF's program work, two main conclusions emerge from the analysis of political economy issues:

  - In fragmented political landscapes (especially
  where governments and congresses are divided), the IMF needs to engage broadly to ensure and help create sufficient domestic consensus on programs. Although the government
  will remain the IMF's counterpart, the IMF
  needs to engage with other key players in the
  political process to ensure needed support for
  program implementation.

  - The IMF needs to be sensitive to the underlying
  institutional weaknesses and political cycles.
  Programs must focus on key policy reforms
  and be attuned to political cycles, which indicate when there are opportunities to introduce
  difficult policy changes and when, on the other
  hand, governments may need to focus more on
  protecting policy gains.

---

[10]The constraints of presidentialist political systems in Latin
America are described in Linz and Valenzuela (1994), and
Urcuyo (2003) reviews the challenges and proposed solutions to
the Costa Rican political system.

References

Agosin, Manuel, Roberto Machado, and Paulina Nazal, eds., 2004, *Pequeñas Economías, Grandes Desafíos* (Washington: Inter-American Development Bank).

De Ferranti, and others, 2003, *Inequality in Latin America and the Caribbean: Breaking with History?* (Washington: World Bank).

International Monetary Fund, 2003, *World Economic Outlook, April 2003* (Washington).

Kalter, Eliot, and others, 2004, *Chile: Institutions and Policies Underpinning Stability and Growth*, IMF Occasional Paper No. 231 (Washington: International Monetary Fund).

Kaufmann, Daniel, Aart Kraay, and Massimo Mastruzzi, 2005, "Governance Matters II: Governance Indicators for 1996–2004," World Bank Policy Research Department Working Paper No. 3106 (Washington: World Bank).

Linz, Juan, and Arturo Valenzuela, eds., 1994, *The Failure of Presidential Democracy: The Case of Latin America* (Baltimore, Maryland: Johns Hopkins University Press).

Loayza, Norman, Pablo Fajnzylber, and César Calderón, 2002, "Economic Growth in Latin America and the Caribbean" (unpublished; Washington: World Bank).

Programa de Naciones Unidas para el Desarrollo (PNUD), 2003, *Segundo Informe sobre Desarrollo Humano en Centroamérica y Panamá* (San Jose, Costa Rica: Editorama).

Rogoff, Kenneth, and others, 2003, "Evolution and Performance of Exchange Rate Regimes," IMF Working Paper 03/243 (Washington: International Monetary Fund).

Transparency International, 2004, *Corruption Perception Index 2004.* Available via the Internet: www.transparency.org/cpi/2004/cpi2004.en.html#cpi2004.

United Nations Development Program, 2004, *Human Development Report, 2004* (New York). Available via the Internet: http://hdr.undp.org/reports/global/2004.

———, 2003, *Human Development Report, 2003* (New York). Available via the Internet: http://hdr.undp.org/reports/global/2003.

Urcuyo, Constantino, 2003, "Reforma Politica y Gobernabilidad" (San Jose, Costa Rica: Editorial Juricentro).

World Bank, 2004, "Honduras: Development Policy Review: Accelerating Broad-Based Growth." Available via the Internet: http://www-wds.worldbank.org/servlet/WDS_IBank_Servlet?pcont=details&eid=000160016_20041215163554.

Recent Occasional Papers of the International Monetary Fund

220. Effects of Financial Globalization on Developing Countries: Some Empirical Evidence, by Eswar S. Prasad, Kenneth Rogoff, Shang-Jin Wei, and Ayhan Kose. 2003.

219. Economic Policy in a Highly Dollarized Economy: The Case of Cambodia, by Mario de Zamaroczy and Sopanha Sa. 2003.

218. Fiscal Vulnerability and Financial Crises in Emerging Market Economies, by Richard Hemming, Michael Kell, and Axel Schimmelpfennig. 2003.

217. Managing Financial Crises: Recent Experience and Lessons for Latin America, edited by Charles Collyns and G. Russell Kincaid. 2003.

216. Is the PRGF Living Up to Expectations?—An Assessment of Program Design, by Sanjeev Gupta, Mark Plant, Benedict Clements, Thomas Dorsey, Emanuele Baldacci, Gabriela Inchauste, Shamsuddin Tareq, and Nita Thacker. 2002.

215. Improving Large Taxpayers' Compliance: A Review of Country Experience, by Katherine Baer. 2002.

214. Advanced Country Experiences with Capital Account Liberalization, by Age Bakker and Bryan Chapple. 2002.

213. The Baltic Countries: Medium-Term Fiscal Issues Related to EU and NATO Accession, by Johannes Mueller, Christian Beddies, Robert Burgess, Vitali Kramarenko, and Joannes Mongardini. 2002.

212. Financial Soundness Indicators: Analytical Aspects and Country Practices, by V. Sundararajan, Charles Enoch, Armida San José, Paul Hilbers, Russell Krueger, Marina Moretti, and Graham Slack. 2002.

211. Capital Account Liberalization and Financial Sector Stability, by a staff team led by Shogo Ishii and Karl Habermeier. 2002.

210. IMF-Supported Programs in Capital Account Crises, by Atish Ghosh, Timothy Lane, Marianne Schulze-Ghattas, Aleš Bulíř, Javier Hamann, and Alex Mourmouras. 2002.

209. Methodology for Current Account and Exchange Rate Assessments, by Peter Isard, Hamid Faruqee, G. Russell Kincaid, and Martin Fetherston. 2001.

208. Yemen in the 1990s: From Unification to Economic Reform, by Klaus Enders, Sherwyn Williams, Nada Choueiri, Yuri Sobolev, and Jan Walliser. 2001.

207. Malaysia: From Crisis to Recovery, by Kanitta Meesook, Il Houng Lee, Olin Liu, Yougesh Khatri, Natalia Tamirisa, Michael Moore, and Mark H. Krysl. 2001.

206. The Dominican Republic: Stabilization, Structural Reform, and Economic Growth, by a staff team led by Philip Young comprising Alessandro Giustiniani, Werner C. Keller, and Randa E. Sab and others. 2001.

205. Stabilization and Savings Funds for Nonrenewable Resources, by Jeffrey Davis, Rolando Ossowski, James Daniel, and Steven Barnett. 2001.

204. Monetary Union in West Africa (ECOWAS): Is It Desirable and How Could It Be Achieved? by Paul Masson and Catherine Pattillo. 2001.

203. Modern Banking and OTC Derivatives Markets: The Transformation of Global Finance and Its Implications for Systemic Risk, by Garry J. Schinasi, R. Sean Craig, Burkhard Drees, and Charles Kramer. 2000.

202. Adopting Inflation Targeting: Practical Issues for Emerging Market Countries, by Andrea Schaechter, Mark R. Stone, and Mark Zelmer. 2000.

201. Developments and Challenges in the Caribbean Region, by Samuel Itam, Simon Cueva, Erik Lundback, Janet Stotsky, and Stephen Tokarick. 2000.

200. Pension Reform in the Baltics: Issues and Prospects, by Jerald Schiff, Niko Hobdari, Axel Schimmel-pfennig, and Roman Zytek. 2000.

199. Ghana: Economic Development in a Democratic Environment, by Sérgio Pereira Leite, Anthony Pellechio, Luisa Zanforlin, Girma Begashaw, Stefania Fabrizio, and Joachim Harnack. 2000.

198. Setting Up Treasuries in the Baltics, Russia, and Other Countries of the Former Soviet Union: An Assessment of IMF Technical Assistance, by Barry H. Potter and Jack Diamond. 2000.

Note: For information on the titles and availability of Occasional Papers not listed, please consult the IMF's *Publications Catalog* or contact IMF Publication Services.